Belonging

Belonging

A DAUGHTER'S SEARCH
FOR IDENTITY THROUGH
LOSS AND LOVE

Michelle Miller

with Rosemarie Robotham

HARPER

NEW YORK • LONDON • TORONTO • SYDNEY

HARPER

A hardcover edition of this book was published in 2023 by Harper, an imprint of HarperCollins Publishers.

BELONGING. Copyright © 2023 by 80th Street Ventures. All rights reserved. Printed in the United States of America. No part of this book may be used or reproduced in any manner whatsoever without written permission except in the case of brief quotations embodied in critical articles and reviews. For information, address HarperCollins Publishers, 195 Broadway, New York, NY 10007.

HarperCollins books may be purchased for educational, business, or sales promotional use. For information, please email the Special Markets Department at SPsales@harpercollins.com.

FIRST HARPER PAPERBACKS EDITION PUBLISHED 2024.

Library of Congress Cataloging-in-Publication Data has been applied for.

ISBN 978-0-06-322044-7 (pbk.)

24 25 26 27 28 LBC 5 4 3 2 1

To the family I made,
Marc, my heart, and our children,
Kemah, Mason, and Margeaux,
you are my everything.

"The desire to go home that is a desire to be whole, to know where you are, to be the point of intersection of all the lines drawn through all the stars, to be the constellation maker and the center of the world, that center called love."

—Rebecca Solnit, *Storming the Gates of Paradise*

Contents

This is a work of nonfiction. The events and experiences detailed here are all true and have been faithfully rendered as I have remembered them, to the best of my ability. The names and identifying details of some individuals in this narrative, including that of my mother, have been altered to protect their privacy. Though conversations come from my keen recollection of them, they are not written to represent word-for-word documentation; rather, the exchanges recounted here represent my best effort to recreate the spirit and substance of these conversations, and may not always reflect the exact words that may have been spoken.

Belonging

First Word:
Where We Awaken

G o and find your life," my father once encouraged me. At the time, I had recently graduated from college, my newly minted Howard University communications degree inviting me to seek my place in American media. My father had another idea. He thought I should take a few months to discover myself first. "Why not go backpacking through Europe and Africa?" he suggested. "Use this time to decide who you want to be."

"Are you serious?" I responded, stunned by this suggestion from my industrious, overachieving father. I had dropped by Dominguez Valley Hospital, where he was chief of surgery, to get breakfast with him. Having just completed an eventful paid summer internship with the *Los Angeles Times,* I was now looking for a full-time job. Daddy and I were walking to the hospital cafeteria when he shared his entirely unexpected idea. He gave a low chuckle as I halted in my tracks, mouth gaping open, not quite sure I had heard him right. This was, after all, the man who from the time I was in elementary school, had taken pains to ensure that my work ethic was unimpeachable. Yet he was now advocating that I blow off finding a job in favor of gallivanting across the world. But as I thought about it more, I realized that his proposition was not as incongruous as it had initially sounded. Far from being a footloose frolic across two continents, in my father's view this back-packing trip would be a continuation of my essential education.

"But I don't have anyone to go with me," I said, my mind already churning through the possibilities, assessing my summer savings, de-vising itineraries, wondering if I could take out a loan or apply for a travel grant to underwrite such an adventure.

"So go by yourself," Daddy shrugged, and in that moment I knew I would dare the journey, carrying my father's blessing in my pocket.

He reminded me that in college he had worked as a biology and chemistry tutor and served food in the campus cafeteria, saving every penny to make the same trip in the year between graduating pre-med from Howard and returning to pursue his medical degree there. He'd often shared that traveling the world alone as a Black man had left him with an unshakable belief that he was equal to whatever life might send his way. In emboldening me now to explore regions as yet unknown to me, he trusted I would strengthen my own resilience and resourceful-ness, too.

I would need those very qualities just one year later, when this man who had been my life's most constant presence told me he was termi-nally ill. His body riddled with the prostate cancer that would eventu-ally take him from me, my father changed his directive. "Go and find your mother," he told me then, his voice rough with the work of trying to live. "You need to know your medical history on her side." It was a doctor's instruction, but after a pause he added softly, "She needs to know you"—and that, I knew, was the wish of a father's heart.

I WAS TWENTY-FOUR WHEN MY FATHER ASKED ME TO SEARCH FOR MY mother, so that I might ask the questions that had burned in me all those years without her. In my two-plus decades as a motherless child, I had learned that identity is shaped as much by those who are absent in our lives as by those who stay by our side. My physical appearance only complicated things as a kid; my lightly toasted complexion and mass of wavy brown hair baffled some people. They might recognize me as Black, but the nod usually came with a wrinkle to their noses, as if to say, *but what else you got mixed up in there, girl?* Other times, if I wore my hair blow-dried straight, people queried whether I was Italian, Jewish, or Hispanic, peppering me with questions about my heritage long before I had examined such questions for myself.

As a child, the only detail I'd known about the woman who birthed me was that she wasn't Black, which, on confronting my light pigment and pointed features in the mirror each day, had left me to assume she was White. As I grew older, the unsolved mystery of my mother inclined me toward chasing the answers. This might explain why a career in journalism called out to me. One story at a time, I wanted to investigate life's unknowns, to engage the larger narrative of my American homeland and witness human experience from the center of its unfolding. Broadcast news in particular appealed to me—I suspect that I secretly hoped that my mother might one day see me on her television screen and come to claim me.

Through the years, my work as a TV news correspondent would place me at the center of epochal moments in Black history, from the tragic aftermath of Hurricane Katrina in 2005, to the shocking massacre of Black worshippers by a White supremacist in a Charleston church ten years later, to the fevered George Floyd rallies in the shadow of a global pandemic, when Americans of all creeds and colors marched together for a brief hopeful moment in the cause of racial justice and the sanctity of Black lives.

Fortunately, in my career as a journalist, I have been tasked with bearing witness to more than Black trauma and pain. There has been triumph, art, and inspiration, as well as stories of pure joy and whimsy, such as the royal nuptials of Prince William and Kate Middleton, and when I donned my tartan and traveled to Scotland to report on the hit TV series *Outlander,* with its romantic time-travel plotline. All of it has shaped me not only professionally, but also personally, amplifying my voice as a Black woman storyteller.

Finding my way into network newsrooms wasn't always easy, however. With my untamed exuberance, transparent vulnerabilities, and penchant for blurting out the right sentiment at exactly the wrong moment, I stepped into my calling in fits and starts, navigating spaces where people weren't quite sure what to make of me. Such encounters never failed to short-circuit me back to a childhood in which I was bused to four different schools in five years, a Black girl integrating White environments, who ached with wondering where she truly belonged.

These days, some might recognize me from *CBS Saturday Morning*, which I cohost weekly with Dana Jacobson and Jeff Glor, guided by our fearless executive producer Brian Applegate. By giving me agency on a national platform, that show changed my whole trajectory in the news industry. Others may recall my time as First Lady of New Orleans, including the spectacle of my wedding to the scion of one of the nation's most powerful Black political families, Marc Morial, then the youngest mayor ever of his storied city, and now president of the National Urban League. Still others know me as a suburban New Jersey mother of three, while to those who remember me from my hometown of Los Angeles, I am the native daughter done good.

But this is more than a memoir of how I got to the place where I now stand. It is also a clear-eyed engagement with our nation's racial story. Indeed, in the fall of 2020, as the country went to the polls to apply the lessons of the George Floyd protests by voting out a divisive president, I was reminded of an observation that behavioral scientist Oliver Sacks once made about the need to bear witness. "The most we can do is to write—intelligently, creatively, evocatively—about what it is like living in the world at this time," he had said. And that is my goal: to offer a narrative of my experience as a mixed-race Black woman in America in a moment when we are finally daring the hard conversations about race and identity, and confronting the multilayered truths of those whom our history has marginalized.

I believe that my own effort to find and know my mother mirrors the quest we all must undertake—to bring together our estranged tribes, to knit something good from a painful past, to invent ourselves anew. As I reflected in "Witnessing History," the *CBS This Morning* segment about my family that aired at the height of the George Floyd racial justice protests in 2020: "Everyone must see in America who she was and who she is, in order to decide who she wants to be. We are living with her original sin. We must face that, and bear witness to change that won't allow a next time."

This book is my witness. In its simplest terms, it is the story of one woman's search for herself. In the context of my mother's early abandonment of me, and my coming of age in the racialized crucible of my American homeland, it is a search that has involved the painful work of constructing an identity that is authentic and purposeful, healed and whole. Perhaps, as my father suggested when he urged me to explore the unknown, this is the task we must each engage—to *find* our lives. We are each, after all, born to a quest whose starting point is set by the providence of where our star is cast, and we must place our feet upon the path where we awaken, and follow it home.

PART ONE

Mother Figures

"Absence is to love what wind is to fire;
it extinguishes the small, it inflames the great."

—Roger de Bussy-Rabutin

ONE

Original Sin

Only hours after I squinted up at my mother's face in the delivery room, she was gone. I had gulped my first mouthful of air at daybreak on a balmy Thursday in Los Angeles, at the end of a historically turbulent year. It was December 1967: I arrived at the crescendo of Dr. Martin Luther King Jr.'s righteous fight for Civil Rights and just as New York senator Robert Francis Kennedy was weighing his fateful decision to run for president of the United States. That afternoon, after holding her light-skinned infant in milk-colored arms, the woman in whose body I was made handed me to my Black father and walked out of the hospital. I have often wondered if she had second thoughts as she left me squalling in the nursery.

When there are gaping holes in your story that you don't yet have the language to interrogate, you begin to color in the missing pieces. This determined act of self-creation is infinitely preferable to walking through the world with a yawning emptiness at your center, into which you might disappear. And so you invent what you don't know as a way to ground yourself, and this desire to contrive your story, to claim your worth in the world despite your own mother leaving you behind, quietly frames how you make sense of everything and who you become.

As a small child, I'd heard my grandmother refer to the woman who birthed me as Caucasian. The context is lost to me now, or perhaps I was too young to grasp what she and my dad were discussing. I did know, however, that Caucasian meant White; that much I had discerned from listening to grown folks talking around me. I had observed from many hours of solitary television watching in my grandmother's house that the people who breathed inside White skin were at the top rung of the ladder of social privilege, and people who looked like my father and grandmother and the rest of our family were often unwelcome or absent in White spaces. And so I had surmised early on that my mother being Caucasian had something to do with her not being around, but it would be years before it dawned on me that my mother's absence from my life might be as much about America's unforgiving racial hierarchy as it was a consequence of the fact that, when I was born, my father was not exactly free to love her.

I don't recall when I first grasped that I was the child of a clandestine affair. I only knew that when Dr. Ross Miller Jr., then a thirty-eight-year-old surgeon, received me from my mother's arms, he already had a wife at home, Iris Rogers Miller, a tall, slender, ochre-colored Southern beauty from a family of prominent Black funeral home owners. But children accept the world as they find it, and so the fact that my father had been married to a woman who was not my mother, simply *was*.

My father's wife knew nothing of my arrival. Iris's parents had raised their only daughter as an African American princess, the belle of Black debutante society in Fayetteville, North Carolina, a young woman whose refined upbringing and impeccable manners everyone assumed would make her a perfect doctor's wife. But Ross and Iris weren't temperamentally well suited: Ross was gregarious and charismatic where Iris was cool and reserved, her demeanor severe in that disdainful way that Black folks refer to as *seditty*. My father's easy conviviality drew everyone to him. As one of the first two Black city councilmen elected in Compton the same year, he considered himself a man of the people, while Iris preferred to mingle only with "the right kind." Their marriage, difficult from the start, became more strained when it appeared that Iris could not conceive. Relatives whispered that Iris would have been perfectly happy to forgo the mess and chaos of young children, but Ross yearned to be a father, and convinced his wife to adopt not one, but two little girls, Cheryl and Adrienne, with the idea that they would be company for each other as they grew.

Both daughters had already celebrated their first birthdays by the time Ross and Iris brought them home. Cheryl, older by three months, was the distracted dreamer, a tiny honey-colored child with a cascade of wavy brown hair and thin features. As a toddler, Cheryl shied away from people, even family members. Adrienne was her polar opposite; inquisitive and precociously bright, she engaged adults readily and could read before she was three. A deep walnut brown like our father, she had short, tightly coiled black hair, alert black eyes, and full lips. Ross, painfully aware that dark-skinned children like Adrienne were less chosen in every realm of American life, had insisted to Iris that at least one of their daughters be of his complexion or darker. But he failed to anticipate that bringing two babies home in the same week would ignite a slow-burning resentment in his wife, who was left to attend to their daughters mostly alone. Ross spent long hours each week at the hospital, with the rest of his time consumed by his community medical practice; his city council work; local school board meetings; and the campaign and networking events he organized as an elected Democratic Party delegate.

My father saw his activism as vital to achieving civil and voting rights for America's disenfranchised communities. Down South in Alabama, Dr. Martin Luther King Jr. was leading protest marches from Selma to Montgomery, with demonstrators braving police batons cracked against their skulls, fire hoses and snarling dogs let loose in the crowd, and the murder of freedom fighters who were only trying to register Blacks and poor Whites to vote. In Los Angeles, where systemic oppression was more likely to hide behind the polite smile of a bank officer declining a Black family's home loan application, or the White realtor telling a Black buyer that a property listed just that morning was no longer available, my father felt an urgency to do his part to help dismantle America's racial caste system.

He had experienced its barriers firsthand. Years before, when he'd tried to buy a house in Compton, the White homeowner refused to sell to him. My father enlisted a White friend to buy the house and deed it to him for a dollar, only to have the local Ku Klux Klan set a burlap-wrapped, gasoline-soaked wooden cross aflame on his front lawn soon after he moved in. The experience left him with the conviction that he could not afford to stand on the sidelines. Though California in the late 1950s was being lauded as a land of liberty and prosperity, attracting hordes of Black Americans fleeing violence and persecution in the Jim Crow South, Ross had seen that Los Angeles was still a very divided town. It was why he had become involved in Democratic Party politics and community organizing, and why he had joined with four other Black doctors to open a practice in an old factory building they had purchased on Compton Boulevard.

The refurbished factory now housed a pharmacy as well as the offices of a pediatrician, an internist, an OB/GYN, a dentist, and Ross, a surgeon who specialized in disorders of the heart and lungs. Conscious of the fact that people of color too often received indifferent medical attention, and armed with studies showing that Black patients had better outcomes when treated by Black doctors, my father envisioned a fully equipped practice that would offer the highest level of care. In many ways, Daddy was a visionary, fighting against social inequities on several fronts at once, staging protests against police mistreatment of Black and Brown people, agitating for more funding for under-resourced schools, and publicly decrying the burning crosses proliferating on the lawns of the city's striving Black families.

In my father's busy life of doctoring and social activism, I had been completely unplanned. Having convinced Iris to adopt little Cheryl and Adrienne one year before, Ross never intended to conceive an out-of-wedlock child. For the first eight years of my life, I knew hardly anything about the woman with whom he'd had an affair, because the details Daddy chose to share about her were so sketchy and elusive that I couldn't seem to retain them. I sometimes wondered whether Daddy had considered asking Iris for a divorce so that he might make a life with his lover, but given how circumspect and emotionally submerged he became whenever I broached the subject of my missing mother, it wasn't something I felt I could ask him, at least not back then.

AS IT HAPPENED, I WAS TO BE KEPT NOT ONLY FROM MY BIOLOGICAL mother, but also from my father's wife, and my sisters, Cheryl and Adrienne, who were now two years old. Though several relatives later reflected that Iris must have had some inkling that her husband's attentions were engaged elsewhere—"A woman always knows," my cousin Reggie maintained—for a long time she appeared to have no idea that he had fathered a child.

I feel only compassion for Iris when I consider her situation. Much later, I would hear gossip that Iris's father had kept a second family across town back in Fayetteville, and Iris had grown up fully aware of her half brothers and sisters, though her mother never spoke of them. Perhaps this explains why she pretended not to know about Ross's affair. The coddled child of wealth and privilege, she had watched her mother studiedly ignore her father's faithlessness, and now she resolved to do the same. As long as my father remained discreet, she would hold her head high and pretend fiercely that all was well, because her mother's example had taught her that a woman without her own means, married to a good provider, must endure such infidelities.

Since my father couldn't simply bring me to the home he shared with Iris, the logical person to care for me would have been my grand-mother, whom everyone called Bigmama. Beatrice Burson Miller lived in South Central in a turreted storybook house that she and my grand-father had purchased in the late 1950s. Ross, who was then doing his surgery residency in Los Angeles, had convinced his parents to move from East St. Louis, Illinois, where they had raised him and his older sister Edna. My grandparents had joined the massive migration of Black Americans moving north and west to escape violence and op-pression, though their new cities were hardly racial utopias themselves.

Still, my grandparents had been content living on that beautiful tree-lined street in South Central, with their son nearby. I arrived too late to meet my grandfather, the first Ross Matthew Miller, who died of a heart attack the year before I was born. Now my grandmother was alone in that well-kept house with its luxuriant garden, except in the summers when Aunt Edna's teenage sons traveled from their home in Birmingham, Alabama, to keep Bigmama company. Though already in her seventies, Bigmama would happily have taken me in, but she was never asked. My dad and Aunt Edna decided, without ever putting the question to their mother, that a newborn would be too much for her to handle on her own. Perhaps my father also worried about having me so close by, in a house that he often visited with his wife and their two daughters. How would he explain the baby girl who appeared out of nowhere in Bigmama's home?

Looking back, I have no idea why my father believed he could keep me hidden. I suspect he simply hadn't thought too far ahead when he enlisted his older sister to have me cared for in Birmingham. But Aunt Edna had her hands full with five children of her own, four sons and a daughter only five years old, as well as full-time jobs teaching at the local business college, Lawson State, and helping my uncle, Thomas Gardner Sr., manage the funeral home that they would very shortly come to own. Her solution was to send a family friend named Mar-garet Tripp to get me from the hospital and bring me to Birmingham.

Margaret became the first mother figure I would ever know, the gentle soul whom my father paid to take care of me. I would live with Margaret, her husband, and their seven-year-old daughter for the first six months of my life, until late in my first spring, when Daddy finally told Bigmama of my birth. Within the month, Bigmama boarded a plane to Birmingham to collect me from Margaret Tripp's home and bring me back to South Central. From that day on, I was hers.

My return to Los Angeles would be brushed by history in the process of being made. Swaddled in my grandmother's sturdy brown arms, I traveled back to the city on June 6, 1968. We had departed Birmingham on a morning flight and landed at Los Angeles International Airport in the early afternoon, just as the body of Robert F. Kennedy was being loaded onto Air Force One. The plane had been sent by President Lyndon B. Johnson to bring the slain senator home to New York, along with almost a hundred mourning family members and friends. In an indelible entry in American history, Bobby Kennedy had been victorious in California's Democratic presidential primary two nights before, and had given a rousing speech that evening in the packed ballroom of L.A.'s Ambassador Hotel. Shortly after midnight, as he exited the stage area through the hotel's pantry, several shots suddenly rang out. When the *pop pop pop* that sounded like exploding firecrackers finally ended, the junior senator from New York lay mortally wounded, a pool of red blooming under his head.

As Bigmama held me to her bosom, shushing my restless whimpers while we waited at the far end of an LAX runway, she already knew that her son had been the first physician to kneel at Bobby Kennedy's side. As a party delegate from Compton, Ross had campaigned with Kennedy during the weeks leading up to the primary, and had been in the ballroom for his victory speech, hope soaring that a true ally of the Civil Rights movement might yet become the nation's next president. And then came the call over a loudspeaker: "Is there a doctor in the house? If there is a doctor in the house, please come to the stage at once." My father pushed through the crowd and started to climb onto the stage, but Secret Service men barred his way, not believing at first that this tall, clean-cut Black man was a physician. When he finally convinced them of his credentials, they grabbed his arm and hurried him to the kitchen, where the candidate and five others lay bleeding on the concrete floor.

Bobby Kennedy would die less than twenty-six hours later, in the early morning hours of June 6, 1968. Whenever my dad recounted the story afterward, his voice thickened with sorrow as he recalled assessing Kennedy's vitals and realizing there was nothing any doctor could do to save him. Of the four bullets that struck the candidate, each fired at close range, one had entered behind his ear, ripping through his brain and sealing his fate. All my father could do at that point was to make the senator more comfortable and try to help the others who had been wounded.

Daddy could never tell the story of that night without also feeling the weight of an earlier tragedy, when another of his heroes, Dr. Martin Luther King Jr. had been assassinated just two months before. Indeed, it had been Dr. King's execution on April 4 of that year that had prompted my father to finally tell Bigmama about me. The world seemed to him to be going up in flames, and who knew how long any of us had left? Suddenly, he couldn't bear the thought that a daughter of his should remain a secret from the loving educator who had raised him.

That afternoon, as I finally dozed against Bigmama's shoulder, waiting for Air Force One to depart, few people had any idea just how historic its passenger manifest actually was. As a reporter many years later, I would run across an obscure news clip noting that the world's three most famous widows of slain leaders had been aboard, two of them offering the newest member of their circle what thin solace they could.

Coretta Scott King had been in Washington, D.C., when news broke of the shooting at the Ambassador Hotel. A family friend later recalled how Coretta broke down in front of her television set, sobbing from the depths of herself at the loss of yet another champion of righteousness. The friend recalled how, after Martin had been cut down on the balcony of the Lorraine Motel two months before, it had been Bobby Kennedy who arranged to fly his widow to Memphis to collect his body. Now, as Coretta finally allowed herself to weep without restraint, no longer needing to project strength for the sake of Martin's movement allies, there was only one place that she wanted to be—at Ethel Kennedy's side. She knew she was one of the few who could understand the public mourning Bobby's widow would now have to perform with a dignity and stoicism that were impossible to truly feel.

Jacqueline Kennedy understood this particular agony, too. She had stood in Ethel's shoes five years earlier, when another hail of bullets had ended the life of her husband, President John F. Kennedy, on a sunny Dallas afternoon. Jackie Kennedy was in London when she learned that her brother-in-law had been shot and would likely not survive the night. She, too, immediately made her way to Ethel's side. Now, at the other end of the airport tarmac from where Bigmama cradled me, Air Force One taxied down the runway and lifted into the air, passing above us as the three widows consoled one another, their stories of loss marking my homecoming.

THE DAY CAME THAT IRIS LEARNED OF MY BIRTH.

Her discovery of my existence was as a result of carelessness on my grandmother's part, although I have always suspected that Bigmama was simply tired of keeping me a secret. Soon after my first birthday, she had brought me with her to afternoon tea at the home of friends, later insisting she had no idea that Iris would also be in attendance. As it wasn't in Bigmama's nature to be intentionally cruel, I believe this to be true. But gossip also swirled among family and friends that there was no love lost between Bigmama and Iris, for reasons I can only surmise. Perhaps it was simply that Iris was standoffish, and Bigmama never warmed up to her. Whatever the cause of their disaffection, there I was, toddling from knee to knee in that room filled with gracious Black ladies sipping from teacups held in perfectly manicured hands. Under my mass of curly dark brown hair, my father's features were unmistakable on my face, and for anyone in doubt, Bigmama's devotion to me made everything crystal clear.

Iris confided to a neighbor afterward that as she watched me with my grandmother that afternoon, she knew exactly who I was, though she said nothing to reveal what she had discerned. Bigmama admitted to me many years later that she had felt remorseful when she noted Iris's stiff posture and lips pressed together in a grim line. She realized that her daughter-in-law was embarrassed and seething, and without a doubt, hurting, too.

At the time, my father was away at a Black doctors convention, otherwise he would surely have stopped what happened next. Iris went home that afternoon, and before the week was out, she had packed up three-year-old Adrienne's belongings and taken my sister back to the agency from which she and Ross adopted her. I cannot begin to understand what she was thinking. Perhaps she told herself that Ross had insisted on two daughters, and damned if she was going to allow him three. Or maybe she had never wanted the darker-hued child, though it pains me to consider such a possibility. In any case, she kept light-skinned, straight-haired Cheryl and divested herself of her dark-skinned, woolly-haired sister. By the time Ross returned home on Friday, his daughter Adrienne was lost to him.

There would be no reversing this devastating event—not for my sister, whom I would now never get to meet, or for my dad. The adoption agency would not return Adrienne to a family in which the mother had demonstrated such a lack of commitment to her welfare, no matter how ardently my father petitioned them. Relatives and friends were aghast at what Iris had done, and the whispers began. As the years passed, it became apparent that my sister Cheryl, though intellectually bright, suffered from undefined social issues; Bigmama, the former teacher, believed that she might be on the autism spectrum, though she was never officially diagnosed. Family members and friends now muttered variations of "Iris kept the pretty child and gave away the sensible one." It was a statement only marginally less harsh than the more usual utterance: "Iris kept the fair-skinned child and took back the little dark one."

It wasn't long before it occurred to me that, to my own mother, I had been "the little dark one," too. Hearing the whispers, I slowly absorbed that it was the difference between my sisters' skin colors that had sealed Adrienne's rejection by her adopted mother, and I tried to work out exactly what role my own complexion might have played in the Caucasian lady rejecting me, too.

For Ross, Iris's cruelty toward Adrienne could not be redeemed. Their union was irrevocably broken. After they separated and Cheryl went to live with her mother, I saw my sister only once a month, on those occasions when Daddy brought her to visit Bigmama and me. Though she was two years older, I felt oddly protective toward her. Cheryl continued to be skittish even around family members. A voracious reader, she preferred to curl up inside the house with one of her chapter books, determinedly ignoring everyone. I was more like our father, energetic and outgoing, and I loved being outdoors, playing imaginary games in Bigmama's backyard. But there was another reason I felt the need to watch over my sister. With a child's understanding, I had fathomed that when Cheryl's mother learned about me, she had done an unforgivable thing. I never stopped worrying that if I made a wrong move—even though I had no idea what such a move might be—my remaining sister might be in jeopardy, too.

I never verbalized this feeling to Bigmama or my father. I doubt I could have articulated it to myself back then. All I knew was that I felt somehow responsible for the loss of Adrienne, as if Iris taking her back to the adoption agency had been my fault alone. Though I now recognize that I was completely innocent in this event, and eventually relaxed into the assurance that Cheryl was in our family to stay, it would be many more years before I grasped the excruciating irony that a girl whose mother had left her behind in a hospital nursery had been the catalyst for another girl losing the only mother she had ever known. As I grew older, I burned with wondering whether Adrienne had ever found a mother who stayed—and whether I would ever again gaze into the face of the mother who did not.

TWO

Bigmama's House

Bigmama was seventy-three when she brought me back to South Central. As I was just six months old, for me this day exists only in the retelling of it by my cousin Lynn, the youngest child and only daughter among Aunt Edna's five children. Lynn was supposed to fly with us from Birmingham. A month away from her sixth birthday, she was excited at finally being old enough to spend part of the summer with Bigmama, as her older brothers Thomas Jr., Reggie, Eric, and Paul had done.

Though Lynn had never spent so much as a night away from her parents, she had been lured by the promise of being able to "play with the baby" at Bigmama's house. With Aunt Edna and Uncle Thomas on either side, she had crossed the hot tarmac ahead of Bigmama and me, a squirming bundle in my grandmother's arms. But as Lynn watched the looming metal stairs being wheeled to the airplane door, she began to have doubts. The three of us ascended the stairs, and Lynn was all buckled into her window seat, peering through the thick oval pane at her parents on the blacktop outside, when she noticed how much smaller they appeared than when she'd let go of their hands and climbed up the stairs just moments before. She remembered the planes she'd often seen streaking overhead, tiny silver bullets in the sky. Reflecting on how the people inside managed to shrink themselves that small, she suddenly realized she had no idea how to pull off such magic.

In one frantic motion Lynn had clicked open her seat belt, clambered over Bigmama's knees, and was running up the aisle and down the steps to her parents. When the stairs were finally rolled away and the plane doors closed, Lynn was still outside on the tarmac, leaving Bigmama and her littlest grandbaby inside the aircraft, the two of us staring into each other's eyes, forging an unshakable alliance as we crossed the continent toward home.

Bigmama didn't bother to get me a crib; she just tucked me in next to her at night, a wall of pillows securing the bed's far edge should I roll away from her. I would share my grandmother's bed until I was almost seven years old, dreaming nightly next to her sleeping form. A stately woman, Bigmama wore her permed iron gray hair gently waved around her face or subdued in a low bun. She was always impeccably dressed in garments ordered from catalogs sent to her by Aunt Edna. Even her nightgowns were soft satiny affairs, yet her demeanor was without frills. My grandmother was a woman of few words, making her seem stern and unflappable, so if you weren't paying attention, you might miss the softness that settled into her features when she gazed on those she loved, or the way her eyes might suddenly dance mid-conversation, as if she was in on a joke that she alone knew. I knew that Bigmama doted on me, the surprise child of her sunset years. As thoroughly as she would correct, caution, and chastise me if she felt the occasion merited it, I rested easily in the tenderness of her expression whenever she turned toward me.

I resided with my grandmother at 1100 West 80th Street in the shadow of Pepperdine University, before it moved its main campus to Malibu ten years after I was born. A romantic central turret and two black-shingled gables crowned the crisp, off-white façade of Bigmama's traditional storybook house, and arched entryways led to spacious rooms and a working fireplace within. The living area was appointed with white lace sheers at the windows and mahogany antiques that Bigmama had acquired through her six decades of marriage. Beatrice Burson Miller and Ross Matthew Miller Sr. had started out as newly-weds in Boston, my grandfather's hometown. After eloping in the summer of 1924, Beatrice and her new husband had moved in with his widowed mother and younger sister. Both schoolteachers with graduate degrees, Beatrice and Ross soon welcomed a daughter, Edna, born in July 1925, with my father, Ross Jr., joining his sister in February 1929.

A year later, the family relocated to East St. Louis, Illinois, where my grandfather had accepted a position as an elementary school principal. East St. Louis sits on the Illinois shore of the Mississippi River, across from St. Louis, Missouri. Though technically in a midwestern state, when my grandparents lived there the city was every bit as oppressive as the Jim Crow South. Sixty-three years earlier, across the river, a Black man named Dred Scott had sued for his liberty under a local statute stating that enslaved persons who traveled to states where slavery was outlawed, automatically became free, even if they later resided in a slave-holding state. Dred Scott had traveled with his master to the free states of Illinois and Wisconsin. On his return to Missouri, he sued his master, arguing that having traveled to non-slaveholding states, he was now a free man.

The landmark case went all the way to the Supreme Court, which in 1857 infamously ruled that a Black man has "no rights that the White man was bound to respect." This ruling would remain in effect until 1868, five years after emancipation, when the Fourteenth Amendment guaranteed full rights of citizenship to all persons born on American soil regardless of skin color. But this grant of birthright did little to counter the racial discrimination that would be progressively encoded in the nation's very institutions through the passing of Jim Crow segregation laws.

Into this separate and unequal world, Bigmama brought all the refinement and stoicism of her genteel Texas upbringing. Her father,

Edward Burson, the son of a former slave, had earned the reputation of being one of the finest Pullman porters in the Lone Star State, a leader in that brotherhood of Negro sleeping-car porters who would later unionize the transportation industry and help to organize the 1963 March on Washington. In the late 1800s and well into the next century, Edward Burson was also employed by the racially exclusive Dallas Country Club in Highland Park. A tall, lean, and dignified-looking figure with a painter's brush mustache, my great-grandfather graciously navigated this playground of wealthy White elites, collecting tips as a server and quietly amassing a small fortune for a colored man of his apparently lowly status. For him the equation was simple: He would endure the slights and indignities of his humble station so that he might provide a comfortable life for his wife, Edna Dade Burson, and properly educate his three children.

My grandmother, the oldest, was born in Dallas in 1895. Her sister, the middle child, would die of scarlet fever at the age of twelve, while her brother, the youngest of the three, would survive into adulthood but bear no children. And so it fell to Beatrice to carry on the Burson line. An academically gifted child, she had roamed happily inside the family's sixteen-room mansion, which she always made a point of reminding me had been equipped with modern indoor plumbing. My grandmother had also been the only Black teenager in Dallas to have her own Neiman Marcus charge card—though she was obliged to wait for nighttime Negro shopping hours to use it. She had attended a prestigious Black boarding school in the South, graduating with her high school diploma in 1912, at the height of the women's suffrage movement. Admitted to Howard University, then the most prominent of the nation's Historically Black Colleges and Universities (HBCUs), she would journey east to Washington, D.C., by train, comforted by the knowledge that her father, Edward, had instructed his fellow Pullman porters to watch over his firstborn and secure her safe passage to the nation's capital.

At Howard, Beatrice blossomed fully into the bon vivant socialite she had always been at heart. In Texas, there had been few outlets for an intellectually brilliant Black girl of gracious tastes, but now she was able to join social clubs, including the legendary Alpha Kappa Alpha Sorority, Inc. She threw herself into helping with neighborhood food drives, tutoring local schoolchildren, organizing fundraisers and fashion shows, and engaging in passionate political debates that were an everyday part of her Howard experience. She amassed a wide array of friends who would go on to become leaders in every sphere of Black American life, and she would keep track of each one for decades afterward, through marriages and births and transitions in career, health, and geography. My grandmother was legendary for never losing a friend.

Upon earning her bachelor's from Howard, Beatrice headed north to attend Columbia University's Teachers College, having decided to pursue a master's in education. It was on a train platform in New York City that mutual friends introduced her to my grandfather, also an aspiring educator, who was visiting from Boston. Ross and Beatrice corresponded for a year after that first encounter, and eloped six weeks after their second meeting.

In East St. Louis, Ross and Beatrice settled with their children in a segregated neighborhood of Black achievers. There, they became friendly with a prosperous dentist and his wife, a classical violinist and music teacher, who lived down the street. The couple's daughter, Dorothy Mae, was the same age as my Aunt Edna, and the two would become lifelong friends. Their son, a year younger than the girls, would defy his mother's wish for him to study the violin, falling in love with the trumpet instead. He would grow up to become the world-renowned jazzman Miles Davis.

Miles was a scrawny and headstrong boy, "always a little bit eccentric," Bigmama told me. She shared that she used to keep chickens in her unfenced side yard, and ten-year-old Miles would career down the street on his bicycle, chasing them on purpose, laughing wildly as he set off a frantic rustling of feathers. One day he ran over one of the chickens. It was an accident; Miles wasn't being mean, Big-mama explained, but he had been reckless. She was so furious that she stormed out to the street and lifted bony young Miles right off his bike and gave him the thrashing of his life. Ignoring his outraged sobs, she sent him on home with an instruction to "tell your mother what you did, and that I spanked you for it." That was my Bigmama. She believed children should be disciplined both in and out of the classroom, and that Black children in particular could not afford to set a foot wrong without being corrected by a caring elder, because the rules were more stringent for us.

My father, Ross, had tried to skirt the line his parents drew. The youngest Eagle Scout east of the Mississippi, as a fourteen-year-old he already had an eye for the ladies. His parents knew it, too, which is why Bigmama had cautioned Ross not to "run behind" a girl from the neighborhood who was two years older than he was and "much too fast" for her own good. My father asked the young woman out on a movie date anyway, figuring that what his parents didn't know couldn't hurt anyone. But as he and the young lady boarded the bus that would take them to the Negro movie theater across town, there sat my grand-mother with hands crossed demurely over her purse in the seat right next to the back door, where Black folks entered.

"Good afternoon, Mr. Miller," she pleasantly greeted her son, pre-tending not to have noticed the young lady.

"Good afternoon, Mrs. Miller," my father croaked before sheep-ishly making his way past her to the farthest row.

His defiance of his mother's wishes was made harder to bear by the fact that when he arrived home that evening, Bigmama said not a word about having seen him on the bus earlier. Her silence on the matter only made him feel guilty and wrong. And, unaware that his mother hadn't mentioned the deceit to his father, Ross waited for weeks and then months for the other shoe to fall. Though both my father and Bigmama considered the whole episode uproariously funny by the time I came along, back then Daddy was convinced that Bigmama had spies everywhere in town, reporting on his movements. He resolved to never again sneak around behind his mother's back, and claimed to have stayed true to that resolution. When he related this story to me many years later, I did not point out that the first six months of my life were a rather notable exception.

My father graduated high school at the top of his class and enrolled at his mother's alma mater at age fifteen, earning his bachelor's degree from Howard in two and a half years, and his M.D. from its medical school by the time he turned twenty-one. After a general surgery internship in Newark, New Jersey, and a residency in thoracic surgery in Nashville, Tennessee, he headed west to Los Angeles in the late 1950s. By then, his old neighborhood in East St. Louis was in steep decline, its once-budding prosperity choked by redlining banking practices and other forms of institutional neglect. It hadn't taken much for Ross to persuade his parents to join him in the shining City of Angels on the Pacific edge of the continent, where jobs were plentiful, the climate mild, homes affordable, and everything seemed possible and new. Already living in Compton, Ross helped his parents purchase the double lot house in an area called Vermont Knolls. My grandparents moved in at the start of a trickle that became a torrent of White flight as more people of color bought homes in the neighborhood. By the time I was born in the late 1960s, Vermont Knolls had been folded in with Compton and Watts to form South Central, which everyone knew was shorthand for "Black and Brown L.A."

Growing up, I never quite understood that our well-tended street was considered to be the hood. In South Central, under Bigmama's care, I spent my earliest years reading and playing imaginary games with my dolls, painting at a card table set up in the backyard, or running through the side garden with my friend Lois from next door. A year younger than me, she helped me stave off the loneliness of being an only child in an elder's home as we laughed and shared secrets among the pink hibiscus, blood red poinsettias, exotic birds of paradise, roses of every hue, and succulents of every description that my departed grandfather had planted. Only when I grew tall enough to pick ripening fruit from the peach, persimmon, avocado, and lemon trees that my grandfather had once meticulously tended, did I begin to notice that other children knew their mothers and I did not, and there were missing pieces to my story.

"BIGMAMA, HOW COME I DON'T HAVE A MOTHER?" I QUERIED MY grandmother one night as she stood over the kitchen sink washing bowls from which we had eaten her okra and tomato goulash for dinner.

I was on the floor near her feet, playing with my doctor Barbie, her cocoa brown skin set off by a starched white coat, pink plastic stethoscope, and Diana Ross cloud of crinkly black hair. At four years old, I had just spent my first week of kindergarten closely observing morning drop-offs, and it had left me with some questions: "All the other kids have mommies, Bigmama, so why don't I have one, too?"

"Oh, everybody has a mother," Bigmama told me mildly, confirming what I already suspected. "I met yours. She was light-skinned, a Caucasian lady."

"Where is the 'Casian lady now?" I wanted to know.

"I really have no idea," Bigmama said, frowning at the glass into which she was now squirting blue dish soap. "Why don't you ask your father?"

Though Daddy had never lived with Bigmama and me, he came by to see us almost every afternoon or evening. And so the next day after school, I perched myself at the top of the steps that led from the kitchen to the side yard, watching for his car to turn into our driveway.

"Where did my mother go?" I yelled out as soon as I saw him. I bounded down the steps and barreled across the yard toward him as he unfolded his tall, brown-suited frame from the driver's seat. "I want to know where my mother is," I repeated breathlessly, hopping from one leg to the other. "Bigmama said you'd know."

As I recall, I would ask my father this question a hundred times that year, seeking an answer concrete enough for my four-year-old mind to understand. Back then, I was neither hurt nor offended that my mother had chosen not to stay. I was simply curious: Other little girls lived with their mommies and daddies, while I lived with my paternal grandmother and had a father who was always around but whose home was elsewhere. Why was I different from other little girls? I think I was asking only that, but it was never the question Daddy answered.

"Well, Michelle, your father met your mother, they fell in love, and then they had you," he told me on the afternoon that I first posed the question. He would phrase his response that way every single time afterward, the same sentence delivered like a recitation, offering up the barest outline of the relationship that had led to my conception. His use of the third person made me wonder whether he was the man in the story, but his care and constancy told me that he must be, which only unearthed more questions.

"Why did my mother leave us?" I pressed him when he showed up on my fifth birthday, bearing my gift of a pristine boxed set of Encyclopedia Britannicas encircled by a big red bow. "Why did she leave me?"

This line of interrogation was new—*where* had evolved to *why*—and I had lobbed the question from left field while my unsuspecting father was bent over stacking the thick black-and-red volumes on a low shelf of the bookcase in Bigmama's study. Daddy straightened up from his task and gazed down at me thoughtfully. Whenever I call back this moment, I can see my father pulling himself in carefully, as if to sequester all memory within the stillness of his posture and the flat look of his eyes behind his black horn-rimmed spectacles.

"Your mother couldn't stay," he said at last.

Until I was nine years old, no matter how many times I posed this particular question, it was the only answer he would ever give me.

THREE

After the Fall

Your grandfather sure did love that garden," Bigmama murmured as she stood at the kitchen window watching Robert, a small, wiry, blue-black man in his forties who came each week to water the riot of plantings, trim the hedges, mow the grass, and prune the fruit trees. "Ross wouldn't let a fallen leaf sit for so much as a minute on his lawn," Bigmama added softly as she turned back to preparing the meal she always made for Robert to eat when his labor was done.

Robert not only tended the garden, he was also a meticulous house-cleaner, finding corners that Bigmama's arthritis would no longer allow her to reach. I understood vaguely that Robert struggled with aspects of human interaction that others took for granted. Like my sister Cheryl, he was excessively shy and reticent to meet anyone's eyes. I thought that might explain why Bigmama felt so protective of him, sighing heavily as she watched him work, as if his very industry made her sad.

Robert was the son of one of Bigmama's tenants in a four-story walk-up on the other side of the freeway. Before my grandfather died, rent collection had been his job, but now the monthly task fell to Bigmama. Later, as gang activity gained a foothold in the neighborhood, my father would persuade Bigmama to sell the building, so she wouldn't have to climb the four stories knocking on doors each month, with drug buys possibly going down in the stairwell. Daddy worried about the escalation in crime, but as far as I could tell, Bigmama never did. Until the day she sold the property, she felt responsible for her tenants, and when one lost a job, or a child fell ill, she would tide them over, letting them make good on the rent the next month, or the one after that.

I usually accompanied my grandmother to collect rent on the first Saturday of the month, and so I had met Robert's mother, a now elderly, rail-thin woman who always grasped Bigmama's hands with an expression on her face that I could not name back then. Maybe desperation came close—a kind of disbelief mixed with gratitude and fear, as if trusting anyone's kindness was a fragile bargain. But Bigmama had decided Robert was a soul in need of her particular attention. Years before, when Robert was a teenager, Bigmama had seen how he struggled in school with limited success despite his diligent soul. The teacher in her folded him into her heart, and at some point when he became an adult she had hired him to help her around the house and yard. Now, as he gardened and cleaned each week, she would cook him a hearty supper of spaghetti and meat sauce, or stewed chicken with candied yams with a big tub of collard greens that she'd soaked all day. Sometimes, she'd make her buttery cornbread with barbecue ribs, always crowning the meal with her delicious peach cobbler.

Bigmama and I ate more simply when it was just the two of us. Dinner might be rice and beans, or my absolute favorite, her goulash with okra, corn and tomatoes, which we'd sop up with slices of soft white bread. And one night a week, we'd eat fast food, McDonald's or Sloppy Joes, but never Burger King. Bigmama had her brand favorites, which I never questioned. Daddy later explained that her rationale was generally based in some social justice detail—for example, she only bought Pepsi, never Coke, because Pepsi had been the first corporation in the country to hire Negro ad men back in the forties and fifties, when the company wanted to challenge Coke's market share among Black Americans in the South. Bigmama was loyal that way, not just to brand names, but also to people.

"Bigmama, you don't cook as fancy for me as you do for Robert," I once complained as I sat at the kitchen table, watching her flurry of activity while the rusty old lawnmower whirred plaintively outside. Bigmama didn't indulge me. "Oh, hush, child," she admonished. "You don't need the kind of nourishing that Robert does."

At the time, I didn't think much about her response, but years later, when her words came back to me, I realized that Bigmama had set herself the task of helping Robert to feel worthy and whole. When Robert finally sat down to eat in the late afternoon, I could see how happy Bigmama made him, serving him second helpings and acting as the most gracious of hosts, fussing over him, as I'm sure no one else in his life ever had. Perhaps ever could. I took quiet notes on my grandmother's intentional way of showing Robert that he mattered, that she saw him as fully worth her singular attention. Watching them, I never let on that deep inside, I felt a bit like Robert myself. I understood how fortunate I was to be growing up under Bigmama's pragmatic care. And yet, when I played hide-and-seek in the garden with Lois, and her mother would lean out the kitchen window and call her home when it started to get dark, I'd watch my friend's small figure retreating across the yard and disappearing into the house next door, a knot of loneliness tightening in my throat.

As I turned toward my own home, where Bigmama waited for me, perhaps cooking dinner in the kitchen, or bent over the dining room table, absorbed in writing letters to distant friends, the awareness of being motherless crept inside me like a whisper. I reflected that even solitary Robert had a mother waiting for him at home, and in those moments, I almost envied him.

I SCRUNCHED MY EYES TIGHT AND WRIGGLED AWAY FROM THE COLD, wet washcloth that Bigmama placed over my face, her usual method of coaxing me awake.

"Bigmamaaa," I whined, drawing out her name.

"Get up now, Michelle," she said, lifting the cloth and looking down at me with a hint of a smile. "You don't want to be late for school."

My grandmother was already dressed for the day as I rolled out of bed to stand obediently in front of her, allowing her to turn my chin this way and that as she vigorously wiped the sleep out of my eyes with the wet cloth. Then she pointed me toward the bathroom to finish washing up. Minutes later, I emerged to find Bigmama sitting in the green armchair next to the window, comb and hairbrush in hand. Laid out on the now-made bed were the clothes I had picked out the night before, a pink floral top with puff sleeves and a pair of apple green capris, coincidentally the colors of Bigmama's Alpha Kappa Alpha sorority. Though pink and green were my favorite colors that year, I was still only in the second grade, and didn't yet know about the proud Black sisterhood my grandmother had pledged while a student at Howard University. My understanding of the group's service on behalf of the African American community, and my sense of the sorority as being synonymous with Black pride, celebration, and joy, wouldn't come until much later.

I settled myself on an ottoman in front of Bigmama, my back pressed against her knees. She dipped two fingers into a jar of creamy white pomade and worked it through my hair from roots to ends, taming the frizz and the flyaways, adding sleekness and shine as she sweet-talked the comb through my tangles. She then drew a swift straight part down the center of my head and gathered handfuls of hair into two fat braids, securing the ends with pink and green bubble elastics to match the day's outfit. Finally, she tapped my shoulder to signal she was done.

I jumped to my feet and slipped into my school clothes quickly, knowing that Mrs. Holmes would be waiting. She lived across the street from us with her husband, and ever since Bigmama had fallen on the side steps of our house and broken her hip some months before, Mrs. Holmes had taken over driving me to first grade in the mornings.

Lorraine Holmes and her husband John were transplants from Louisiana, Black Creoles with skin the color of red earth and accents rich with the Bayou. Every morning, Mrs. Holmes would put out a slice of cinnamon raisin toast and a glass of grapefruit juice for me while she and Mr. Holmes finished getting ready for their day. I would sit at their kitchen table daydreaming that I was part of a regular household with a mom and dad, eating breakfast before school like the kids I saw on *The Brady Bunch*.

But as much as I enjoyed the homey tableau in my neighbors' kitchen, I found it hard to forget the events that had brought me there—the chilly morning when Bigmama had tumbled on the stairs.

Standing at the top of the steps leading from the kitchen to the side yard, Bigmama had sent me back to get a sweater before proceeding down the stairs on her own. Normally, I would have been at her side, holding her hand as she navigated the steep concrete steps, seven of them set against the house like a three-sided pyramid. With no railings on any side, the stairs could be treacherous for a tall, big-boned woman pushing eighty. Sure enough, that day Bigmama missed her footing. When I came back out, sweater in hand, I found her sitting midway down the pyramid.

"Bigmama, what are you doing?" I asked, confused to see her seated there.

"I fell," she said through teeth clenched over a grimace. Now I noticed that her face was contorted with pain, though when she slipped she hadn't made a sound.

"Bigmama, you were supposed to wait for me!" I cried, racing to her side. Terrified, I knelt at her shoulder and took her hand into my lap, looking around wildly for someone who might be able to help us. Fortuitously, Mrs. Holmes's father, who was visiting from Louisiana, was out walking in the yard and had seen Bigmama fall. He rushed across the street to offer assistance, but quickly assessed that maybe Bigmama had broken something, and was better off sitting where she was until the paramedics came. I smoothed strands of Bigmama's hair off her damp forehead as Mrs. Holmes's father ran into the kitchen to call an ambulance. By this time, more neighbors were filing into the yard. Soon the Smiths from across the street, and Mr. Tolson from down the block, and the Cannons, an elderly White couple who lived on one side of us, were all standing in a circle around Bigmama and me. My chest heaved and tears pooled at the sight of my strong, capable grandmother so stranded and in pain. I tried to swallow the sobs breaking from me, in vain. *What if Bigmama is so hurt she can't take care of me anymore?* I thought, my panic rising. *Where will I go?*

Noticing my escalating emotion, Bigmama began stroking my hand. Speaking with some effort, she suggested that perhaps Leon, the Smiths' sixteen-year-old son, might be able to drive me to school. Mr. Smith left to go and get Leon, and soon the family's white Chevy was pulling into the yard with Leon slouched at the wheel, sporting his fledgling Afro and perpetually bored countenance. Still fretting and hyperventilating, I kissed my grandmother's hand and obediently climbed into the back seat of the Smiths' boat of a car. Kneeling on the seat and peering out the rear window, I watched the cluster of people in our yard grow smaller and more distant, and then disappear. I felt relief when an ambulance screamed past, heading toward Bigmama.

Leon continued slowly up our street as I turned from the rear window and sat still as a statue in the middle of the plastic-covered back seat. I stared straight ahead as the car made the first left onto South Mariposa Avenue. As soon as Leon rounded the corner, a new set of sirens split the morning, and a police cruiser tucked in behind us. Leon pulled over at once, glancing back at me nervously, his bored expression gone, his eyes wide and boyish face frozen. He shut off the ignition and placed both hands in plain sight on the steering wheel.

Even though I was only in first grade, I already knew to be wary of the police. Once, when a public service announcement promoting an Officer Friendly had played on our television, Bigmama had looked at me and said, "Don't ever go to a police officer if you're in trouble, Michelle. You just come to your father or me instead." She spoke sternly, using the voice she reserved for lessons she sincerely wanted me to absorb. It dawned on me now that the only time I had ever seen the police in my neighborhood was when there was a problem, and they never appeared friendly. And now, here we were, with police officers pulling Leon over for no reason my five-year-old mind could fathom, their blue uniforms filling the car windows, ruddy faces scowling at me in the back seat.

The cops took Leon's license and walked back to their cruiser. We waited an eternity for them to return. I sat in the back seat praying they would let Leon go, but just in case, I began mentally retracing my steps to home in case I had to run back and let everyone know the police had taken Leon. In the midst of my contingency planning, the cops walked back to the car, handed Leon his license and waved us on. As he restarted the ignition and drove me the remaining six blocks to Marie Fegan School, the silence inside the car was heavy.

School that day was a blur. All I remember was a single cord of fear strumming inside me: *What if Bigmama can't take care of me anymore?* And a prayer: *Please, God, let Bigmama be okay?* How selfish of me, I think now. Somehow, though my father still came by to see me and Bigmama several days each week, and I had occasionally stayed over at his sparsely furnished one-bedroom condo on weekends, I had no desire to move in with him full time. With his days consumed by hospital rounds, clinic hours, community events, and city council meetings, home for him was a mere pit stop, definitely not a place for me to settle in and feel safe and attended to as I did at Bigmama's house. No,

I was convinced I needed a mother or an older woman to wipe the sleep from my eyes every morning, to help me lay out my clothes for school and tame the unruly mass of my hair before sending me off for the day, pressed and pristine.

Bigmama usually picked me up at the end of classes, sometimes driving, sometimes walking. But that afternoon, Mrs. Holmes came to get me, explaining that my father had called and asked her to keep me at her home for a few hours, until doctors at the hospital finished doing whatever it was they needed to do to fix Bigmama's injury. I cannot describe to you the joy that flashed through me when at about seven o'clock that evening, my Aunt Edna's substantial form walked through the Holmeses' front door to collect me. She explained that she'd flown in from Birmingham earlier that afternoon, and planned to stay with us for a few weeks to help out while Bigmama healed.

I grasped her hand much too tightly, swinging our clasped fingers back and forth as we crossed the street back to our house. At the top of the driveway, before going inside, Aunt Edna paused. Bending toward me, she put one finger under my chin and lifted my face.

"Now, Michelle," she said, her voice gentle. "I don't want you to worry about Bigmama. She fractured her hip when she fell, but it wasn't a very bad break. Your grandmother is going to be just fine."

"Yes, Aunt Edna," I mumbled, chastened all over again that I hadn't been at Bigmama's side, holding her hand and helping her down the steep stairs.

On entering the living room, I ran to Bigmama and threw my arms around her neck, exhaling at the sight of her lying in her recliner, a quilt over her legs as she smiled and gestured for me to come and kiss her cheek hello.

The next several weeks would stand out for me as a particularly charmed interlude of my childhood. In that time, Aunt Edna started to become more real to me. No longer was she this lady in Birmingham whom I loved simply because she was my father's sister. As she walked me to school every morning, and picked me up every afternoon, she became the woman I laughed with as we dashed into the road to avoid the barking dog on our street, the one who invited me to pore over clothing catalogs with her as she instructed me in the finer points of style and how to spot a good deal. She also told me stories about my father as a boy, and shared the proud history of her extended Miller and Gardner clans.

From Aunt Edna, I learned that we were related by marriage to Arthur George Gaston, then the richest Black man in the American South. Raised in poverty in a rural Alabama log cabin, A. G. Gaston had later wed Aunt Edna's sister-in-law Minnie Gardner, one of sixteen siblings in Uncle Tom's family. With Minnie's help, A.G. had launched one successful business venture after another in Birmingham, using his wealth to support Civil Rights initiatives throughout the south. The A.G. Gaston Motel was a known safe house for movement allies, a place where they could gather to plan marches and other acts of civil disobedience. And when Eugene "Bull" Connor, Birmingham's notoriously racist Commissioner of Public Safety, had had Dr. King arrested for his movement activities in 1963, Aunt Edna's brother-in-law had paid the Civil Rights leader's bail of $160,000 from his own pocket.

I curled up next to my aunt and listened attentively as she traced the entire lineage of relatives I had met or would meet in her home, but whose backstories I had not known. She wanted me to understand that even if I didn't know my mother's people, I was connected to a proud legacy of Black achievers on my father's side. Among the family members she told me about was Carol Jenkins, the daughter of another of Uncle Tom's sisters. Carol had just been hired by NBC-TV in New York to host *Positively Black,* one of the first talk shows devoted to African American issues in the country. Carol would later write *Black Titan,* a biography of her maternal uncle A. G. Gaston, and though I had no idea of it back in 1973 when Aunt Edna first mentioned her name to me, she would also support my own future journalism aspirations, inviting me to visit her in New York City while I was in college, showing me around the NBC studios and introducing me to some of her colleagues.

It was during Aunt Edna's extended visit after Bigmama's fall that I was finally convinced to move out of my grandmother's bed and into my own bedroom down the hall. Aunt Edna helped me arrange my Barbies and books in my new quarters, and softened my transition to sleeping alone by reading to me every night until I fell asleep. I don't recall how long she stayed with us in South Central, but by the time Bigmama was once again walking with the help of a quad cane, and Aunt Edna was packing to return to her husband and children in Birmingham, she had become so much more than my favorite aunt. I had anointed her my "other" mother, a flesh-and-blood replacement for the one who had walked away from me at birth.

Aunt Edna would become the first of many women who, throughout my childhood and adolescence, I would look to for the kinds of instruction that girls normally get from their mothers, everyday lessons on *who* and *how* to be. Most of these women never suspected that I had adopted them as maternal surrogates, folding them with sweet longing into the secret places of my heart.

FOUR

Xernona and Me

I was peering into the hall mirror, trying to fix my own hair. It was a Saturday morning, and my grandmother had just informed me that Daddy was bringing a woman friend to meet me. Bigmama was still a little frail from her fall and hip-repair surgery several months before. Watching her carefully plant her quad cane as she picked her way across the living room to her favorite chair, I was already inventing for myself a hopeful story—which was that Daddy wanted to introduce me to someone who might become my new mother. If so, I had to make myself presentable, hence my effort to gather the wildness that grew out of my scalp into a ponytail that would be more decorous.

Suddenly, a stylishly attired woman appeared behind me in the mirror. I hardly noticed my father at her shoulder, so transfixed was I by his companion. He introduced her to me by the name of Big, which seemed to my child's mind entirely fitting. She was magnificent, a slender, caramel-skinned goddess of a woman with a shiny upsweep of hair, lively kohl-lined dark brown eyes, and red lips curved into an enigmatic smile.

"I want my hair to look like that!" I declared, turning and pointing to Big's up do. "Can you make my hair like yours?"

Big later confessed that she had been immediately taken with me. *This girl is decisive,* she recalled thinking. *She's not yet six but she knows what she wants, and she's not taking any less.* What I remember is Big smiling warmly and squatting down on her blue kitten heels to meet me at eye level.

"Okay," she said obligingly. "Why don't we try?"

That day as Big brushed and gathered my hair into a high ponytail tied by a yellow ribbon she pulled from her purse, I fell completely in love. She and my father wouldn't actually begin dating for another few months, but even I could sense the energy snapping in the air between them. I sat on the cool stone ledge of the fireplace and observed them as they laughed and chatted with Bigmama and me, and by the time they got up to leave, I was convinced I'd found the perfect new mother.

"Bigmama, I'm going with them," I declared, running to my room to retrieve my shoes. I needed to make sure Daddy knew I wanted Big to be my mother. But Bigmama seemed to have no idea of the moment's urgency.

"Not today, Michelle," she said when I came back into the room, my pink plastic sandals in hand. "You'll see them another time."

"No, I want to go now!" I insisted, becoming visibly upset. But no matter how much I held my ground, there was no convincing my grandmother—or my dad for that matter—to let me tag along as a third wheel.

"I'll tell you what," Big interjected after a few moments, trying to ease my disappointment. "I'll come back later this week and take you to lunch, just you and me. We'll fix up your hair just the way you want it, and we'll have a girls' date. How does that sound?"

Even as a young child, I had never been enamored of future prom-ises. I wanted things to happen *right now.* Only then could I be sure they would come to pass. But I calmed down somewhat at Big's sugges-tion of a girls' date. And every morning that week, as soon as Bigmama woke me from sleep, the first words out my mouth were, "Is this the day Biggie is coming to get me?"

Our date had been set for Thursday afternoon, and after what felt like an interminable stretch of days, it finally arrived. Big later reported to my father that I gave her the third degree, grilling her with "one hundred questions," asking how old she was, whether she was married (she had been, but wasn't now), and the big one: "When are you going to marry my dad?"

Fortunately, Big was more amused than offended by my interrogation. Years later, she shared what she'd been thinking: *Well, her father has strong views on everything, so why would I expect his child to be any less demanding? She's his daughter; she doesn't have a choice. Besides, when you get right down to it, she's actually a lot like me.* But recognizing the similarities we shared was no reason for Big to indulge my impropriety—I had, after all, crossed all sorts of lines with a grown woman, demanding answers to questions that weren't mine to ask. Even so, she was gentle.

"Whoa, hold up now, Michelle," she said, laughing and raising both palms in front of her face in mock defense. "Let's not get ahead of ourselves, okay? Why don't you and I just get acquainted first? Let's spend time together, and then we can see what happens down the road."

BIG'S ACTUAL NAME WAS XERNONA CLAYTON. SHE LIVED IN ATLANTA, but visited Los Angeles often to see her twin sister, Xenobia, whom everyone called Little. Xenobia and her husband Tony Smith were my father's closest friends, and their son Bradford, a year older than me, was like a brother. Most Saturday mornings, Daddy would pick me up and bring me with him to Little and Tony's house, where the party was always happening. My father's friends and their children assembled regularly at Little and Tony's for backyard barbecues, festive pool days, and impromptu Saturday night sleepovers. Often, when Daddy came to collect me for these gatherings, he would bring along his current romantic interest, and she would pay extra special attention to me, the two of us tacitly agreeing that she would be my pretend mother for the occasion. Some of these women I grew to dearly love—though few so ardently as Big. I wished that my father would hurry up and propose to her, but for a long time after his divorce from Iris, Daddy seemed to have decided that he was no longer the marrying sort.

It was no secret that Daddy enjoyed the ladies, and the ladies had a thing for him, too. Though in adolescence I would grow more critical of the way his romantic relationships often overlapped, as a child I saw all these affiliations as pure possibility. Each woman my father dated was a potential new mother for me, or so I believed with all the faith and simplicity of childhood. Anyone could see that Daddy cut a dashing figure; in the vernacular of courtship, he was definitely a catch. Tall, handsome, and knowledgeable about an endless range of topics, he had recently become head of surgery at the hospital, even as he continued his political activities within the Democratic Party. He had extensive social connections, especially among Black leaders and trailblazers. He had attended Howard University with many of them, and was sought after to help organize Civil Rights marches on the West Coast and throughout the country.

As admired as my father was, I felt special being his daughter. With him at my side, I could rest in the expectation of being welcomed into just about any room we entered. However, the social occasions I most enjoyed with my dad took place on weekend afternoons when I joined in the merriments at the home of Little and Tony. They lived about twenty minutes away in View Park, which was then considered the Black Beverly Hills. Little and Tony adored my dad as much as he loved them, and they welcomed me into their lives as if I were theirs by blood. My father was also their doctor, as both husband and wife suffered from chronic health problems. Xenobia had been diagnosed with multiple sclerosis as a young woman, and though she and her sister were identical, by the time I met them, Little was frailer of body than Xernona, her arms thin, her gait unsteady. In contrast, Tony appeared more robust, but whenever he shrugged off his shirt to join guests in the pool, you couldn't fail to notice the long, jagged scar snaking down the center of his chest, evidence of very serious heart surgery. Yet both Little and Tony moved through life with an infectious joy, making their home a hub of entertainments, fostering a familial atmosphere.

It was at Little and Tony's house that I learned how to swim alongside Bradford, with whom I had an easy, bantering rapport. His parents owned the first microwave I ever saw, and served me the first meal I ever ate warmed by this newfangled contraption, a plate of lasagna. And, in the company of Little and Big, I developed a taste for good coffee. I could think of nothing more sublime than being in the kitchen with these two impossibly chic and riveting women, sipping the aromatic brew. I wanted to be just like the sisters. And since Little was already married to Tony, Big was the one I prayed every night that my father would have the good sense to marry, thereby granting me a dazzling new mother.

Xernona Clayton was a giant of a woman, all four feet, eleven inches of her. As small as she was, she was mighty. Deeply involved in Civil Rights causes in Atlanta, she worked tirelessly to advance the agenda of Dr. King's organization, the Southern Christian Leadership Conference (SCLC). Big floated rather than walked across any room she was in, effortlessly holding everyone in thrall. As a couple, she and my dad were a formidable pair, intellectual equals, verbal jousting partners, each other's standing plus one at social events and political fundraisers whenever Big happened to be in town.

Xernona and Xenobia, née Brewster, were Oklahoma girls, born in 1930 to civil servant parents in Muskogee. With their vivacious optimism and identical tumble of dark curls, both twins later attended Tennessee State University together, where they were nicknamed "Miss Co-Everything." Xernona's star wattage was undeniable, and Xenobia, the younger twin by minutes, was content to let her sister hold center stage. They both pledged the AKA sorority in college, as my grandmother had done, and after graduation, they both moved to Chicago and worked undercover as investigators, exposing workplace discrimination for the local branch of the National Urban League.

Big married the nationally acclaimed journalist Ed Clayton in 1957, and two years later, the couple relocated to Los Angeles, where Ed had been charged with setting up West Coast offices for *Ebony* and *Jet* magazines. After Little was diagnosed with MS, Big convinced her to move closer to her in L.A. so she wouldn't have to face her health challenge alone. Not long after, a mutual friend introduced Xenobia to Tony, who oversaw security for a department store chain, and within the year they were wed. Given the twins' involvement in social justice causes, they and their husbands became a part of the same circle of Black activists and striving young professionals as my father. They attended the same charity events, supported the same Civil Rights initiatives, and marched shoulder to shoulder at national protests.

Around this time, Dr. Martin Luther King Jr. was trying to broaden his organization's membership umbrella in the fight for equality, and he began asking around to find someone who could elevate the SCLC's national public relations campaign. Several people recommended Ed Clayton, who flew to the Kings' home in Atlanta to explore how they might work together.

When Coretta Scott King explained to Ed that she planned to use her education and training in voice, piano, and violin to help raise money for the movement, Ed immediately suggested that she perform concerts in Black churches, whose congregations would be a natural launching pad. He recommended his wife Xernona to help with the logistics, and a few weeks later Big and Coretta were traveling to large urban centers and small rural towns on their first musical tour. In hotel rooms across the country, the two women shared their deepest hopes and confidences, and grew close. By the end of the tour, Xernona had consented to relocating to Atlanta with her husband to help manage operations for the SCLC.

Big was a natural born organizer. She could convince anybody to do anything, so it naturally fell to her and the team she put together to cover the logistics of planned marches and nonviolent acts of civil disobedience. Before all major protests, she ensured that attorneys were at the ready should participants run afoul of law enforcement and require legal assistance. She helped map the protest routes, provided water for the marchers, made sure adequate funds were raised to bail people out of jail, and had medics at the ready in case anyone got hurt. Big took care of all the myriad behind-the-scenes details to which few people ever gave a thought. She was essential to everything and everyone.

But in 1966, a little more than a year after Big and Ed moved to Atlanta, Ed suffered a heart attack, and died unexpectedly. As Xernona mourned her late husband with Coretta Scott King at her side, the women had no idea that in two short years, it would be her turn to support Coretta after her husband was gunned down on the balcony of the Lorraine Motel in Memphis. It was Xernona whom Coretta asked to sit next to her as she told her children that their father had been assassinated, and Xernona who made the arrangements for Coretta to fly to Tennessee and retrieve her husband's body. Big even convinced a local dress shop to provide a rack of appropriate garments for the grieving widow to wear for what would become several emotionally strenuous days of memorial appearances and services.

Years later, I would sit in Little and Tony's living room listening raptly as Big recounted the story of how she had been forced to reapply Dr. King's mortuary makeup as he lay in state at Spelman College in Atlanta. Xernona, standing beside the open casket, had been disturbed to note what looked like a daub of red clay on Dr. King's right cheek that had been left unblended by his undertakers. She appealed to the mortician to correct the unsightly blob, but the man insisted there was nothing he could do.

In her inimitable way, Xernona swung into action. She surveyed the chapel and noted the slain leader's dark-skinned mother sitting in the first pew, and then she looked over at Harry Belafonte's wife, who was White. She approached each woman and asked to borrow their face powders, which she then mixed together to create "a little roux" that more closely matched Dr. King's medium brown complexion. "Belafonte was standing there watching me," Big recalled. "And we put his handkerchief around Martin's neck to protect his shirt collar, and I proceeded to tone down the red clay blob with the powder I mixed up. It blended more evenly with the rest of his face and made such a difference." From the front pew, Coretta smiled gratefully.

CHILDREN SELDOM DREAM OF BECOMING WHAT THEY'VE NEVER SEEN, so perhaps I am a television news correspondent today because of the niche Big would create for herself as talk show host, and at my own future network no less. The year I was born, she had become the first Black woman to host her own television show in the South, *The Xernona Clayton Show*, which aired on the CBS-affiliate station in Atlanta. Famously, in 1968 when she interviewed Calvin Craig, then the Grand Dragon of the Georgia chapter of the Ku Klux Klan, she convinced him to subsequently quit the organization and renounce all that it stood for. She would later join the staff of Turner Broadcasting, becoming vice president for urban affairs in 1988, before going on to found the Trumpet Awards in 1993 to honor distinguished African Americans.

This was the sort of woman Big was. In the face of everyday bigotry or epic tragedy, she still managed to sweep regally into every space, scattering her light, forcing everyone around her to stand up straight. I particularly recall the times she took me to see her tape her talk show. How magical it was to watch everything come together behind the scenes, to sit at her side during hair and makeup, and then to stand in the darkened area of the studio as she walked onto the lighted set—glamorous, commanding, powerful.

Gazing at Big as she interviewed her talk show guests, I would fantasize about a future in which I, too, could boldly ask people whatever I wanted, knowing they would engage my questions. Oh, I was brimming with questions! I wanted to know everything about the world around me, but I was still only a child, and being actively coached by Bigmama not to overstep acceptable bounds. I could hardly wait until I was as old as Big, and able to ask anybody anything. It wasn't hard to figure out that my thirst for answers was rooted in the riddle that was my mother. Since transferring my maternal hopes to the person of Big, however, I had stopped pressing my father for details about the woman who had given birth to me, knowing by heart the frustratingly incomplete story he would offer in response.

On some level, I understood that my father felt that the full, unvarnished details of my mother's disappearance from my life weren't suitable for my hearing. Perhaps he worried about undermining my perception of him as the wise and benevolent father, as if I couldn't hold that truth about who he was alongside another reality I had already recognized: when it came to the women in his life, he was impossible to pin down, a player, a heartbreaker, a charming rogue. What he failed to understand was that, by withholding the facts from me, he had unwittingly implied that my beginnings were somehow shameful, a secret to be kept at all costs, the reasons dire and unknowable for a mere child.

I often felt like a traitor for missing my mother, for wanting so badly to unravel the reasons for her leaving, especially given that I was so well loved and cared for by my grandmother, my Aunt Edna, and now by Big, too. And yet, the mystery of my mother's whereabouts had only become larger with each passing year, to the point I sometimes thought that I might suffocate from the *not knowing*. But now, here was Big, who entertained my incessant questions in a way that felt open and unburdened, and who took me to see her work, modeling for me a life in which all of my agency could be laser focused on seeking—and receiving—*answers*.

I'm going to be like Big when I grow up, I remember thinking as I watched her on set in the television studio. *I'm going to do what she does.* As the future began to crystallize in imagination, I saw myself striding into the spotlight and asking guests *all the questions*, one after another after another until the well of not knowing finally ran dry.

DURING THE THREE YEARS THAT BIG AND MY FATHER WERE OFFI-cially a couple, one of my favorite parts of the summer months I would spend visiting my Birmingham family was when Aunt Edna and Uncle Tom would drive me to Atlanta to stay for a couple of weeks with Big. It would be just Biggie and me in her sprawling home, the two of us venturing into the city to explore. Some nights, Big would host her lively dinner parties, allowing me to stay up long enough to greet her guests, many of whom knew my father. Big would then put me to bed with instructions not to leave my room. This, I obeyed, though I would lie awake for as long as I could manage, enjoying the intermingling voices and bursts of laughter reaching my ears from the living room.

Invariably, I would run into Big's room much too early the following morning, leaping onto her bed and chattering about breakfast. After Big had stumbled to the kitchen to pour cereal and milk into a bowl for me one too many times, she decided I needed to learn how to do this for myself. Before her next dinner party, she led me to the kitchen, took down a box of corn flakes from the cupboard and placed it on the counter, showed me where the carton of milk was in the fridge, and explained that I would no longer need to wake her in the mornings as I was now old enough to handle breakfast on my own. I had watched her pour the cereal and milk into a bowl so many times, she was quite sure I would know what to do.

Feeling very grown up, I did as she had instructed the next morning, carefully re-closing the corn flakes box and returning the milk carton to the refrigerator before slurping down every last spoonful of cereal in my bowl. Deciding to go the extra step, I pulled a stool over to the sink and climbed onto it to wash the bowl and spoon, placing them carefully in the drying rack. Pleased with my initiative, I scampered down the hallway to Big's room and burst through her door.

"I did it, Biggie!" I cried happily. "I made my own breakfast just like you showed me! And I washed up everything, too!"

Big lifted a drowsy head and propped open one eye to take in the sight of me excitedly twirling beside her bed. She closed her eye again, moaned, and rolled over, pulling the covers over her head. "Very good, Michelle, I knew you could do it," she mumbled through the sheets. "But I rather think you missed the point of the assignment. Now go on and watch some cartoons until I come find you."

One year, during my scheduled time with her, Xernona had been asked to give the keynote speech at a conference in New Orleans. Rather than cut short our time by taking me back to Birmingham, she decided to bring me with her to the Crescent City. On the plane, I kicked off my shoes and socks and squatted on the floor in front of my seat, using it as a stage for my Barbies. I was clueless of the fact that, the way our flight had been scheduled, we would have very little time to spare for Big to check us into a hotel and freshen up before being whisked to the conference center. As our aircraft began its descent in preparation for landing, Big instructed me to get back in my seat and buckle my seat belt. I did as she asked, sweeping my Barbies onto the floor, my feet still bare. After the plane pulled up to the gate, Big urged me to return my dolls to my purple backpack so we'd be ready to disembark with no delay.

"But I have to find my shoes," I said.

"Your shoes—?" That's when she noticed my unshod feet. "Well, put them on quickly, Michelle. We have to get moving."

But my shoes had slid backward under several seats, my socks tucked inside them, and so we had to wait until everyone had exited the plane before I was able to track them down. By the time we got through baggage claim, found the man holding a sign that said "Xer-nona Clayton," and followed him to the black town car sent to collect us, Big was harried from hurrying and herding me, and I was huffing and puffing from running through the terminal on six-year-old legs. At last, we were finally settled in the car, our luggage in the trunk, as we headed to our hotel in the French Quarter. Exhausted from our early start in Atlanta that morning, and all our scurrying through the airport, I leaned my head against the window of the town car and fell promptly and deeply asleep.

At the hotel, Big and the limo driver were unloading our bags from the trunk when a bell captain approached the vehicle, reached for my door, and opened it. As the back windows were tinted, he hadn't noticed me leaning against the door. He jumped aside with alarm as I rolled right out of the seat and onto the sidewalk at his feet—and continued sleeping. Big was at her wits' end. She rushed over to me, hastily handing off her bags to the bell captain and bending to lift me into her arms. Petite as she was, I was almost her size, yet she managed to carry me bodily into the hotel, the limo driver and the bell captain following behind with our suitcases. I remained asleep on her shoulder, my feet almost touching the floor, as she stood at the front desk checking us into our room. I didn't awaken even when with a great sigh of relief she deposited me onto the bed.

With less than half an hour before she was due at the conference center, she went to freshen up her makeup and hair and then shook me back to consciousness and tidied me up, too, as there was no question of leaving me behind in the hotel room. At the conference center, we learned that only the keynote speaker and the person introducing her were to be seated on the stage. Big tried to convince the organizers to place a third chair beside her own, so that I could be seated next to her.

"I'm sorry, Ms. Clayton," the organizer said. "But it won't work for the pictures."

"But Biggie, I want to sit with you," I whined, still tired from my eventful morning.

"My daughter is only six," Big explained. She often referred to me as her daughter back then, and I loved nothing more. "I'd feel better if she were on the stage next to me. Trust me, the photographer won't care. Besides," she added, trying to lighten the negotiation, "look how cute she is."

But the event organizer would not be convinced, and so it was decided that I would sit in the first row of the auditorium, with a clear line of sight between Big and me. I agreed to this in principle, but as the event got underway, and I sat watching Big waiting her turn at the podium, I couldn't think of a good reason why I shouldn't be up there with her. I had grasped that the man Big had talked to didn't want the photographs ruined by having me sit next to Big, but now I had another idea.

The next thing everyone knew, I was climbing the steps onto the stage. As the person introducing Big kept speaking, Big watched in amused horror as the pretty floral outfit she had dressed me in disappeared into a wing of the stage, then reappeared dragging a gray metal folding chair behind me. I had previously noticed the row of chairs backstage, and now I pulled the one I had grabbed over to Big and positioned it carefully behind her. There. I had solved it.

The organizer hadn't wanted me sitting next to Big, but he had said nothing about me sitting behind her. Before climbing onto the chair, I put my lips to Big's ear and whispered helpfully, "Don't worry, Biggie. I'm going to sit right here, but I promise I won't interrupt anybody." Then, when seated, I learned forward again. "I'm okay right here," I assured Big. "Are you okay?"

The audience was clapping. It was time for Big to take the podium, but not before she turned and answered me thoughtfully. "Well, no, Michelle, I'm not really okay, but I think we should leave things as they are. I think this will be easier, because I don't know what else you might do if this fails." Every time Big recounted this incident afterward, she would laugh ruefully and add, "Those pictures would have looked a lot better with Michelle sitting beside me on stage rather than behind me."

Big tells that story now as a way to illustrate how much she loved me, even when I strummed her last nerve. The two of us were a mutual admiration society—of course I wanted this endlessly fascinating woman to be my mother! How could I not? In Big's company, the unspoken ache I felt for the woman who hadn't stayed all but disappeared. But unfortunately for me, Xernona marrying my dad simply wasn't in the cards.

Four decades later, when I questioned Big about exactly what had ended their relationship, she let out a soft chime of laughter and said with a wink: "Your father's life was complicated. Let's just say, he and I decided that we were better off as very dear friends."

The truth of this statement had broken my heart. I had just turned seven when my father shared the news that Big would be getting married again—but not to him. I hadn't even realized that she and Daddy were no longer together until I learned that she had recently become engaged to a prominent judge in Atlanta, and had requested that I be a flower girl at her wedding. Daddy did not attend. Instead, he put me on a plane to Atlanta in the care of Little and Tony, to be met by Aunt Edna when we landed.

I can still see myself in a cloud of yellow chiffon, scattering rose petals along the carpeted aisle of a gloriously bedecked hotel ballroom, and then watching from the front as Big, radiant and otherworldly in white lace and tulle, glided toward the man who was not my father. I felt as if my chest would crack wide open, because every step she took toward where I stood put her farther and farther away from ever becoming my mother. That evening, when the vows and the speeches and the toasts had all been made, and the dancing began, for reasons I could not begin to express to any of the aunties who tried to comfort me, I hugged my yellow chiffon knees and sobbed.

FIVE

The Colors of Us

It happened on a day when Bigmama was down with the flu. Barely able to lift her head from the pillow, she had gestured to the comb and brush and jar of pomade on the dressing table, instructing me to fix my own hair for school. Now seven years old and in the third grade, I had begun to do this sometimes, though Bigmama would always take the brush when I was done to smooth the flyaways and add a little magic. But on this morning, she was soundly asleep as I dragged the comb through my wayward volume of hair. By the time I got it somewhat untangled, I was running late for Mrs. Holmes, and so rather than trying to part the hair into sections so that I could braid or twist it, I decided to leave everything loose.

As I quickly wriggled into my clothes, I swiped at the strands fluffing around my face, two wings of hair brushing my cheeks and the rest billowing halfway down my back. That whole day at school, the entire uncontrolled mass grew larger and more unruly with each passing hour. My hair and I had finally made it through to the last period of the day, when halfway through social studies class, my friend Kendra ambled over to my table and mentioned that she liked my new hairstyle.

"Thanks," I said, preoccupied with trying to locate the capital cities of all fifty states in an atlas so I could plot them on an outline map our teacher had given us.

Kendra lifted a section of my hair and spread it across her palm. "Maybe I'll wear my hair loose tomorrow, too," she said.

I looked up to assess the small braids secured with colorful plastic barrettes covering Kendra's head. "Well, your hair is short and you have tighter curls," I observed. "You'd look really nice in a low Afro."

I thought I was only being helpful. It was 1974, and Afros were not just a hot style trend, they were also a proclamation of Black pride. Many mornings, I'd stand in front of the bathroom mirror trying to make my hair stand up the way it should to achieve a perfect orb. Instead, it flopped under its own weight, and by second period every day my braids or ponytail were a frizzy mess, whereas Kendra had exactly the right texture to pull off a flawless 'fro.

I completely missed the meaning of the moment when Kendra abruptly removed her hands from my hair and took a full step backward, a strange expression on her face. I didn't understand the look, but it wasn't my nature to dwell, and so when she turned on her heel and walked away from me without another word, I simply shrugged and went back to searching for state capitals. But twenty minutes later, after class let out and I set off on foot for home, Kendra and three other girls from our grade fell in step beside me. I greeted them brightly, suspecting nothing amiss until a few paces on, they suddenly surrounded me, blocking my path forward.

"What?" I asked innocently. I thought they were playing some game that I hadn't yet caught on to.

"You have such pretty hair," one of the girls said sweetly, but out the corner of my eye I noticed Kendra smirking. It was at that moment that the air shifted. Next thing I knew, each of the girls had grabbed a handful of my hair and were pulling on it—*hard*.

"What are you doing?" I screamed, as they yanked my hair in every direction, my head bobbing wildly. "Why are you doing this?"

"How'd you like if we rip out all this pretty hair," one of the girls muttered, panting from the exertion needed to achieve exactly that.

"Stop! You're hurting me!" I cried. "What did I do?"

"You think you're better than us 'cause you're light-skinned with White girl hair!" another one of the girls yelled.

"I don't think that!" I wailed, trying to catch their hands with my own. "Why would you say that? It's not true!"

"You said I have short hair!" Kendra yelled then. She hurled the accusation with such visceral wrath that it seared me. I realized with shock that she had been offended by my comment earlier about her hair being just right for an Afro—*but why?* I thought her colorfully adorned braids were beautiful, and besides, why would I ever want to insult her? She was my friend.

From the storefront of a hair salon across the street, a woman alerted by my screams noticed the commotion and ran out to pull the three girls off me. By then I was sobbing desperately, feeling violated and betrayed. "What did I do?" I wept after the girls released me and ran away. "I don't know what I did wrong. Why'd they jump on me like that? Why would they do that?"

The woman bent toward me, dabbing at my tears with fingers tipped by wine-red nails. "Come, baby. Stop crying now. We'll call your grandmother," she said gently. Circling my shoulders with one arm and holding me to her side, she guided me back across the street to the salon. I let my wet cheek rest against the green plastic hairstylist's apron she wore over a simple white T-shirt and jeans. I wished fleetingly that she might be my missing mother, swooping in like an angel or superhero in my moment of need. Starting around the time that Bigmama broke her hip, I had developed a habit of looking into the faces of strange women, secretly wondering if one of them might be the woman whose body had carried me. Of course, I knew the salon lady couldn't really be my mother. Her skin was a deep brown, much darker than my own pigment, and her natural hair could not have produced the mix of straight, wavy, and frizzy strands that sprung from my own head—and which had just provoked such violence from a girl I had thought was my friend.

As we entered the salon, the black-and-white-tiled interior was oddly familiar, and it dawned on me who the Good Samaritan was who had rescued me—she was Bigmama's regular hairdresser. I had sat reading Nancy Drew or Hardy Boys books in a corner of her shop on many Friday afternoons as she permed and styled my grandmother's hair. Her name was Miss Sandra, I remembered her now, and mumbled a polite thank you as she helped me up into one of the silver client chairs before paging through her phone book for Bigmama's number. I listened as she described to my grandmother the scene she had witnessed. It sounded even meaner in the telling. After she hung up, she looked at me kindly, assuring me Bigmama was on her way. "Now let's fix this hair a bit," she said as she lifted styling implements from the mirrored counter and began to reclaim my torn and matted hair.

On the way home from the salon in her blue Datsun, Bigmama didn't ask me any further questions about what had happened with Kendra and the other girls. Perhaps she saw how raw I still felt, and so she simply instructed me to go and wash my face as soon as we got inside, while she made me a bologna and cheese sandwich to tide me over till dinner. In the bathroom, I stared at myself in the mirror for a long time, trying to assess what made Kendra turn on me so viciously. My face looked blotchy and my eyes were swollen from crying, contradicting the effect of my hair, newly attended to by Miss Sandra, who had styled it in two smooth braids over my shoulders. I didn't recognize the miserable girl in the mirror. By nature, I tended toward irrepressible cheer, but now, it felt as if some sort of protective skin had been ripped away, so that everything, even my own face, looked unfamiliar and wrong. In a sudden, angry rush of self-loathing, I spat on my own arm, cursing my complexion and the too-straight texture of my hair, which I now understood to be the cause of my unwitting offense to Kendra.

I thought about the Caucasian lady who Bigmama had said was my mother, and understood with a clarity that had somehow escaped me before this moment that she was to blame for my light skin and long, loosely waved hair. Why hadn't I consciously grasped this before now? Wasn't it only a few days ago that I had curled up next to Bigmama on the living room couch as she was watching the nightly news, put my arm against hers, and asked why she and I weren't the same color, and why didn't I have the same kind of hair as her and my cousins in Birmingham?

"Well, your birth mother was White," Bigmama had reminded me, lifting her pecan-brown arm over my head to circle my shoulders and pull me closer. "That's why you look the way you do," she added. "I suppose strictly speaking you *are* mixed, even though the way your family sees it, you're every bit as colored as the rest of us."

At the time, I was only making idle conversation, and the import of this exchange had failed to truly land as I'd moved on to a drawn-out story about playing capture the flag with my friend Lois from next door. But now, staring at my face in the bathroom mirror, Bigmama's words came back to me, leaving me with the strange sensation that I was wholly unknown to myself, because I couldn't even picture the face of the woman who had given me one-half of my genetic code, the Caucasian lady who had bestowed my light tan complexion, and then walked away. She hadn't stuck around to armor me against a world in which I was both too brown to be White and too light, I now realized, to be unquestioningly embraced as a Black girl.

Though I didn't have the language to explain it back then, some part of me had already fathomed that had I been dark skinned with short woolly hair like Kendra's, I could have made the very same comment to her as I had that morning, and she would have received it differently, as mere observation, perhaps even as an expression of sisterhood. But it would be many more years before I grasped that what had come at me like a tornado that afternoon had been a little Black girl using anger as a salve for her own deep-seated feelings of hurt and shame. Just as I had absorbed truths about America's racial hierarchy from television shows and magazine spreads without even knowing I was doing it, Kendra had internalized the message that having short, tightly coiled hair and dark brown skin put her far outside of society's ideal of beauty and worth.

Ironically, the pain inflicted upon Kendra by this messaging would have the effect of making me despise my own features, too. My classmate's hurt had rudely and irrevocably introduced me into the ugly colorism that to this day pervades the African American community, a legacy stretching all the way back to the institution of slavery, when plantation owners first devised a strategy to deliberately "divide and conquer" the Black race. These White men came up with the idea of instilling a color hierarchy among enslaved Africans by selecting light-skinned Blacks to tend their homes, cook their meals, and raise their children while relegating dark-skinned Blacks to punishing heat and the sting of the overseer's whip as they worked long days in the fields. After centuries of such sinister psychological conditioning, colorism had become so woven through our culture as to provoke reactions to skin pigment even among Black folks, the root causes of which might not always be fully conscious.

The only antidote, I now understand, is for us to call out the insidiousness of "light privilege" wherever it appears, to reject attitudes about skin color that are born of this nation's most pernicious history, and to hold each other as sisters and brothers in repudiation of the divide-and-conquer ethos of the White gaze. Of course, this kindred embrace was nowhere in evidence on the afternoon that Kendra and her friends surrounded me, as none of us had any conscious awareness then of the cruel conditioning governing us.

Kendra never did apologize for what had transpired between us on that terrible afternoon. At school the next day, she seemed concerned, as if waiting to see whether I would tattle to our teacher and get her in trouble. I acted as if I didn't even see her, and gave her and her friends a wide berth. If Bigmama or Daddy ever spoke to the school administrators about the hair-pulling incident, I never knew anything about it. But from that day on I became careful. I had discovered that for some, my appearance marked me as a racial imposter, a girl who didn't truly belong. I surmised that my safest course was to stay vigilant at all times, and so I learned to read the way the air in a room might stir around me, betraying the slightest hint that someone in my orbit might find fault with me for no reason other than the light pigment of my skin or the too-loose texture of my hair, physical attributes not of my choosing, bestowed upon me at birth by a woman whose face I couldn't even conjure.

SIX

The Woman in Blue

One Saturday as my friends and I were splashing and playing in Little and Tony's pool, my pretend brother Bradford piped up: "Michelle, where's your mom? How come I've never met her?"

At nine years old, I had already been asked this so many times by kids at school that the question no longer caused me to flinch, at least not visibly. I would merely toss out my stock answer, which I now gave Bradford, too.

"I don't have a mom," I said flippantly.

I had learned that this response usually shut down any further interrogation, as people either felt too sorry for me to press for details, or too uncertain of what they might uncover should they continue to probe. For good measure, I added a nonchalant shrug before swimming away from Bradford, freestyling to the other side of the pool. My father had been standing on the patio talking to Tony, and from the corner of my eye, I had noticed him pause mid-sentence, as if listening for how I would answer Bradford's question. Now, as I swam past him, I saw his eyes narrow as they tracked me pushing aside the blue water, his forehead gathered in a frown.

I wasn't the only child at those weekend pool parties who was growing up outside a traditional nuclear family. Another girl, Chrystal, was a daughter of divorce. She was being raised by her mom, Dodye Evans, a single parent and speech pathologist who had been a brilliant dancer in her day. Chrystal was four years older than I was, and had taken me under her wing when we were younger, making sure I was included in the backyard fun. No doubt she'd noticed we were the only children without two parents present, for reasons only the adults seemed to understand. Chrystal and I never talked about our missing parents. In fact, we both acted as if this shared detail of our young lives was of no consequence. Yet because I knew how the fact of it weighed on me, I thought it must weigh heavily on Chrystal's heart, too.

When Chrystal's mom and my father began seeing each other romantically, I prayed I would gain a big sister, and that her beautiful and gracious mother Dodye would become mine as well. Each night, as I knelt with Bigmama beside her bed to say our devotions, I silently pleaded with God to move Daddy's heart to ask Dodye to marry him and make their daughters whole. What could have been more perfect? Of course, nothing is ever that simple. As with Big, Daddy dated Dodye for years, but their relationship never moved to the next stage.

The other children at Little and Tony's weekend house parties were oblivious to my sensitivities in this regard, which was why Bradford hadn't hesitated to ask why my mother never came around the way everyone else's mothers did.

That evening, as Daddy was driving me back to Bigmama's house, he mentioned very casually that he'd heard me tell Bradford that I didn't have a mother. Trying to anticipate where this line of conversation might be headed, I shifted in my seat so I could see his profile. Deep purple shadows filled the car, and the red glare of taillights from vehicles in front of us glinted off his glasses, making it hard to read his face. When he didn't speak again for several moments, I looked back at the road, and waited.

"Michelle, you *do* have a mother," he said finally. The casualness was gone now, and in its place was a tone of resolve, as if he considered it imperative that I grasp what he was telling me. "You are *not* motherless, and I don't know why you told Bradford that. Your mother just doesn't live with you."

I studied the dark freeway disappearing under the wheels of his silver Mercedes. I wasn't sure what he wanted me to do with this information that I already knew. *Yes, I have a mother somewhere,* I thought grudgingly, *but I have no memory of her, so what is the point of having her?*

Suddenly, with a force that pinned me to my seat and left me breathless, I realized that I did have one memory of the woman who had given birth to me. Years before, when I was five years old and visiting Daddy at his condo, he had pulled an album from a closet and opened it to a single black-and-white photograph. In the glossy, studio-lit portrait, my father and a striking raven-haired woman sat on either side of a serious-faced toddler. The child's eyelids were puffy, her lashes wet and eyes forlorn, as if she had stopped crying just a second before the photographer clicked the shutter. Now, in the dark car with my father, I suddenly understood that the toddler in the photograph had been *me*.

As Daddy covered the miles toward home, the raven-haired woman's face came back to me, clear in all its details—her dark eyes glistening, the alabaster whiteness of her skin a stark contrast to my father's darker hue, her lips poetic in shape, as if painted by a Renaissance master, the overall effect being one of sultry and alluring beauty. The memory was almost too much to bear, and I hugged myself to contain the astonishment that I did, after all, know what my mother looked like, though not from life, but from the sole picture of the three of us that—as far as I know to this day—ever existed.

"What is my mother's name?" I asked almost shyly.

Now that I had dredged up from the depths of memory an artifact proving the existence of the Caucasian lady Bigmama had mentioned, I needed to attach a name, a label of sorts, something irrefutable that would record my mother's face in my permanent memory.

"Laura Hernandez," Daddy said.

He glanced over at me warily, before turning his eyes back to the road. Perhaps he was wondering why he had never shared such a fundamental detail, but at that moment, I wasn't dwelling on all the facts about my mother that I didn't yet know. I was too enthralled by the memory of the family photograph that I had apparently buried in my unconscious all these years, only to have it surface with such startling force now.

"Laura Hernandez," I repeated softly, memorizing the syllables, letting them play on my tongue, slip down my throat, and find a permanent berth inside me.

My mother's name is Laura Hernandez.

And now I know her face.

THREE WEEKENDS LATER, AS WE WERE HEADING BACK TO BIGMAMA'S house at dusk on a Sunday evening after spending the weekend with Little and Tony, Daddy took an unfamiliar turn.

"How would you like to visit your mother?" he said calmly, as if this were just a regular conversation.

My head whipped around to stare at him. *Was he serious?* I croaked out a sound that passed for consent, and we said nothing more as he merged onto the freeway, driving for some time before taking the exit for Ladera Heights. The knot in my throat became a rock as Daddy pulled up in front of a nondescript beige apartment building, two stories high. He parked and got out of the car, waiting at the curb for me to join him, and taking my hand in his as we walked up a concrete path to the front door. My jeans suddenly felt uncomfortably snug at the waist, and I tugged my yellow T-shirt down nervously. At the same time, I felt as if I was floating outside my body, looking down on the scene, jotting mental notes to take out and study later on.

We climbed a flight of stairs to the second floor and walked down a short open-sided hallway to a plain wooden door. Daddy knocked, and a woman opened. She appeared startled to see us standing on her threshold, uncertain about greeting us. She wore a slim-fitting turquoise blue shift dress with wavy white trim at the collar, and her thick black hair tumbled loose around her shoulders. *My mother is so pretty,* I thought. And then I noticed the lake of unhappiness in her eyes. I was quietly taking her in as the three of us stood in silence until finally she stepped aside, allowing us to enter. Daddy put his palm on my back and guided me into the living room. I knew the woman was staring at me. I could feel the heat of her gaze on my skin but, anxious about whether I would pass muster, especially since I hadn't passed muster at birth, I did not meet her eyes.

"Would you like a drink, Michelle? Some water?" she asked.

I nodded, the sound of my name on her lips lingering in my ear. The woman turned and walked into the kitchen, and my father followed her, leaving me alone in the small living room with its bright orange couch set off by satiny pink cushions and a white shag rug. I wasn't sure whether to go and sit on the couch or stay where I was. After a few moments, I inched a little to the left to give myself a better view of the kitchen. The woman who Daddy told me was my mother was standing with her back against the sink. Despite the shadows the overhead light cast in the wells of her eyes, I saw that she was crying. I couldn't hear what she and my father were saying, but their heads were close together, and the woman was shaking her head, *no, no, no.*

I guess we surprised her, I thought, giving her the benefit of the doubt, hoping it might help me push down a feeling of loneliness so familiar that I hadn't, until this moment, connected it to the woman in blue. Was she the one I had been aching for all this time, I wondered then, not Big or any of the other women my father dated? In that moment, it seemed that the woman wearing a dress the color of the ocean was the only one who could fill that empty space inside me. And yet, judging from the way she and my father were desperately whispering back and forth in the kitchen, it was clear that she still had no wish to gather me in her arms and bring me home.

I was sure now that the last thing she had expected that evening was for us to show up at her door. She seemed, more than anything else, unnerved and frightened to have the child she had left behind nine years earlier, suddenly reappear. Right then Daddy came back into the living room.

"Come on, Michelle, we're leaving," he said, his face impassive.

He opened the apartment door and gestured for me to follow him. We didn't speak as we walked down the breezeway, descended the stairs, and stepped outside. The woman didn't come out of the kitchen to tell us goodbye, which made me wonder if she really was my mother after all. But when I got to the curb and opened the car door to climb inside, I glanced back toward the apartment building, and there she was at the second-floor window, a blue smear behind glass, face ashen—a ghost.

Daddy didn't look back. He just slipped into the driver's seat, turned the key in the ignition, and rolled away. His jaw was set, a small muscle working there. His hands gripped the steering wheel tightly. I sensed that something momentous had been settled between him and my mother during those minutes in the kitchen, and not to his liking. Now, as he drove me back toward Bigmama's house, he seemed depleted. He made the effort to ask me about school, my friends, and whether I'd like to join him and my older sister Cheryl for a housewarming at his friends the Gibsons' new home in Brentwood next week. I didn't mention the woman in blue or inquire as to why our visit to see her had been cut so short. An avalanche of questions rumbled inside me, but I knew the moment wasn't right to ask them.

My restraint would be rewarded, because after we turned into Bigmama's driveway, Daddy shut off the engine and swiveled in his seat to face me. His posture was looser now, as if he had come to a decision on the way home about what I should know.

"Your mother's getting married and moving to South America with her new husband," he told me quietly. "He's a diplomat, and I have no idea how long they will be living abroad. I took you to see her tonight because I knew it might be your last chance."

"Is she a White woman like Bigmama says," I asked quietly.

I already had a sense of the answer, perhaps from staring in the mirror at my own face. There had been something about the weight of the woman's ink-black hair, the barest hint of bronze rather than pearl as an undertone to her pale skin, the faintest almond-shaped points at the outer corners of her thick-lashed eyes. She definitely wasn't Black like Daddy and Bigmama and me, but I had intuited that she wasn't entirely Caucasian either, at least not in the European sense of the word.

"Well, she looks White," my father said. "That's how the world sees her, and she doesn't tell them any differently. Her parents emigrated from Mexico before she was born, so I suppose that makes her a White Chicana."

I swallowed hard. My father had just handed me one more piece of the puzzle that was my mother—one more detail about my heritage. So I was Black and Mexican. I was possessed of an equal share of DNA from the two most vilified racial groups in Los Angeles, the ones who routinely drew the ugliest epithets of all, the "niggers" and the "wetbacks." This was the contempt that both sides of my family had to endure, making me doubly reviled in the country of my birth.

And yet, along with this harsh new awareness, another sentiment rose in me, a soft feeling, something almost tender. I was remembering all the times people had asked me if I was Latina, Hispanic, Chicana, Spanish, all the different names for what my mother was, and I'd told them no. I thought about the afternoon that Kendra and her friends had surrounded me on the street and furiously yanked my hair, rejecting the very notion of me as a regular Black girl. It was the moment when I'd realized that others might not see me as I saw myself. Since that time, the feeling of being an outsider had stalked me, the sense that I didn't quite belong made all the more painful by the fact that whatever made me appear less Black to others than I felt inside remained a mystery.

Now, having seen with my own eyes where my physical attributes had come from, I felt more *known* to myself, and infinitesimally closer to my mother—even though she'd been distressed by us being in her home.

"Why was she crying?" I asked, unsure if I really wanted to know the answer.

Daddy shrugged and didn't respond for some time. In the furrow of his brow, his tightly pressed together lips, I could see him dismissing one option after another about what he might say. "It's too much for her," he said finally. "You and me, we've just always been too much for her."

"But *why*?" I pressed him. "Why were we too much for her?"

It was the question that had haunted me for years, even after I stopped asking it out loud, and now I held my breath, praying that enough was already different about this day that Daddy might finally answer it. He said nothing for such a long time that the tiny hope fluttering inside me began to wilt. But then he spoke.

"Her family discovered she was seeing a Black man, and her mother and brother insisted she end the relationship," he said, his tone almost robotic. "I was married at the time, but her family didn't know that, and I had told her I would get a divorce so that we could be together. But she couldn't go against her family, especially her mother. Even if I had been free, you see, I was still Black."

And I was, too, I thought.

I had long suspected that my mother's reason for leaving had had something to do with the difference in our skin color. Now my father had just confirmed that Laura Hernandez had been unwilling to yoke herself to raising a Black child, to be relegated to second-class citizenship and possibly ostracized from her own kind. I felt an odd sense of triumph at finally scoring from my father a concrete explanation of why my mother had walked away. But in the wake of that I was flooded with a new kind of pain.

My mother didn't want me.

My skin wasn't light enough to make her stay.

I became aware that Daddy was frowning at me, as if unsure whether he had done the right thing in giving voice to this long overdue—and in retrospect glaringly obvious—truth. "It doesn't mean your mother didn't love you," he said softly.

I forced a bright smile, intended to reassure him that I was less shaken than I actually felt. He wasn't fooled. He wiped a large, well-tended surgeon's hand down over his face, and sighed. He seemed beyond exhausted now, resigned and sad. "I'm so sorry, Michelle," he said at last. "Come, let's go and find your grandmother."

If I had known that my father would never mention this night again, perhaps I would have stalled before going inside so that I could ask a few more questions. At the time, I thought we had arrived at an opening, but in fact, that was the day Daddy seemed to slam the door shut on the story of how the woman in blue had come to birth me and then abandon me—because this is how I now thought of myself, a child abandoned, unchosen by the one person on earth who nature dictated should love me. As more time passed, that surreal visit with my mother faded to a mere shimmer. Maybe this suppression of memory and experience was an act of self-preservation, willful and necessary, at least for a time. Whatever the case, for years afterward, I would look back on the Sunday evening when my father took me to see the raven-haired woman in blue, and I would wonder if it really happened.

SEVEN

Girl on the Bus

On the first morning after school let out for the summer of 1977, I meandered into the kitchen for breakfast, only to hear Bigmama clear her throat in a particular manner I recognized. The sound signaled to me that some important announcement was forthcoming. Bigmama had been stirring eggs at the stove, and now she turned to me, skillet in hand as I slipped into my usual chair opposite the door. "Thank you, Bigmama," I said reflexively, as she spooned the egg scramble into a plate set out in front of me. I retrieved a slice of toast from the bread bowl already on the table, watching with interest as my grandmother settled herself in the seat next to me. I knew this, too, was significant, as she usually sat across from me at the kitchen table.

Without further preamble, she informed me that I would be changing schools in the fall. In her no-nonsense teacher's voice, she explained that I had scored in the highest percentile on a recent aptitude test given at my school, which had led my father to decide that for fifth grade, I should attend Hamlin Elementary's newly integrated gifted program. Bigmama advised that she herself was in full agreement with this plan. She went on to share that I would become part of the first wave of students to be bused from our South Central neighborhood to schools in the mostly White and comparatively more wealthy communities of the San Fernando Valley.

Desegregation had come to the Los Angeles Unified School District after a 1970 court ruling mandated that the city's public schools be fully integrated. In the LAUSD's drive to reshuffle the racial mix of its academic programs, large numbers of schoolchildren were designated "Permit With Transportation" or PWT students. The goal was for Black and Brown inner-city kids to be bused to White residential neighborhoods in the Valley, with a comparable number of kids from the Valley assigned to travel in the reverse direction. To accommodate the expected influx of upper-middle-class students who were used to more enriched academic environments, the LAUSD had pledged to shore up funding and extracurricular programming at under-resourced schools in minority neighborhoods like South Central and East L.A.

But White parents weren't having it. No way were they letting their kids travel beyond their own neighborhoods. In protest, legions of San Fernando Valley parents pulled their children out of the public school system and enrolled them in expensive private institutions, while others avoided the busing mandate by relocating to other parts of the state. In the end, the PWT kids would travel in one direction only, with LAUSD buses ferrying children from poor neighborhoods to more prosperous campuses in the Valley. Eventually, the school board would vote to abandon its PWT initiative altogether, replacing it with a voluntary magnet program that facilitated students being bused long distances from their homes to attend specialized academic programs to which they had been admitted. With majority White schools continuing to be infinitely better funded than schools in minority neighborhoods, the advent of busing, and the citywide slate of gifted and talented programs it brought within reach, reoriented everything for students of color like me.

Bigmama later confessed that she had fully expected me to grumble and resist the plan to put me on a bus every morning to a school far away from home, so she was pleasantly surprised when I simply nodded in acquiescence and went back to my eggs and toast.

"Good girl, that's settled then," she said, smiling and patting my shoulder.

I smiled, too, because I enjoyed pleasing my grandmother. But the deeper truth was that I'd felt an immediate thrill at the prospect of starting fresh in a place where there would be no mean girls to keep in my peripheral view. For the rest of summer, I nursed a secret hope that I might find my place in the new setting, among students with whom I had no history. To be fair, I was only ten years old and not yet well versed in the racial fault lines of the city I called home.

My new school was an hour away in the neighborhood of Wood-land Hills, its square campus bordered by a grid of residential streets in an overwhelmingly White part of town. The first day, the other kids being transported with me from South Central gaped at the landscaped properties gliding past outside the bus windows. I was less in awe. I had often played with the children of my father's friends in such houses. Far more impressive to me were the birthday parties for my little cousin Tommy that I had attended at Diana Ross's estate in Beverly Hills. Aunt Edna's firstborn son, Thomas, had married the singer's sister, Rita Ross, and Aunty Diane, as I called her, used to invite me to her nephew Tommy's birthday celebrations at her home, as well as to parties for her daughters, Rhonda, Tracee, and Chudney. In star-struck L.A., I would often find myself staring at some of the celebrities and their kids at Aunty Diane's parties, where stars like Cher, one of my idols at the time, were among the guests.

The former lead singer of the Supremes, the most successful American girl group of all time, Diana Ross in the mid-seventies was at the height of her solo career, and every one of my grade-school classmates had known who she was. So it was with some excitement that I would go back to Loren Miller Elementary on the Monday morning after Tommy's party and tell my friends that I had been to Miss Diana Ross's house. "She lives in Beverly Hills," I'd say before going on to describe the wonders of my cousin's birthday festivities on her expansive compound. My friends would look at me dubiously, because I was just a regular South Central kid like they were, and families like ours didn't hobnob in rich celebrities' homes.

"Come on, you did not do that," they would tell me, laughing derisively. "Michelle, you know you're lying."

"I'm not! It's true!" I'd insist, not understanding till many years later what I was really reaching for as I shared this experience with my friends. They all lived with their mothers and fathers, and I didn't, so I had to find something else that might elevate me—not in their eyes, I realize now, but in my own.

One of my classmates went home and told her mother that I had claimed to be at Diana Ross's house, and the next morning, the girl said to me: "My mom says to tell you she called Diana Ross, and she does not know you."

"No, she does!" I said earnestly. "Tell her I'm Tommy Gardner's cousin!" It never occurred to me that mother and daughter were just having a joke at my expense.

Now, in fifth grade at Hamlin, I would be attending classes with mostly White students for the first time. I had counted three Black girls, including myself, and one Black boy in my otherwise entirely White class of about three dozen kids, with me as the only Black student who would leave the group for honors curriculum classes on Fridays.

One of the other Black girls in my homeroom was named Michelle Woods. When our teacher took attendance the first day, and Michelle and I realized we shared a name, we grinned at each other across the classroom and nodded our heads in solidarity. Even so, when we met up by unspoken agreement to get lunch at recess, I watched closely to see if my mixed-race appearance might affect her response to me. But Michelle seemed to care not one bit about how I looked, and by the end of the day, we were inseparable.

We were both rather portly girls in a room full of sylph-like kids who had been going to school together for years. Michelle's skin was a medium shade of brown, and her short hair was bone-straight from a recent perm, with thin flyaways at the temples and skinny pigtails forever coming undone. Her big dark eyes were warm soulful pools, all the more endearing to me because of the slight droop of her left eyelid. I admired the way she bodaciously loved every aspect of herself and never questioned that she was beautiful, even before the operation she would undergo that winter to correct her drooping eyelid.

We both quickly realized that our teacher was unsure how to navigate the new experience of having Black kids in her classroom. Michelle and I weren't rude in any way—neither her mother nor my grandmother would have tolerated misbehavior from us—but when we sat near each other, we invariably ended up chatting and giggling irrepressibly, distracting each other from the work that had been assigned. When we became unruly, we would catch our teacher staring at us, her expression pained, and that was enough to put us in check for a few minutes, because none of our previous teachers would have let us get away with being so giddy in class.

But Michelle and I were exemplary students compared to the third Black girl in our group. She would sing to herself throughout the lesson, getting up to stroll to the back of the classroom and sharpen her pencil several times each period, sometimes even sauntering out of the room, we assumed to go to the bathroom, without asking if she might be excused. No matter what this girl did, our teacher would just gape at her, her face frozen with alarm as the other kids snickered and then laughed outright at her relinquishment of classroom control. *You better say something to that girl,* I would think, knowing that our teacher's refusal to discipline the Black kids only made us seem disrespectful.

At Hamlin, Michelle became my protector, my saving grace. Not only did she move through our new and overwhelmingly White environment with a buoyancy and confidence I tried to emulate, but she was also the first person in any school I had ever attended whom I trusted to see me *as me*. Ever since those girls at Loren Miller had grabbed handfuls of my hair, I had been stumbling to recreate myself as a girl who lived easily inside her skin, who belonged to herself, regardless of what others thought of her. While the brief encounter with my mother had given me an understanding of where my racial ambiguity had come from, Michelle's friendship now created a space where I could begin to heal the self-doubt that plagued me in classroom settings. In her company, my sense of separation eased somewhat. Watching how she moved through the world, I was learning that rather than shrinking myself to accommodate others' preconceived notions about who I should be, I could decide my own truth, and live large into it. Michelle showed me that you didn't have to be rich, White, and skinny to be happy and fulfilled in exactly who you were.

The safety and acceptance I found in Michelle, and that she also found in me, were critical for two Black girls at a place like Hamlin, where for the most part our classmates looked right past us, as if we were invisible to them, or more accurately, irrelevant. That year, as often as Bigmama would allow it, I would take the bus home with Michelle and hang out with her after school. I think our friendship also put Bigmama's heart at peace somewhat. She was not quite as robust as before, and wasn't able to ferry me around as she once had. In fact, my father and Aunt Edna had recently arranged for Vondela Pilot, a family friend who was a registered nurse, to come by several nights during the week to check on Bigmama and me. It was Vondela who picked me up from Michelle's house in the evenings when my father had hospital rounds or meetings and couldn't make it.

The Woods family lived in a modest home, with a well-kept living room, a cozy eat-in kitchen, and two bedrooms leading off a short passageway. Michelle, the middle child of three, shared one of the bedrooms with her older sister and her younger brother, while her mom and dad slept in the other room. Their house might have been small, but it felt like a kingdom to me. I reveled in the freedom I felt in the company of Michelle's family, with whom I could shed my careful good girl persona and be wackily and gleefully myself.

All the Woods siblings were academically brilliant. Michelle's brother Norman was seven years old and already in the third grade, and her sister NéeNée, though not yet thirteen, was in the eighth grade, after having skipped a year. It was clear to everyone who met her that NéeNée in particular was destined to go far, yet she wore her precocious intellect graciously, never showing off that she was usually the smartest person in the room. Most afternoons, I would join Michelle and her siblings in their shared bedroom to do homework—or at least NéeNée would be diligently studying, while Michelle and I whispered about boys as we lolled and laughed on the top of the bunk bed the sisters shared. Below us on the bottom bunk, NéeNée would roll her eyes at our foolishness, while Norman stretched out on his cot under the window, reading superhero comics and ignoring us all.

At about five-thirty each evening, when Michelle's mom got home from her job as a pharmacy technician, we would crowd around the kitchen table to eat bologna sandwiches amid a riot of chatter. An hour later, their father would arrive home from his job as an oil company supervisor, and the family scene would be complete. I could feel my world expanding as they all shared opinions and insights on everything under the sun. Other times, Michelle, NéeNée, and I would play rousing games of Jacks on the kitchen floor with Mrs. Woods reading or sewing nearby, or we'd dribble a basketball in the front yard, sometimes with Mr. Woods and Norman joining in.

Michelle's parents' involvement with their kids' lives was unlike anything I had ever seen up close. My own father, though he would transport me wherever I wanted or needed to go, was more likely to engage me in grownup conversation than to kick off his shoes and punt a ball around the yard with me. And when Michelle slept over with me some weekends, Daddy would drop us off at Bob's Big Boy burger joint, or at a movie, or he would send us off to have fun in the pool at his new condo on the marina in Long Beach, while he watched us from the balcony and caught up on city council business or clinic files.

His presence was constant, his attention to my schooling and the development of my intellect unceasing, but compared to Michelle's father he was more distant. I understood how hard my father worked, how many different hats he wore, so I coached myself to appreciate being his clear priority, and to accept his version of parenting. But sometimes, when I was with the Woods family, I would step outside myself for a few moments to recognize how completely joyful I was feeling, and it was always too soon when Vondela or Daddy arrived to pick me up or Michelle's mom announced it was time to drive me home.

Years later, Michelle reflected that I had given her an experience of family that she, too, had craved. Both her grandmothers had died before she was born. And so when she slept over at my house, she relished sitting around our kitchen table chatting with Bigmama, who would tell us stories about her time at Howard, the AKA sorority soirees they had held and community service they performed. My grandmother also warned us away from teenaged boys—"They and their salamis will try to fill your head with all kinds of folly," she'd say as we giggled and covered our faces with embarrassment. She counseled us to put our focus on getting good grades instead. "That will take you much further in life than those silly boys," she pronounced. It was a beautiful exchange while it lasted—Michelle's lively close-knit family one weekend and my wry, plainspoken grandmother the next.

I attended Hamlin for only one year, after which Michelle and I moved to different schools for sixth grade. Though we would remain friends, no longer was I able to spend idyllic afternoons at Michelle's house, basking in domestic moments with her family. For a long time, I thought of the Woods household as the American dream, come to life. To me they seemed perfect, and the longing I'd always felt to be part of a family in which a mom, a dad, and siblings all shared one roof eased when I was with them.

But nearly a decade later, Michelle's family was beset by tragedy. Her parents had divorced by the time that a horrific act of domestic violence came to their home. An abusive man Michelle's mother had dated shot and killed Michelle's older sister NéeNée and seriously wounded her mother. I wasn't there. I only know what Michelle told me later, sobbing in my arms.

The tragedy eviscerated everyone, though Michelle and her parents did manage to secure Michelle's then two-year-old son and NéeNée's infant son, both of whom had been present at the scene of such violence. Both grandsons would grow up to be fine young men, and Mr. and Mrs. Woods would once again become close, the best of friends, Michelle said, though they would choose not to remarry. But Michelle's mom would never get over her grief and remorse at having brought into their lives the man who would so cruelly rob them of the bright light that was NéeNée. And I would never get over the shock and sorrow that even the most perfect and loving of families could be blown to smithereens in a nanosecond.

For so long, as I'd mourned the absence of my mother, I'd also been grieving my own loss of an intact nuclear family, with the Woodses as my picture of what that looked like. During the year I had spent in their midst, I'd seen my own parents' separation from each other on the day of my birth as depriving me of the close-knit rambunctious joy I'd experienced within Michelle's home. But now unimaginable tragedy had visited the door of this family I loved, forcing me to reckon not just with the devastating loss they had suffered, but also with the fact that no family, not even the Woodses, was immune from the fragility and unpredictability of life.

I had sat with Michelle for a long time after she told me what had happened to NéeNée, and shared how her family had coped in the aftermath. As I left her that night, I fully grasped, perhaps for the first time, that family wasn't a storybook ideal. Family was the people who rallied to your side, come what may, whether they gave birth to you or not. In this new light, the Woodses were still incredibly beautiful to me, even though my understanding of what made them so had changed. Despite Michelle's parents being divorced so many years before and in the face of indescribable pain, the family members had made a chain of hands across turbulent waters, refusing to allow anyone to go under, determined to pull each other through. Their survival had shown me that you didn't need to be a nuclear household or even to share a gene pool to perform such lifesaving work. All you really needed was commitment—and abiding love.

EIGHT

Our Matriarch

My new school, located in the middle of the San Fernando Valley, was even farther away from home than Hamlin, an hour and a half on the yellow school bus that picked me up each morning from Normandie and Adams. Once again, I was the Black girl from the hood plopped down at a resource-rich institution, which invariably meant the setting was predominantly White. This time, I was one of only three students of color in my sixth-grade honors program.

Though I was sorely missing my trusty sidekick Michelle, I resolved to overcome my perennial oddball status and find a place at Saticoy Elementary. My first strategy was to apply myself and shine academically, so no one, not the teachers or the other kids, would have any doubt that I belonged. But if anyone questioned my presence, they never said. No one was mean to me exactly. Instead, each morning when my school bus rolled up to the campus, expelling me into a world where nobody else looked anything like me, I would become invisible, so incidental to everything and everyone at Saticoy that no one bothered to take note of me at all. I spent weeks moving like a shadow through the hallways, trying to figure out how to breach what felt like a completely closed circle of fellow students.

I still prickle with embarrassment at one particular misbegotten attempt to become one of the cool kids. I had noted that some of the popular girls never wore a bra, their budding twelve-year-old breasts sitting up perkily under the tank tops or breezy summer dresses they wore. Deciding to emulate their free-spirited choice, I picked out a green polka dot sundress to wear to school the next day, and snuck out of the house quickly to catch my bus, before Bigmama could notice I had ditched my bra. The problem was, I was more developed than the willowy blond girls who went braless, which meant I bounced around much more abundantly than they ever did. For most of that day, I hugged my books to my chest, trying to disguise my miscalculation, relieved for once to be invisible to my classmates.

My teacher took note, however. She had become enamored of my grandmother after Bigmama made a point of connecting with her at a PTA event. Now, she took me aside to inquire gently about my attire.

"Does your grandmother know you came to school without a bra today?" she asked me. I shook my head miserably. "Oh, Michelle," she said almost sadly, "I think your grandmother would be so disappointed to see you dressed in this manner."

I understood from her tone that she wasn't criticizing me so much as she was trying to protect me, so I refrained from asking why she had never taken any of the White girls aside to ask about *their* strutting around braless. Of course, I knew the answer lay in the difference in our anatomies, and besides, I was far too humiliated to prolong our exchange. Obviously, emulating the popular girls' fashion choice wasn't going to get me noticed except by our teacher. Yet I remained determined to decipher Saticoy's social code and stayed on the lookout for another way.

One day, instead of watching as I usually did while the other kids played dodgeball at recess, I decided to go out for the teams. The rule was, every student who showed up had to be allowed to play. Predictably, all that first week I was picked last by the team captains, and I couldn't say I blamed them. I was horrible at the game, a large, clumsy girl who practically magnetized the ball. The other kids were paying attention to me now, and not in a good way. They took to calling me Raquel Welch Junior because of the way my boobs leaped around as I played. "Here comes Raquel Welch Junior," someone would snicker when I walked into the classroom after recess. I acted nonchalant, as if their name-calling didn't bother me, but after my mortifying day of going braless, the moniker stung. I had always been a stocky child, taller than most of my classmates, girls as well as boys—and now I was *busty* as well. However, I did pause to note that at Saticoy it wasn't my mixed-race appearance that made me feel outcast, as it had at Loren Miller, where I had been too light, and at Hamlin, where I had been too dark. Now I was the outsider because of the size and shape of my body, which did me no favors on the dodgeball court.

As I ruminated on my situation, I began to see that it would be entirely up to me to transform the perception of me as a big-bodied loser in the game. My skin and my hair I could not change, but my athletic prowess I could work on. Almost overnight, I turned fierce on the field. I refused to be the shy, clumsy girl being regularly walloped by the ball. Instead, I became aggressive. As it happened, when I concentrated on mastering the motor skills required to play dodgeball well, I discovered I could be really agile, my aim deadly and sure. Soon, I was a triple threat—I could dodge, throw, and catch—and I was *killing* it. Oh, I was *fearless*. I might still be the fat girl on the team, but now I had some cred as a top player as well. The Raquel Welch Junior taunts tapered off, and now when we lined up to choose sides at recess, all the other kids wanted me on their team. Instead of getting picked on, I was getting picked first, and people began talking to me off the field, too. No longer the invisible Black girl, I had cracked a particular code about the ecosystem of school, namely that regardless of your background, athletic ability earned you power and respect. But just as I began to trust myself to navigate the new order of things, my world transformed itself yet again.

I had noticed for some time now that Bigmama tired more easily than before, her vitality ebbing slowly. She still looked out for me in every way possible, though her eyesight had dimmed, and Daddy had convinced her to give up driving her blue Datsun. That was also about the time that Vondela Pilot began sleeping over on weeknights, cooking our meals and helping Bigmama get ready for bed, and then getting her bathed and dressed come morning. Though I presented my usual cheerful face to the world, a hum of anxiety ran through each moment, a crackle no one but me could hear. Even so, I would not allow myself to imagine a reality in which my grandmother was no longer my legal guardian.

I began to more consciously appreciate her company as we sat together in the evenings, after we had all eaten dinner and Vondela had retired to her room. I would be at one end of the mahogany dining table doing my homework, with Bigmama at the other end, a dignified presence rhythmically tapping the keys of her electric typewriter, composing exquisitely beautiful letters that were legendary among her relatives and longtime friends. This hour after dinner had lately become my favorite part of each day, Bigmama engrossed in her letter writing and me solving algebra problems, constructing social studies arguments, or studying for an upcoming biology quiz, neither of us feeling any need to speak as evening slipped softly between the curtains. "Go turn on the lights, sweetheart," Bigmama might say when the shadows inside the house grew deep, and I would jump up from the table and do as she asked, before the two of us settled into companionable silence once more. I could hardly bear the thought that the day would come when I could no longer sit with Bigmama and bask in her presence in this deeply nourishing way.

One night, when Vondela was away from the house doing grocery shopping, and a theater project had kept me after school, Bigmama picked up her silver quad cane and painstakingly made her way out to Normandie Avenue, where she knew the late bus would drop me off.

The intersection was half a mile away from our house, an easy fifteen-minute walk for me, but Bigmama's progress past the manicured front lawns of our street and out to the bustling four-lane boulevard took almost an hour. Her bones ached all the time now, and her proud, erect shoulders had begun to stoop. But she was as determined as ever, and on this night, she meant to meet my school bus so I wouldn't have to walk home alone in the dark.

Exhausted by the time she reached Normandie, Bigmama perched herself on a fire hydrant and wiped her perspiring face with a lace-edged handkerchief she retrieved from her sleeve. At that exact moment, our neighbors Mr. and Mrs. Holmes happened to drive by on their way home. Astonished to see my grandmother hunched over her cane and breathing heavily as she mopped her brow, they stopped the car and went over to her. When Bigmama explained that she was waiting for me, Mr. Holmes prevailed on her to allow him to stay and meet my bus while Mrs. Holmes drove her back to the house.

After this incident, Daddy began to stop by most afternoons to check on Bigmama. He would take her vitals and inevitably counsel her to get more rest. My older cousin Reggie, who had spent summers with Bigmama in East St. Louis before I was born, also began to come around more often. He had relocated to Los Angeles in the late seventies to do his medical internship and residency at Martin Luther King Jr. Hospital. Reggie was the grandchild who perhaps knew Bigmama better than the rest of us. Seventeen years older than I was, he had experienced a different grandmother than I had. He recalled her wicked wit, her rollicking sense of fun. But there was also something else. Bigmama had recognized that Reggie was a sensitive soul, a boy who had to try harder in school than his brothers, and she poured her heart into him, bolstering his confidence and assuring him that he was equal to his dreams. It worked, too: Reggie grew up to become the doctor in the family, and arguably the most successful of our generation, professionally speaking.

Don't get me wrong: It wasn't that Bigmama hadn't poured her whole heart into her other grandchildren, as well. But she was older when I came along, and a stricter disciplinarian, perhaps because she knew she couldn't simply indulge me and then send me home for my parents to straighten me out. Besides, I was a scrappy and endlessly curious kid, much as I tried to contain my spiky energy so as not to disturb my grandmother's peace. I also seldom let on that I ruminated on my missing mother as deeply as I did, lest Bigmama feel she hadn't given me everything a growing girl might need. To all appearances, my grandmother had molded her youngest grandchild into a cheerfully obedient preadolescent, even if I did wear her out with my incessant questions and opinions, and often drew admonishing looks for sudden and inappropriate fits of laughter in settings that required more decorous behavior.

Then came the day when Bigmama threw up her breakfast of soft-boiled eggs and tea, which Vondela had served to her in bed while I was down the hall getting ready for school. I heard the commotion and ran to her room, where I found Vondela already cleaning up my grandmother, wiping her face, neck, and arms with a soapy rag and handing her a cup of Listerine so that she could swish out her mouth. After slipping her soiled nightgown over her head and guiding her arms into a fresh garment, Vondela settled Bigmama into the armchair by the window, then turned to strip the bed sheets. I plopped cross-legged at my grandmother's feet, taking her hands in mine and remembering with a sharp ache the mornings when she would wipe my face with a damp rag much as Vondela had just wiped hers. Presently, Bigmama reached an unsteady hand toward me and I leaned forward so she could cup my chin in her palm and lift my face to hers, her faded eyes bathing me in love.

Outside, I heard a car screeching into the driveway. When Reggie burst into the room, I realized Vondela must have called him. He rushed over to Bigmama and in one smooth motion scooped her up bodily into his arms, one elbow under her shoulders, the other under her knees as he carried her out to his car. Noticing the ease with which he lifted her, I saw with a pang that my big-boned grandmother had become thin, her brown arms roped with veins, every line of her body shrunken and fatigued. Reggie settled Bigmama in the back seat of his car and tenderly strapped the seat belt around her. Vondela and I followed them out to the driveway, Vondela explaining to me that Daddy had asked that Reggie bring Bigmama to the hospital so that she could be properly assessed, just to be on the safe side.

"Your grandmother is in good hands," she assured me as Reggie reversed out of the driveway. We watched them leave, Vondela's brow creased with concern, one arm circling me, a sixth grader already taller and bigger in body than she was, the two of us a mismatched little unit. We both caught the moment Bigmama let her head fall back onto the car seat, eyes closed, face twisted into a grimace, her spirit utterly worn.

Vondela put a hand on my shoulder and turned me toward the house's arched front door, its polished wood gleaming in the early morning sunlight, setting off of the central storybook turret that had sheltered me since infancy.

"Go and finish getting ready," she said gently, as if reading the dark turn my thoughts were desperately trying to avoid taking. "It's too late for you to catch the bus now. I'll drive you to school."

NINE

Shape Shifting

The house was unnaturally silent without her, yet you could feel Bigmama's presence the moment you stepped through the door. It was a visceral thing, as if my grandmother were just in the next room and would sweep in at any moment, the material of her dress swishing softly, her musical laugh gentling the air.

After being discharged from the hospital following a week of tests and medical treatments, Bigmama had returned home just long enough to pack a suitcase before flying with cousin Reggie to Alabama, where she would be cared for by her only daughter. Daddy assured me that, for the time being, Vondela would stay on at the house with me, overseeing my school and extracurricular activities, and I would fly to Birmingham to see my grandmother during the holidays.

I was relieved that he made no mention of my going to live with him in his three-bedroom condo on the marina in Long Beach. I had absolutely no desire to leave Bigmama's house, especially when Daddy was so busy with work and his community activities that he barely saw his apartment except to sleep most days. I couldn't imagine anything drearier than being in that place, wondering when he would get home. Not that I would have been alone as I waited. Daddy's new love, Maria, a New Yorker of Puerto Rican descent who worked as a social worker at the same medical center where he was chief of surgery, had recently moved in with him, along with her son and daughter.

I had met Maria and her kids for the first time a couple of years before, when they were still living in their home in Hawaiian Gardens. The way Daddy had engineered our introduction had left me with an uneasy feeling of déjà vu, because just as when he had taken me to see my mother when I was nine, he had given me little warning. At the time, I was approaching my eleventh birthday, and Bigmama was still moving about the house on West 80th Street mostly under her own steam. During the week, Daddy had called to say he would be picking me up on Saturday and taking me to see the new *Star Trek* movie, along with my sister Cheryl, my friend Michelle Woods, and the children of one of his friends. I'd been immediately thrilled by the idea of this outing. As I'd climbed into my father's car with Michelle, who had slept over with me the previous evening, I relished the crush of kids, which in addition to my then twelve-year-old sister Cheryl, included a boy about my age and a girl about Cheryl's age. The boy and the girl were obviously siblings, both with the same glossy black hair and café-con-leche skin.

After the movie, we all piled back into Daddy's car. I was having too much fun to consider where we were headed next, and didn't think much about it when we pulled up in front of a modest single-family home. Daddy explained that the boy and the girl I had just met lived there, and their mother was inside, preparing a meal for us. That's when my sixth sense about my father prickled, and in a flash I knew, without him telling me, that whoever the mother of the new kids might be, Daddy was romantically involved with her.

Suddenly, nothing felt quite as entertaining as it had been before, because I was aware that Daddy was also in a long-term relationship with my friend Chrystal's mother, Dodye, whom I loved. Right then, I resolved not to like the woman I would meet inside, who to be fair, knowing my dad, probably knew nothing about Dodye. A tall olive-toned beauty with short, stylishly cropped black hair, Maria could not have been warmer to Cheryl and me, despite the fact that my sister and I were distinctly chilly in return, Cheryl because she really couldn't have cared less who Maria might be to my father, and me because I couldn't have cared more.

A year later, the woman who had prepared a delicious spread of rice and beans and stewed chicken for us that afternoon, would give birth to my little brother, the third Ross Matthew Miller, just weeks before Bigmama took a turn for the worse. After the baby arrived in March 1980, Maria, her newborn, and her older kids would move into my dad's apartment permanently. My second brother, Jonathan, would join our family three years later.

And so, when Bigmama left Los Angeles to be cared for by my Aunt Edna in Birmingham, the last place I wanted to be was at Daddy's home, which was already crowded with more bodies that it could reasonably hold. Besides, I refused to believe that my grandmother would not soon return to the spacious rooms we had shared my whole life. Every night before bed, as I prayed for her recovery, I told myself that she was only in Birmingham for a little while, so that Aunt Edna could nurse her back to health, and as soon as she was strong enough, she would once again be back with Vondela and me on West 80th Street, running the show. In the meantime, Vondela and I would keep her beloved home in order, awaiting her homecoming.

Despite the terrible emptiness inside the house, the days with my interim guardian soon settled into a predictable routine. Newly diagnosed with diabetes, Vondela was scrupulous about how we ate. She cooked lighter meals and served smaller portions than Bigmama ever had, and made sure I consumed my proper allotments of fruits and vegetables daily. I knew she was concerned about my girth—at five-foot-six I already topped one hundred and sixty-five pounds—though she never suggested outright that I lose weight. She didn't have to. I was now thirteen years old and in the spring semester of eighth grade at my third school in four years, Walter Reed Junior High, where I was weary of being the conspicuously big-busted Black girl among all the slender, bud-chested White girls in my classes.

One evening after finishing homework, I was sprawled on my bed browsing through the latest issue of *Seventeen*, which had arrived in the mail just that afternoon. I turned past one fashion spread after another, each page showcasing thin, glamorously bedecked young women. By the time I got to the classified ads at the back of the issue, I was aching with the certainty that I would never look like any of those models. And then a small notice caught my eye. It was an advertisement for a summer weight-loss camp for teen girls that billed itself as a "fat farm." Slated to run for seven weeks on the University of San Diego campus, the program would house all attendees in the student dorms.

I sat up abruptly, visualizing the possibilities. Maybe this was the very thing I had been seeking, though I hadn't consciously decided to transform myself. But with Bigmama gone, and the woman who gave birth to me somewhere in the wind, I had felt my motherlessness more intensely of late. As a kind of defense, I was becoming adept at compartmentalizing my feelings, keeping my missing mother in a locked room in my mind, while hanging onto the hope of Bigmama's eventual return. Looking back, I can see this was where my tendency to build walls around my sadness truly began. Instead of looking inward to confront the self-doubt that claimed me without Bigmama there to bolster my confidence, to mirror in her loving gaze a vision of myself as worthy and right, I turned my attention outward, casting around for a way to clamber out of the dark hole, to recreate myself as someone who could withstand the scrutiny of light.

To my mind, that meant becoming a person who could walk into any room and *look* as if she belonged. Even if I didn't feel it exactly, even if I still secretly doubted my right to be there, at least I could muster a passable impersonation of a girl who was confident in where she stood.

And so I set about the task of becoming someone who—despite being motherless and holding two vilified races in one skin—would be welcomed by peers, accepted, invited in.

I got out of bed and padded to the hall telephone to call my father. It was almost 10 P.M., but I didn't want to wait another minute to find out whether he'd consent to my attending a summer sleepaway weight-loss camp. When I was done explaining the program to him and making my pitch, Daddy gave a low chuckle and said, "Well, I certainly applaud your initiative, Michelle." And he agreed to underwrite my plan.

I HAD NEVER BEEN AWAY FROM HOME FOR SEVEN WEEKS BEFORE. NOR had I ever experienced such complete immersion in an environment of stunningly entitled girls, more than three hundred of them, with me as the only Black girl in the group activities each day. To make matters even less hospitable, my roommate was a straight up mean girl, though I took far too long to discern this. She was much larger in girth than I was, but appeared to have none of the insecurity that often comes with being a big girl in a fat-phobic world. She came from money—her father owned a chain of auto-parts stores that harvested parts to car dealerships, and the business had done very well for him. My roommate, having grown up as her daddy's little princess, had learned to wield her wealthy White privilege like a bludgeon, and that summer, her chosen target was me.

I didn't realize at first that she was trash-talking me behind my back, telling the other girls that I acted like I thought I was better than her just because I had less weight to lose than she did, and because my father was a doctor and hers was an auto-parts dealer. When I discovered she was actively disparaging me—one of the younger girls in the program took me aside one day and told me—I was crushed. I had gone out of my way to be pleasant and accommodating with my roommate on those rare occasions that we found ourselves together in our room. And the difference in skin color aside, I'd assumed that with a girl who shared the particular experience of living inside a heavy body, I'd at least find a kindred soul. We were three weeks into the program by the time I realized that this wasn't going to happen, and that my own roommate was the reason the other girls shot me unfriendly looks when I entered the cafeteria, classrooms, or gym.

It probably made things worse that I had been dropping weight more quickly than many of the other girls. This wasn't dumb luck— I worked *hard* for every pound lost, rising an hour before breakfast each morning to run four miles around the campus. After that, I would attend the nutrition and cooking classes I'd signed up for, faithfully taking notes on what our instructors told us, before heading to the gym for my daily weight training sessions. I interspersed these classes with calisthenics workouts and team sports like soccer and volleyball, with a period of free time in the late afternoon.

I forced myself to stay sociable, chatting with whoever would talk with me, smiling at jokes cracked by any member of a group I happened to be standing in, ignoring the antagonism directed toward me from my roommate. But at lunch one day in week four, one of the girls splashed water from her hydration bottle at me, soaking my face, shirt, and hands, which I had raised instinctively to block the spray. I assumed this girl was being playful—my default would always be to give others the benefit of the doubt—so I laughed and wiped my wet hands on the back of her sports jersey, thinking I was getting her back. She jumped away from me as if horrified.

"Michelle touched my butt," she yelled, insinuating something sexual.

I looked at her, speechless for a few moments before finding my voice. "No, *you* threw water on *me,* and I was just drying my hands on your jersey as a joke," I hastened to explain. "I thought we were just kidding around," I went on. "It definitely wasn't a come on."

I should have saved my breath. Water bottle girl just huffed indignantly and stalked away from me, her clique of mean girls falling in line behind her, my own roommate included. After that, whispers went around that I was a lesbian, and if the other girls knew what was good for them, they'd stay far away from me. The mass banishment made me sad, not because they called me a lesbian, but because it was a lie. It didn't bother me one bit if they thought I liked girls. In fact, it was amusing to me when I remembered Bigmama telling Michelle Woods and me to stop being so boy crazy and attend to our school- work instead. But it was upsetting that the girls at camp had decided I was somehow wrong in my very being, unworthy of being part of their group, and they were choosing to vilify a whole group in order to disparage me. Well, I'd been an outsider before, and I knew there was nothing else to do but keep my head down.

A counselor named Susan saved the summer for me. In her twen- ties, she saw what was happening and went out of her way to befriend me. One evening after dinner, we were sitting in the music corner of the common room, heads nodding and shoulders bouncing along to Michael Jackson's *Off the Wall* album spinning on a blue plastic turn- table. When the record ended, Susan picked out Sheena Easton's *Take My Time* album, the one featuring her pop single "Morning Train," which was on everyone's lips that summer. But before placing the rec- ord on the turntable, she turned to me, the vinyl disc held between her palms like an offering.

"Hey, Michelle, I wanted to talk to you about something," she said. "All these girls are calling you a lesbian because they want you to feel bad. But you need to know that the name they're calling you isn't any- thing to feel bad about."

"I know that," I told her.

"Do you?" she said. "Because even if you did like girls that way, that would be nothing for you to be ashamed of. You need to know that, because what's happening to you right now isn't fair."

I saw she was righteously angry on my behalf that the girls had turned a blameless descriptor into an ugly epithet designed to wound me. "It's not the word," I assured her again. Somehow, despite the era, I knew that being different in that way wasn't wrong. At the time, I may not have understood the why of it, but having been an outsider all my life, I sure wasn't about to discriminate. "I don't care if they think I'm a lesbian," I continued. "So what? The thing I hate is how they act toward me. They're just so mean."

Susan nodded, perhaps sensing this wasn't my first time feeling like an outcast, and that the girls' spite had slipped into a well-prepared groove. "You know what, Michelle? You just be proud of who you are, no matter what other people do," she said. "You're a good person, and you're working so hard on the program. Maybe some of them are jealous that you're losing weight and getting fit and they aren't, but don't let that discourage you from the progress you're making. Just keep doing what you need to do. And no matter how they act, just keep being you."

"Thank you, I will," I said as she bent to place Sheena Easton on the record player, carefully positioning the needle on the "Morning Train" track. Sheena's bright soulful voice filled the room. *I wake up every mornin', I stumble out of bed/ Stretchin' and yawnin' another day ahead. . . ."* We sang along, swaying to the snappy, hypnotic tune. At a certain point I realized that I was feeling lighter and easier than I had in months, as if a burden I didn't know I was carrying had fallen from my shoulders. I suspected that Susan was battling the feeling of being stigmatized as a lesbian herself. I didn't know this for a fact, but I did know that this possibly queer young woman had shown empathy for a kid who wrestled with the feeling of being different. It was a coming-of-age moment of allyship that I would remember always.

In the end, despite the mean girls, I judged my seven weeks at fat camp to be an unqualified win, because I finished the program twenty pounds lighter than I had begun it. But by far the most healing experience had been the friendship and encouragement Susan extended to me when she saw that I needed to feel more at home in my skin. I wasn't there yet; it would take years for me to fully incorporate the lesson, but I believe that along with Michelle Woods when we were at Hamlin, that summer it was my sole camp friend who helped me along the path to accepting myself exactly as I was, no matter the verdict of the world.

I WAS MISSING BIGMAMA, REMEMBERING OUR LONG-AGO NIGHT-before-school ritual as I carefully laid out what I would wear on the first day of ninth grade. But for the fact that she was now too weak to hold up her end of phone conversations, I would have called her in Birmingham to tell her my choices—a blue silk floral long-sleeve blouse and skinny blue jeans that made my legs look as if they went on forever, especially when paired with my brand-new, impeccably white K-Swiss kicks. The next morning, I painstakingly blow-dried my hair into glossy straightness, parted on one side, front wings neatly tucked behind earlobes adorned with thin gold hoops. Since that fateful day in third grade when I'd worn my hair loose, I'd learned to tame my incipient frizz by running palms lightly coated with coconut oil over my heat-straightened strands.

My summer of exile aside, I held out hope that maybe this would be the year I finally broke out of my odd-girl persona and ascended to the ranks of the cool kids. The year before, I had been one of only two Black kids in Walter Reed junior high's Individualized Honors Program, and my friend group had been small, consisting of the only other Black kid in my advanced placement classes, an outgoing athlete named Otis Livingston, and three regular stream students, a biracial Black and Jewish girl named Kelly Pierson, her friend Laura Marquez, who was Mexican, and a Filipino girl named Magdalena Gillo. Paul Lucas, a husky Jewish boy, sometimes joined us. So did Dorian Johnson, a well-liked Black kid who was friendly with everyone, yet often hung with our little crew. Except for Dorian, we were a scrappy band of misfits who helped each other feel less weird.

As much as I relished my posse of oddball kids, I still hankered to be *seen* by the rest of my classmates—not an unusual desire for a girl on the verge of fourteen, who'd spent much of her academic life feeling invisible. Year after year I had arrived for the first day of classes as a new girl bused in from the hood, looking for a crack that would allow me access to a culture in which most students had known each other since kindergarten. But now, in ninth grade, I was no longer new, and that had to count for something.

Yet my sense of always being the odd girl was so deeply ingrained that for months I failed to grasp how dropping significant poundage had propelled me into the ranks of the "cute girls." I remained remarkably oblivious of my new status even when a boy I'd noticed on the first day of my Graphic Arts class began taking an interest in me. This boy, who I'll call Anthony, was of Italian and Jewish parentage, with an overgrown spill of light brown curls and a courtly manner. Within weeks I was crushing on the kid, charmed by the way he always sought me out as soon as I entered the art room, and how he was always maneuvering to partner with me on class projects. Even so, I took an unreasonably long time to get that this boy might actually like me, too. We were more than halfway through the fall term when I finally figured out that Anthony and I were engaged in a giddy adolescent flirtation.

One afternoon a few weeks before Thanksgiving break, the two of us were occupied with silk-screening a design onto a textile. Heads close together, we were bent over a table in the school's art room, intermittently chatting as Anthony held the wooden frame steady while I used a blue plastic wedge to swipe photosensitive emulsion onto the mesh in the center of the frame. We were both concentrating so intently that neither of us noticed when Otis and Paul entered the room, the two of them deep in conversation. But as they ambled toward us, we both heard when Otis said very audibly, "Why don't we ask Michelle? She's Black. She'll know."

Perhaps it was the sharp intake of breath that made me look up at Anthony curiously. He had turned as white as the paper in our notebooks lying open on the table next to us. I understood in that moment that everything was about to change. I knew it so clearly that I calmly laid down the blue plastic wedge and stood waiting. I didn't exactly brace for what I knew was coming so much as I began to prepare myself for how I would need to respond. I was intensely aware that, above all else, in this moment I needed to be definitive.

Anthony swallowed hard, the bony knob in his throat bobbing up and down.

"Michelle, you're Black?" he said in a whisper.

"Of course, I'm Black," I said brightly, making my voice cheerful, forcing a smile. "What did you think I was?"

"Yes, what did you think she was?" Otis echoed.

"I-I-I thought she was J-J-Jewish," Anthony stammered, clearly unnerved by the sudden attentiveness to his question by Otis and Paul.

"Okay, well now you know," I said, shrugging and picking up the blue wedge, getting back to swiping emulsion as if this little exchange were no big deal. Yet I knew without a doubt that the four of us had just etched a line in the sand, and Otis, Paul, and I stood on one side of it, Anthony on the other.

My silkscreen partner said nothing more, his silence conveying everything I had already surmised. To this day, I cannot recall what Otis and Paul wanted to ask me, or how I responded. I only know that as I turned back to coating the mesh for our silkscreen design, I could see the fresh tension in Anthony's arms as he gripped the frame. I knew he was counting the seconds until the period was over, so he could escape the art room, its atmosphere now thick with my confusion and his fresh and inexplicable contempt. As soon as class ended, he rushed out of the room, and in the days following he effectively ghosted me, declining to speak to me unless I addressed him directly. Even then he would reply grudgingly, with an exasperated grimace and sigh of disdain.

I eventually put it together that Anthony believed I had willfully deceived him about my race, an idea that was shocking and illogical to me. All my life, I had encountered people who would take note of my light skin, long wavy hair, and pointed features and be curious about my ethnicity. "What are you exactly?" they might ask. "I'm Black," I would tell them, cheerfully removing their confusion. Sometimes, if I was in the mood to claim my mother's contribution to my heritage, despite her absence from my life, I might say, "My father is Black, and my mother is Hispanic." Never before had my response provoked the level of hostility now being directed at me from Anthony. It stunned me to realize he actually thought I had been *trying* to pass for White.

I wanted to confront him and let him know that I was *proud* of who I was. Why would I ever choose to hide my race? Why would I deny the bonds of kinship with my father's family and everything that connected me to the resilience and achievements of Black people in this country? It never would have occurred to me to pretend to be anything other than what I was, my father's daughter, the purpose and pride of my grandmother's final years, a Black girl to my core. And yet, in a split second, I had become a pariah in the eyes of a boy who had previously presented himself as a friend simply because *he* had misinterpreted my physical appearance.

So this is how racism cuts you, I remember thinking. It was disorienting, baffling, isolating, humiliating. *I'm still me!* I wanted to scream at him. *Nothing's changed!* But he acted as if I was no longer the same person as I had been before.

Never again would Anthony and I partner on assignments in Graphic Arts class. In fact, I had to complete our joint silkscreen project on my own. After that, I ignored my former crush even more industriously than he ignored me, refusing to give any indication that I was bewildered by his behavior or that I even cared. But I had learned my lesson, which was to never in life be caught in that situation again. I promised myself that no one would ever again have to wonder about my ethnicity. If I detected a question from anyone on the matter, I would be unequivocal, erasing all doubt. On the racial battlefield that was

America, I could not appear to be straddling the middle ground. I had to choose a side and plant my feet there.

That day with Anthony in the art room became the watershed moment when I released my mixed-race story and claimed my Black identity in full. I was still hungry for details about my mother's side of the family, still quietly roiled by her absence. But no longer would I accord her half of my identity, when she had given me nothing of hers. From that day on, I let my hair fluff and curl with abandon around my head, but the deeper change was internal, invisible to anyone but me. I now understood more acutely than I ever had that in the country of my birth, there was no room for ambiguity. Black people's ongoing fight for equality demanded my commitment.

IT WAS WITH A WEARY SENSE OF RELIEF THAT I ESCAPED LOS ANGELES at Thanksgiving, traveling to Birmingham to spend the holiday with my Alabama family. Both excited and apprehensive to see my grandmother, when I finally stood at the door of her room, I ached to see how much more frail she had become since leaving South Central. Her sunken eyes stared at the ceiling as caregivers and family members came and went from her sick chamber, but when she became aware of me hovering, a smile flickered up from the depths of her white-ringed irises, and she lifted a skeletal brown arm to beckon me closer and bring my cheek down to hers.

All this time I had thought that Bigmama was merely getting old— she had celebrated her eighty-sixth birthday that year. But now I saw very clearly that she was dying. Aunt Edna took me aside and explained that our beloved matriarch was being stolen from us by late-stage ovarian cancer, which had already metastasized throughout her entire body by the time she was diagnosed. Yet I still wasn't prepared to lose her only four short months later. In early March 1982, Uncle Tom telephoned us one morning to tell us that Bigmama had slipped away in the night. Holding the receiver out to Vondela, I felt disconnected from myself, so outside of my own body that I was barely aware of the tears rolling down my face. When Vondela and Uncle Tom began talking about possible funeral dates and flying Bigmama's body back to Los Angeles from Birmingham, I left and went to sit alone in my grandmother's room. I sank into her favorite green armchair by the window, where for so many years we had sat with my back leaning against her knees as she patiently detangled my hair.

I felt strangely orphaned, despite the fact that I still had a father—and even a mother somewhere. The eventuality I had dreaded my entire life, and had repeatedly repressed, now rose and ransacked me, hollowing me out. Sitting in Bigmama's chair, a weak watercolor sun filtering in through the curtains, nothing felt real, nothing but the secret shame that my grief at losing my grandmother was already being grotesquely hijacked, swamped by the resurgence of a long-held fear: *Without Bigmama, what will happen to me now?*

TEN

Naming and Claiming

I couldn't hear myself singing the words of "Amazing Grace." The world seemed muted and at a distance. It didn't seem right to be in Bigmama's church without her voice warbling the hymn beside me, as she had done almost every Sunday morning of my childhood. Standing between my father and my Aunt Edna in the front pew of Manchester Baptist Church on South Vermont Avenue, I could barely take in that this was the last time I would be inside that whitewashed stucco sanctuary in the physical presence of my grandmother, who lay in repose in an open casket on the crimson carpet of the altar. Her terrible stillness in that dim sanctuary, filled as it was with vibrantly colored flowers sent by family and friends from around the country, seemed impossible to fathom.

After the funeral, the first I had ever attended, everyone reconvened at West 80th Street for the repast. Neighbors and friends had brought most of the dishes that now covered the dining table, a feast provided for the hordes who had come from far and wide to attend Bigmama's homegoing service. I curled up in one corner of the living room couch, noticing that the sounds filling the house were distinctly festive, a rising hum of conversation punctuated by chimes of laughter from different corners, with small children ducking between clusters of grownups, playing hide and seek in rooms over which Bigmama had once presided. I was sure that my grandmother would have approved of the merriment that accompanied the many recollections of her now being shared, but for myself, I couldn't muster any joy at all. I had no idea what came next, where I would live, who would take me in, and I was worn out with wondering and worrying about it. And so I just sat in a corner and let my thoughts float.

Meanwhile, out of my earshot, conversations were happening about me. I became aware of this when Daddy, Aunt Edna, and Vondela called me away from our guests, beckoning me to follow them down the hallway to Bigmama's room. Once there, Daddy explained that he and Aunt Edna had asked Vondela to move into Bigmama's house permanently to care for me, and she had agreed. I looked from his face to Aunt Edna's and finally to Vondela's, my heart lifting with relief as I met her smiling eyes.

I already loved Vondela and appreciated how she had kept everything going when Bigmama could no longer manage on her own. A slim, attractive brown-skinned woman in her mid-forties with a short Jheri curl, Vondela had the calm and proficient air of one who could be trusted to handle whatever arose. Why she had agreed to be my mother surrogate, I could only guess, though I had long suspected that she harbored an unrequited love for my dad—something about the melancholy look in her eyes whenever she regarded him. Whatever her reasons, I knew that I would infinitely prefer staying on at Bigmama's house with Vondela to moving into my father's already overcrowded Long Beach condo.

The truth was, I was still resisting any closeness with Maria. Even though Daddy and his previous partner, Dodye, had remained good friends after their inevitable parting, I still felt as if I would be betraying her and her daughter Chrystal by taking Maria into my heart. After all, my dad had dated Dodye on and off for most of my preadolescent years, and I'd wished for every one of those years that he would marry her. In fact, when I'd first learned that he and Dodye had broken up when Maria was already several months pregnant, I had been incensed at my dad, failing utterly to recognize that my anger was really profound disappointment masquerading as something else. Anger at my father felt easier to express than the hurt, disillusionment, and regret that had attended the news that he and Dodye would never marry.

Later, I would understand that Maria truly loved my dad, but back then I was a grieving, hormonal teenager and far less charitable. I saw Maria as an interloper who had come between my father and the woman I had long believed was his soul mate. I'm ashamed to remember those feelings now, rooted as they were in my confusion at some of the questionable choices Daddy had made when it came to romantic relationships. The way I saw it, he'd already lived this particular story, getting a woman to whom he was not married pregnant, while already in a committed relationship with someone else—which of course was how I came to be. And even though Daddy had been an unfailingly attentive and loving parent to me, my own situation now felt anything but secure. I never stopped worrying that the remaining threads holding our little family unit together would suddenly fray, as indeed so many threads had already given way when Bigmama got sick and then died.

"Why would you do this?" I had accosted my father some months after my little brother Matt was born. We were standing next to Bigmama's dining table, the two of us alone in the house. "Why would you betray Dodye like this? She's always been there for you, your best friend. You know each other's scars; you keep each other's secrets! Why would you cast aside a woman like Dodye just to make the same mistake a second time?" I didn't point out that Maria was Latina and light skinned, like my mother, while Dodye, being African American like us, seemed a more appropriate marriage partner. Somehow, I knew hurling this particular opinion at my dad would have been a step too far.

"Michelle, calm down," he told me with exaggerated patience. "You don't really understand any of this."

"What don't I understand?" I demanded.

Daddy looked at me for a long moment, calculating his answer. Finally, he sighed and pulled out a chair. "Sit down, Michelle," he said. "It's really none of your business, but I'm going to explain it to you." He waited for me to settle myself across from him at the dining table that had once graced his childhood home, before he spoke again.

"Try and see it my way," he said as I glared at him. "I want more children, I always have, but Dodye is already settled professionally and not in a phase of her life where she wants to start a new family with me. I get that. And she gets me. We both completely understand each other. I will always love Dodye, and I know you will, too. But it's different with Maria. With her I have a chance to have more kids."

"But you're not married to Maria!" I had shrilled, my eyes blazing. "Just like you weren't married to my mother, and you see how that turned out!"

To his credit, Daddy stayed calm in the face of my rank teenaged impertinence and disrespect. "Maria and I are getting married," he told me then. "Maria is going to be your new mother."

"No, you're wrong about that," I had shot back, my voice low and fierce. "Maria will never be my mother!" With that, I had pushed back from the dining table and stormed out of the room.

In years to come, I would grow to love Maria unreservedly, and to appreciate her for giving me my two brothers and remaining devoted to my dad, who even I could see was not an easy man to live with. As progressive and egalitarian as he had always been with me, within his own home he was something of a lord, demanding that everyone else's living arrangements conform to his preferences and needs. That meant he expected Maria to oversee all things domestic—cooking, cleaning, and caring for the children as he came and went on his own unpredictable schedule. As I grew older, I would come to view Maria as a saint

for so graciously dealing with my father's unwillingness to be more accommodating within the marital home. But back when Bigmama had
just died, I refused to allow her any quarter to win me over. Belatedly, I
would understand just how cruel and unfair I had been to her, though
I was never anything but polite to her face. I knew that had she been
alive, Bigmama would not have tolerated any whiff of rudeness toward
Maria on my part.

My father was another matter. Perhaps I dared to challenge him
because I knew he was committed to me, and wasn't going anywhere,
no matter how badly I behaved. And, as emotionally unraveled as I had
been after losing Bigmama, I was devoid of the inner resources to politely measure my words. I'd been a solitary child in my grandmother's
house for so long that whenever I stayed over with Daddy and Maria in
the condo, I had felt tense and rattled by the clamor and chaos around
me, and I didn't hesitate to let them know how eager I always was to
escape back to the peace and quiet of my childhood home—as empty as
it seemed without Bigmama. Now, I was grateful and relieved that my
father had seen fit to make an arrangement with Vondela that would allow me to continue living in the place I loved for the foreseeable future.

MY GRANDMOTHER MIGHT NO LONGER BE WITH US, BUT IN THE
months that followed, thanks to my new guardian, the house on West
80th Street remained my sanctuary. For so many years, as I'd integrated
one academic institution after another, Bigmama's home had been my
refuge from the isolation of being the new girl in yet another majority White school. My outsider status would abruptly change, however,
when I entered tenth grade at Palisades High. On this new campus, I
would finally start to connect with a diverse and accepting community
of friends with whom I could be my full self—and all because I had
fallen in love with the music of Prince.

I had my cousin Lynn in Birmingham to thank for this fortuitous turn of events. Even though Bigmama would never again be in Birmingham, until I left home for college I would continue to fly south to spend school breaks with Aunt Edna and her family, with my dad joining us at Thanksgiving or Christmas whenever he could get away. The December that I turned fifteen, I finally felt old enough to court the attentions of twenty-year-old Lynn. Though I had for years tried to follow her everywhere in the house, she had never taken much more than a polite notice of me. But this trip would be different. On this visit, she would introduce me to the artist named Prince.

I was sifting through records in the den one afternoon, and came across the *Controversy* album just as Lynn walked into the room. Unfamiliar with the beautiful, androgynous-looking man sporting a pink suit and perfectly permed bob staring out at me from the album cover, I turned to my cousin. "Who *is* this?" I asked her.

"Oooooh, that's Prince," Lynn said, her eyes suddenly dancing. I didn't understand her excitement until she played the record for me on the turntable.

"Oh my God, I love this!" I exclaimed, shimmying in time to the artist's wild percussive sound. I studied the album cover, intrigued by Prince's full painted lips and dark mascara-rimmed eyes. "And he's wearing makeup!"

"Prince might wear more makeup than you or me," my cousin responded in an exaggerated Alabama drawl, "but honey, Prince ain't nuthin' but a straight-up *maaan.*"

And then Lynn had a brainstorm. In just a few days, on Sunday, December 19, 1982, Prince would be playing a concert with The Time and Vanity 6 at Birmingham's Civic Center Arena as part of his *1999* album tour, and Lynn had tickets to attend with one of her friends. "You should come with us!" she announced, pulling me up from the floor and twirling me around. "You need to be at that show!" Since Lynn was in college at Hampton University, my aunt sprang for my ticket, delighted to see the girl cousins excitedly simpatico about something at last. It would be my first live concert ever, and in the days leading up to it I was so dizzy with anticipation, everyone would tell you I was just about losing my mind.

On the night itself, I melted into the rhythm pulsating from the stage, with Prince's band The Revolution, The Time, and Vanity 6, all lit by electrifying pyrotechnical displays. The man himself pranced in his bedazzled costume as he belted out the lyrics to songs like "Delirious" and "Little Red Corvette," all the tracks on his *1999* album, every one of which I now knew by heart. Singing along with the rest of the audience, I was ecstatic. Between sets, I kept grabbing Lynn's arm, gushing, "Thank you! Thank you! Thank you!" until my cousin laughingly peeled my fingers from her arm, saying, "Okay, Michelle! I get it! You're happy!" And I was. For a girl who had been relatively sheltered by Bigmama's old-school childrearing ways, Prince and the Revolution launched me into the stratosphere.

Still, I had no idea of the magnitude of the gift Lynn had given me with that Prince concert until the spring semester of tenth grade at Palisades High. With a scenic campus overlooking the Pacific Ocean, Palisades was the city's number one public high school. I had excelled academically at Walter Reed, which had allowed my father to reach out to his Board of Education contacts to secure me a place in the gifted program at Pali. But on this, my fifth time entering a new school, I had more than good grades on my mind. I was determined to use everything I'd learned about being the new girl to finally work my way into the popular crowd. This would prove easier than I imagined, because even though the neighborhood around Pali High was predominantly White, the school had taken the LAUSD's integration mandate seriously, busing in large numbers of teens from across Los Angeles, giving me a ready-made community of students of color on the very first day.

The campus itself remained fairly segregated socially, with Black and Hispanic kids mostly hanging with each other, White kids with their own, Asian kids together, and so on. But there was enough mixing among the different groups through sports and other activities like cheerleading and theater club, that students were able to forge and maintain relationships across ethnic lines. In my three years at Pali, I don't recall a single incident of racial conflict. Finally able to relax my hypervigilance at school, I became something of a chameleon, a sunny, bohemian-dressing Black girl floating among many different groups, traversing the student body spectrum at Palisades High.

During quiet evenings in my room at Bigmama's house, I would often pause in the midst of homework to wonder at my new social range, and how, for the first time at school, I had found my place not just in one group but in several. My entrée to this new world had all started with Angelique Faulk, a bushy-headed beauty who sashayed into our tenth-grade Geometry class decked out in a beige three-piece skirt suit and black pumps, carrying a briefcase. *Who wears a three-piece suit to high school,* I recalled thinking. *Where does this girl think she is?* And she had arrived late to class, too, the teacher already explaining formulas as she chose the empty desk behind mine. I confess I really wanted to hate the girl, with her flawless complexion and precocious poise. But then she tapped me on the shoulder halfway through the class and whispered, "Excuse me, but do you understand that formula on the board?" I turned to see her face scrunched with worry, and something completely guileless and open in her demeanor, and everything in me softened. "Yes, sure, I can explain it to you afterward," I whispered back, and by the time we walked out of class together, we were on our way to becoming fast friends.

Angie ran with a crew of girls who had transferred with her from junior high; they all clopped around the campus in three-piece suits and low-heeled pumps, looking like mini moguls. I hung with them for two weeks or so, wearing a sky-blue business suit to school myself, but I couldn't sustain it. I quickly realized I was far more comfortable in flowing dresses, sweatpants, T-shirts, jeans, and sneakers. Even so, Angie and I would remain close.

Shelli Alexander, Pali's top tennis star who sat next to me in Health class, was another day-one friend. Her comedic timing was peerless. As our teacher lectured us about the birds and the bees as part of the state's Sex Ed curriculum, Shelli would roll her eyes and pretend to flick her short-cropped mass of ringlet curls over her shoulder like a White girl tossing her hair, all while giving a hilarious running commentary under her breath—"Um, I think we already know that goes there, Sir."

At the end of tenth grade, I went out for the flag team. My fellow cheerleaders Christine Greene, Karen Addams, Gayle Stephens, and Dana Flanagan quickly became my weekend running buddies, bouncing from one party to the next with me, the five of us socializing to within an inch of our young lives while always making sure to keep our places on the honor roll. Later, an effervescent girl named Chris Thomas would also join our pep squad, relinquishing her role as the school mascot, a dolphin, to be a flag twirler, and becoming one of my lifelong friends.

Among the guys on campus, I was closest to Sheldon Hambrick, a physics nerd and avid photographer who could break down and rebuild his father's DeLorean with as much skill as any trained mechanic. At Pali, the nerds were the real in-crowd, especially Black nerds like Sheldon, who had an extra air of swag about them. Most of them also played sports, and in addition to being popular athletes, they were politically liberal, academically brilliant, and culturally grounded. Everyone wanted to hang with them, to bask in their cool, and there I was, accepted into their midst right from the start.

It didn't hurt that I had another credential that had put me squarely on everyone's radar—I'd been to a Prince concert. At the time, Prince's *Purple Rain* album was playing everywhere, and the single fact of having seen him perform live gave me instant street cred, and not just among the Black and Brown kids but the White ones, too. With Prince playing on repeat at after-school hangouts and on weekend beach days and dance parties, I had achieved a status in the student hierarchy that was entirely new to me. Marveling at my new standing as part of Pali's in-crowd, I decided to *be* the girl they thought I was, the one who was hip and trendy enough to have seen Prince perform in the flesh.

It had taken me all the way to tenth grade to find an academic setting in which I could feel as if I might actually belong, and I intended to enjoy all the perks and possibilities. I was finally coming into my own, successfully moving among many different kinds of friend groups and secretly thrilling to the fact that they seemed to *want* to be friends with me, too. No longer the shy girl perennially on the margin of her school's social compact, I could finally stop reining myself in. I could *breathe.*

MY SISTER CHERYL, NOW SEVENTEEN, SEEMED TO BE ON A REVERSE social trajectory from the one I had so recently embarked upon. With each passing year, she had become more reclusive and set in her ways. She remained the opposite of me, quiet where I was boisterous, restrained where I was irrepressible, socially retiring where I was eager to rush out and immerse myself in every activity that my father and Vondela would allow. Cheryl visited us on West 80th Street much less than when Bigmama had been alive, when Daddy had brought her to the house to see her grandmother. These days, I only saw my sister when she came to spend occasional school holidays with Vondela and me. Given the difference in our core natures, we had never been particularly close, at least not in the way I had once fantasized that sisters could be. Now, in adolescence, we simply accepted each other's presence. We were family, and therefore we loved each other, even if we were both fairly indifferent to interrogating how our distinct experiences of life had created who we had been as children, and who we were becoming in the hormonal surge of adolescence.

One evening, I was sitting at the dining table doing homework when Cheryl called to speak to Vondela. I looked up curiously as

Vondela's tone grew increasingly concerned, her brow furrowing deeply over the course of her conversation with my sister.

"But why are you at a strip mall at this hour?" I heard Vondela say. I glanced at the wall clock. It was just past nine and dark outside.

As Vondela listened to whatever Cheryl was saying on the other end of the line, she was shaking her head unhappily, her lips pressed tight.

"Does your father know?" she asked at one point.

And a few moments later, "You know this isn't safe, Cheryl." Her tone was more distressed than censuring. "What on earth are you thinking? Okay, okay, just stay where you are. I'm coming to get you."

Vondela sighed as she put down the phone, her square, capable fingers massaging her brow. She crossed the room to retrieve her car keys from a drawer in the curio cabinet. At the front door, she paused and looked back at me. "Your sister's at the 7-Eleven down the street from your dad's condo," she told me. "I want you to call your father and let him know where she is and that I'm on my way."

Moments later, I heard her silver Audi reversing out of the driveway and watched through the window as her taillights receded up the street. I then picked up the phone and did as she had instructed me, informing Daddy of Cheryl's whereabouts. Clearly disturbed, Daddy explained that my sister had been staying with him and Maria at their condo for the past few months, and he hadn't even realized that evening that she was not in the house. He thanked me for calling and got off the phone quickly, I guessed to go and find his eldest child.

A few hours later, Vondela returned home with my sister next to her in the passenger seat, and immediately behind, Daddy's car swung into the driveway. We all helped Cheryl unload two large suitcases, a backpack, and random shopping bags stuffed with her belongings from the trunk of Daddy's car, carting and depositing everything in the empty bedroom next to mine. That was the night that our little two-person household became three.

The next morning, Vondela told me the backstory. Cheryl, who had lived with her mother in Brentwood ever since Iris and Ross divorced when she was four, had been having continuous conflicts with Iris. My sister had been refusing to do her chores, finish her homework, or engage with much of anything other than sitting in her room reading and watching television. Nothing Iris did or said seemed to pierce her recalcitrance. Rather, it seemed to amp up her resistance to the point that she had run away from home. What she had actually done was walk to the payphone at the end of their block and call our father to come and get her, which he did, bringing her back to the condo he shared with Maria and their children.

Daddy phoned Iris to let her know that Cheryl was safe with him, and he suggested that Iris allow her to stay at his apartment until the tension between mother and daughter cooled down. They agreed he would come by that night to collect a few clothes for Cheryl to wear in the interim, but when he arrived at Iris's townhouse, she had packed every last item of her daughter's belongings, and declared to Ross that Cheryl was now his responsibility—don't bring her back. That's when things got real. Daddy's three-bedroom condo, with his once again pregnant wife, two teenagers, and a two-year-old, proved far too hectic an environment for Cheryl, whose nerves had always been easily jangled. After months of what must have felt to her like utter mayhem, my sister ran away again, this time calling Vondela from the first payphone she found.

My father had now decided that the best place for his older daughter was with Vondela and me. Neither Vondela nor I demanded much of Cheryl, who took meals with us mornings and evenings, attended classes in between, and mostly stayed in her room at other times. I remembered the whispers within the family about Iris sending away our other sister, the bright spark Adrienne, "the little dark one" as everyone seemed to refer to her back then. Though Cheryl and I had practically nothing in common, I was relieved and grateful that when Iris finally turned her back on Cheryl, too, Vondela and I had been there to offer my sister a far gentler landing than Adrienne's had been. Still, Cheryl's arrival put a fine point on the ways in which our family situation continued to be unusual, the differences seemingly more pronounced with each passing year.

In twelfth grade, I chose to be presented as a debutante, participating in the formal ball held by the junior chapter of my grandmother's sorority. I remember I'd very much wanted to be presented to Black American society, not only to follow in Bigmama's footsteps, but also because I'd thrilled to the pomp and circumstance when I'd attended Lynn's debutante cotillion in Birmingham back when I was in junior high.

I can still recall how on the night of my own ball I posed for pictures, resplendent in my white gown with its scalloped detailing at the neckline and sleeves, and my elbow high white gloves. My father, spiffy in a black tux, stood on one side of me, and Vondela in a red ruffled silk dress was on the other. I remember feeling happy as the photographer snapped the pictures of us, satisfied that the record of my cotillion would look the same as the record of every other debutante being presented—a girl in white standing between an older woman and an older man, whom everyone would assume to be the girl's mother and father. Not for a moment did it occur to me that my parental figures were both dark skinned, and could not by the laws of genetics have produced a seventeen-year-old who looked like me. As far as I was concerned, the three of us posing to mark my debutante cotillion were picture perfect.

Of course, I remained keenly aware that my family configuration was unlike that of any of my friends, but at Palisades High I found that I didn't mind being different as much as I once had. So what if my home life with Vondela and Cheryl, and my father living elsewhere, was somewhat unorthodox when compared to the rest of my tribe? After a mostly solitary childhood and early adolescence, I was finally out in the world, and I rushed at my new life, always hungry for what might be around the next corner. I wonder now if I was running headlong toward the next turn, unconsciously hoping she would be there, the woman whose body had made me, searching for me, too.

PART TWO

Chasing the Dream

"If you surrendered to the air, you could ride it."

—Toni Morrison, *Song of Solomon*

ELEVEN

The Mecca

Crossing the yard to my dorm, Aunt Edna and my cousin Paul beside me, I thought I might literally burst from exhilaration. The three of us were carting my belongings in two oversized suitcases and a black steamer trunk to Room 201 Frazier Hall. As we walked, I took in the redbrick grandeur of the sprawling campus with its Georgian buildings and splendidly arched windows, the arrow-straight paths traversing the main quadrangle, the manicured lawns and gracefully placed trees. I thrummed with excitement as I surveyed the clusters of freshmen getting to know one another, some faces eager and animated, others laid back, too cool for school. No doubt this was the atmosphere on college campuses across the country, but at Howard University, the sense of rapturous anticipation was reflected on faces from every corner of the African Diaspora, with students of every shade and description, from almost every state in the union and many nations across the world.

The gorgeous diversity of Black people alone was thrilling. Never before had I seen a more magnificent assortment of women and men gathered in one place. As I stood in line for registration later that afternoon, my eyes landed on a copper-colored Adonis a few spots ahead of me. Tall and athletic, he flexed inside his white Oxford shirt and pressed Levi's, a copy of *The New York Times* neatly folded into reading-sized quarters in one hand, his other hand slipped into a back pocket. In front of him, a chocolate brother turned and smiled directly at me with a gleaming set of pearly whites. Everywhere I looked, I saw handsome men of every color, and alongside them, the most spectacular array of women. Bold or retiring, every student strutted the campus with the singular sense of having landed somewhere special.

We had arrived at The Mecca!

I already knew several people on campus, including my friend from Pali High, Chris Thomas, who'd told me that she had decided to attend Howard when she learned I would be going there, too. Then there was Wendy Raquel Robinson, my assigned roommate. When I'd first entered our dorm room and found her unpacking her belongings with her poised and genteel mother, Wendy's reserved manner had made me wary. An aspiring actress who would go on to achieve marquee success in Hollywood, back then Wendy could pull off urban-punk glam while rocking regular jeans and Converse, her asymmetrical braids beaded at the ends and framing one side of her face. She seemed uninterested as Aunt Edna, Paul, and I introduced ourselves, and I worried that she might be just too cool to be bothered with the likes of me. A little while later, though, as Aunt Edna and Wendy's mother became absorbed in conversation, I shyly asked my roommate where she was from. That was all it took. We both squealed with excitement as we realized we were both from L.A., and that we had grown up just two streets apart in South Central. Soon we were laughing and jumping up and down like long-lost friends, with Wendy confessing she'd initially feared I would be prissy and stuck-up, a girl used to relying on light-skinned privilege. Relieved to discover that our first impressions of one another were so far off the mark, we hugged warmly before heading off to say goodbye to our families, both sensing that we'd found a sister for life.

Familiar with being the new girl at the start of the school year, I could already tell that Howard would be different. Despite the fact that for the first time in my life, I was well and truly on my own, I felt none of the apprehension I had always thought would attend this moment. I was aware only of surging excitement to be among peers whom I wouldn't have to convince of my right to be there.

When my high-school guidance counselor had asked me to name my first-choice college, there had been no contest. I wanted to attend Howard University, as my father and Bigmama had done. I wanted to experience the place that the school's alumni still proudly call The Mecca. Possibly the most prestigious of the nation's HBCUs, the institution is famous for educating and nurturing a long roster of "firsts" among African Americans. Through its dedication to developing generations of Black excellence, today Howard counts among its alumni illustrious men and women who include Nobel Peace Prize–winning statesman Ralph Bunche; renowned soprano Jessye Norman; literary lights Zora Neal Hurston, Toni Morrison, Isabel Wilkerson, and Ta-Nehisi Coates; the nation's first Black Supreme Court justice, Thurgood Marshall; beloved actors Chadwick Boseman, Debbie Allen, Phylicia Rashad, Taraji P. Henson, and Ossie Davis; singers Roberta Flack and Puffy Combs; top chef Carla Hall; Civil Rights leaders like Andrew Young and Stokely Carmichael; Congressman Elijah Cummings; and the first Black, South Asian, and woman vice president of the United States, Kamala Harris, who as it happened, was entering her senior year at Howard as I began my freshman year. This is not even close to an exhaustive list of celebrated Howard alumni. Like all these Black achievers, among so many others who came before, during, and after me, I wanted to be a Bison.

Before Howard, I'd only ever observed an institutional commitment to the idea that Black is Beautiful in the pages of *Essence, Ebony,* and *Jet* magazines. And, apart from time spent within my community of family and friends, I'd only experienced the fact of it during National Medical Association conferences with my father. These retreats were a yearly immersion in Black purpose and pride, giving the lie to the abasement of our culture in mainstream media. I would soon discover, however, that Howard's commitment to Black being beautiful, brilliant, proud, and prepared was deeper and more comprehensive than I could have anticipated. On the day in August 1985 that Aunt Edna and my cousin Paul dropped me off on the campus in Washington, D.C., and waved goodbye, I entered a bubble that celebrated Blackness and Black people in ways that our larger society had never even *tried* to envision.

Of course, Howard didn't only admit Black students, or hire only Black faculty and administrative staff. Every ethnicity was represented on campus. But having attended majority White institutions for most of my life, I relished the experience of being in a majority Black academic environment for the first time since elementary school. I understood the Hispanic, Asian, Native American, and mixed-race students also wanting to be where people of color were well represented, but I was surprised by the White people I saw moving through the crowd of students, who had chosen Howard, as well.

Granted, the school offered a top-notch education. Yet the incessant media messaging pervading the wider culture was that anything Black was essentially inferior, and so I could not help wondering how the White students at Howard had managed to escape that societal indoctrination. As one who had grown up with enough mystery about her origins that pursuing answers had become almost a reflex for me, I didn't hesitate to ask some of the White kids outright what—aside from its academic rigor and prime location in the nation's capital—had led them to attend college at Howard. Each person told me about someone in their lives who had made them question the American notion of White privilege, and the idea that anything not White was of lesser value. They'd wanted to experience a Black environment and Black culture in their own right, to test for themselves the received notion of White supremacy.

As I was considering a future in journalism, I decided to write a story about the White kids who had chosen Howard for the campus newspaper, *The Hilltop*. One sophomore I talked to was from a very small town in Vermont and had never before been in a diverse environment. I'd noticed him at a campus demonstration against apartheid in South Africa and was curious about what had brought him to a majority Black school. A week later, we met up for coffee in the Punchout, the campus food court and student center. He told me he'd loved every moment so far of his time at Howard. "There are all kinds of people here," I remember him saying, "and everyone is just doing their thing, and reacting to everyone else based on who they are and how they act, not how they look. At the same time, being a Black person in America gives you a kind of connectivity, a sense of belonging. Being here in the midst of that, allows me into that sense of community, too."

He went on to express how his immersion in the history and diversity of Black culture had, as he put it, "blown" his mind. And then he said something I will never forget. "You know," he reflected, "there are all kinds of Black people, just like there are all kinds of White people. But White people, when they think about themselves, they imagine the CEO, the movie star, the wealthy socialite, and no matter who they are or what their circumstances, they define themselves by that. But when they think about Black people, they imagine the person in jail, the person who can't read, the person whose life may have been derailed by traumas they don't care to see, and they define all Black people by that. They never stop to realize there are White people in those circumstances, too. Instead, when they meet Black people who don't fit the stereotype they have in their heads, they're like, 'Oh, you're the exception. You're not like all the other Black people.' They might never have met a single Black person in their lives, yet they're so sure of their conception of Blackness. I wish every one of them could spend a semester at Howard, being exposed to the breadth and diversity of Black people and Black culture. The history of Black achievement in this country alone would astound them, if they would only allow themselves to hear it. Sadly, most of them never will."

I'd just been schooled by a White kid and felt so enlightened by his perspective. Thirty-five years later, as I recall this conversation, our nation's news outlets are filled with stories on whether or not Critical Race Theory, or CRT, should be taught in schools. Critical Race Theory, a term coined by African American scholars Derrick Bell and Kimberlé Crenshaw, examines the intersection of race and law in American life, assessing the social and legal realities Black people have been forced to confront since their arrival in this country. As of this writing, CRT is being deployed by right-wing political forces as the new racial dog whistle. Heaven forbid White children should learn about slavery, reconstruction, Jim Crow, the Civil Rights movement, the genesis of the movement for Black Lives. Feigning ignorance of the fact that this examination of institutionalized racism is primarily taught in graduate schools, right-wing conservatives insist that such learning would only serve to make White children feel badly about themselves for events that unfolded before they were born. Given that many White Americans refuse to acknowledge their own biases and allow the notion of Black inferiority to stand in place of historical truth, my respect for the White students who chose to immerse themselves in a Black college experience has only grown. I saw it back then, but recognize it with an even greater clarity now: The White students who were my classmates at Howard were unusually inquisitive and boldly aware.

My teachers, too, were of every race, nationality, and creed. My Black Diaspora professor was Portuguese; my Tae Kwon Do teacher, Korean; my English professor, Nigerian. At Howard, the "miseducation of the Negro" was being purposefully dismantled, meaning just about everything the mainstream media had taught us—that we are not beautiful, we are not smart, we are not worthy—was being revealed as the lies our people had labored under simply by virtue of being Black in America. From day one of my classes, all of it was very intentionally being spun into a new understanding of ourselves, and the vastness of our achievements in this country, so that every one of us would learn to proclaim, "Yes, we can!" long before it became the electrifying rallying cry of America's first Black president in 2008.

At Howard, I would experience unconditional acceptance in an academic setting for the first time in my life. Though I had been able to create a diverse community for myself at Palisades High, and had been more socially comfortable there than at any of my previous schools, being in a nurturing majority Black environment would have the effect of fully grounding me in my core identity as a proud and ambitious woman of color. I had come of age in the racial soup of my American homeland as a Black child whose caregivers were determined to expose me to the most enriched academic environments possible, which in Los Angeles in the seventies and eighties had translated to my attending majority White schools.

But now, immersed in an environment expressly designed to support not just Black intellectual growth but also Black mental and emotional health, I saw with excruciating clarity just how limited Black children in White school settings inevitably are, simply by virtue of being Black in a culture that prizes whiteness above all else. I didn't blame my father and grandmother for sending me to White schools, and for insisting that, no matter how socially alienated I might feel, I should challenge myself to be academically excellent. But I was deeply grateful for the corrective experience of attending an HBCU, where, somewhat ironically, I could take off my race lenses whenever I chose, and operate unfettered by even the most well-meaning White person's unconscious biases about my kind.

Before Howard, I hadn't even noticed I was wearing racial lenses, yet every Black person in America inevitably does, and every mainstream experience is filtered through them. But now, released from America's restrictive racial story, I could explore more fully who I wanted be. At Howard, this newfound freedom from White expectations made me unafraid to dare. I was eager to step out of my comfort zone, buoyed by the idea inculcated in students that failure is essential to success, and is only fatal when we don't pick ourselves up, heed the lessons, and apply ourselves once more. Safe from the judgment and bigotry of the White gaze, students at Howard and other HBCUs find the experience so deeply restorative it's no wonder that a disproportionate number go on to break through barriers as African American firsts and to populate the ranks of professional achievement.

Hoping to make my own mark in this pantheon of influential men and women, I had decided that the way I would do so would be through a career in journalism. My natural curiosity about people's stories had led me to join the staff of *The Hilltop*, and to sign on to host a weekly talk show on the campus radio station, WHBC. The first time a producer pinned a microphone to my lapel inside the small studio, and I began asking questions of an anti-apartheid campus activist who sat across from me, I knew I was where I wanted to be. I pictured Big, and remembered the excitement I had felt when she had taken me with her to the TV studio. The thrill of watching her work came rushing back, filling me with a sense of inevitability, despite the fact that my interest in journalism had lain dormant since that time. Though it had never occurred to me to join my high school paper or senior yearbook staff, the desire to enter the field of journalism now arrived full blown, as if it had been waiting all along for me bring it into consciousness. *I am meant to do this*, I told myself. I remained convinced of this even when my father tried to convince me to take another path.

Daddy had flown to Washington, D.C., to take me out to dinner and hear how I was settling in. That evening, I sat across from him in the white-tablecloth establishment he had chosen, and eagerly spilled that I had finally figured out what I wanted to do. I intended to become a journalist.

"You're choosing a hard road," he had said, his expression concerned. "You know there are hardly any of us in newsrooms or on television, and there's no guarantee you'll be able to break through that barrier. I always hoped you'd become a doctor like me," he had added, "but it's been clear to me for some time that you have no interest in medicine. So why don't you go into business instead?"

"Journalism doesn't feel like a hard road to me," I had assured him. "It feels right. And besides, the fact that there are so few Black people reporting the news is the reason I *should* do it, not the reason I shouldn't."

I understood that Daddy only wanted my future to be financially secure and he believed my entering the business world would ensure that. But the thought of becoming some sort of corporate drone left me completely cold. On the other hand, having a pass to ask questions of people, to fully investigate the stories that made them who they were, was galvanizing, especially for a girl who had spent the first decade of her life trying to fill in the sketchy outline of her own story.

Daddy did not connect those dots, however. Instead, he saw my burgeoning interest in journalism as having been influenced by the high-profile careers of Bob Woodward and Carl Bernstein, the two *Washington Post* reporters who in 1972 had uncovered the Watergate scandal, forcing President Richard Nixon to resign two years later. Since then, he said, "Every Tom, Dick, and Harry wants to be a reporter."

"Not just Tom, Dick, and Harry, but Michelle, too," I shot back wryly. But he was off target about the Watergate scandal having been a significant factor in my choice. "Woodward and Bernstein have nothing to do with it," I told him. "That's not even the kind of journalism I want to do. I want to be in broadcast news, something like what Big used to do."

"That's not news, that's entertainment," he replied, almost derisively. "Ask Big. She'll tell you."

"Okay, I *will* ask her," I said, deciding in that moment not to waste any more breath trying to convince him of the worthiness of my goal. I already knew that whatever argument he raised, I would not be turned aside.

I didn't have to wait long to sit down with Big, as she traveled to the city on business only a month later. She had called and asked me to meet her for dinner at the Capital Hilton, where she was staying. I was excited to see her. As an executive with CNN's parent company, Turner Broadcasting, she was in a perfect position to give me valuable insight into every aspect of the business of TV. But as I would quickly discover, that wasn't her mission. As soon as we reached for our dinner napkins, she shared that my father had called and asked her to talk me out of trying to become a broadcast journalist.

"Why would you want to do that?" I asked her, sincerely surprised and not a little bit disappointed.

"Honestly, Michelle, it's a tough field for women, and especially Black women," she began. "There are so very few of us. I mean it all looks very glamorous on the surface of it. You get to be on television, your family will see you, your friends will be impressed, boys will flock to you, but the truth is, behind all that, the romantic image we have of journalists is really kind of false. You have to work like hell to get in front of the camera, especially now with so many more people trying to break into the profession. You're so bright. You could do anything else you wanted, go in almost any direction. I'm with your dad. I don't want the TV world for you. As a woman in that spotlight, you have to look a certain way, act a certain way. It can be chauvinistic and brutal. And what if you don't make it, what will you do then?"

"Well, damn, Big," I said when she was done. "I sure as heck won't make it if I don't even try. I'm not afraid of failing. If I have to, I can always find my way to something else. But I have to give it a shot."

More than three decades later, when I already had several years and awards under my belt and was the host of *CBS This Morning*'s Saturday show, Big would ask if I remembered the time she had tried to talk me out of going into television news, and whether I held it against her. Noting the regret in her tone, I rushed to reassure her.

"Absolutely not," I said, sharing that my conviction about the path

I had chosen had only grown stronger with each passing year. "If anything, sitting across from you that night, knowing you had brilliantly conquered that world, despite everything you were telling me about why I shouldn't go there—well, Big, it only made me more sure."

OF COURSE, THE WAY FORWARD WOULD NOT BE SMOOTH SAILING FOR me, as I would be obliged to build my own networks in the field I had chosen. Unwilling to rely on Big's hard-won connections, given that she had tried to dissuade me from pursuing broadcast news, I had no other legacy contacts or friends to offer me a leg up. As filled with possibility as I felt at Howard, it would take me a couple more years to find reliable mentors and advisors, and I would make my fair share of mistakes during that time.

The problem was I had no filter, especially now that I felt liberated from the eternal vigilance I had adopted ever since the day four girls in my class grabbed handfuls of my hair. But in my joy at being in a place where I felt safe letting down my guard, I sometimes failed to read the room, rushing headlong into controversy I should have seen coming. Perhaps most disheartening was how my eagerness to gain experience as a young journalist had caused me to fumble my chance at becoming a member of the very Alpha Kappa Alpha sorority chapter my grandmother had pledged some seventy years before. Here's how that sorry little episode unfolded.

Knowing that pledging season for the school's Greek organizations would be coming up, I pitched an exposé on hazing to my editors at the paper. At the time, Greek rushing rituals on predominantly White and historically Black college campuses were a hot topic, following a string of hazing-related deaths of pledges related to alcohol intoxication, heatstroke, heart failure, and drowning. That year, as I set about interviewing the leaders of every sorority and fraternity on campus about secret hazing practices, I was *intense*. One afternoon, I even followed a line of AKA pledges into their sorority meeting room, and asked them to please have a representative come out to meet with me.

An attractive soror dressed in an apple green linen jacket and wearing a single strand of pearls appeared. With perfect composure, she took my elbow and calmly steered me back outside.

"I'm Majella Chube," she said as we walked down the front steps of the building and strolled to a bench situated under a cherry tree. "What is it I can do for you?"

I knew at once who Majella Chube was. A friend from Birmingham had told me all about her the previous summer. Herschell Hamilton had graduated from Howard the year before. When he discovered I would be enrolling there, he'd waxed on about the girl on campus who had commandeered his heart. The naturally exuberant part of me wanted to throw my arms around Majella Chube right then and there, because I felt as if, through Herschell, I already knew her. I managed to resist the urge—I was there as an investigative journalist, after all, and such giddiness would be unseemly. And so, after explaining that I was doing a story for *The Hilltop* on hazing among the Divine Nine Black Greek organizations, I barreled forth with my pointed and perhaps even antagonistic line of questioning.

"So tell me," I said, "how does AKA haze its pledges, and what measures do you take to protect them from being injured?"

"Oh, there's no such thing as hazing in our organization," Majella responded dismissively, with no hint of a smile. I pressed on with my questions, taking earnest notes as she gave her practiced and scrupulously polite denials. I remember admiring her poise. *Maybe I'll pledge AKA next year,* I thought. It was a moment of naïve disconnection, with me believing I was fulfilling my role as a hardnosed journalist and that Majella and her fellow AKAs would understand I was just doing my job.

Before we parted I did let her know that our mutual friend had said glowing things about her. "Herschell Hamilton," I clarified. "He thinks so highly of you."

"Oh," she said, her ice queen composure thawing ever so slightly as a quizzical smile touched her lips. "How do you know him?"

"I know him from Birmingham because that's where my aunt and my cousins live," I told her. "Our families are good friends. He told me to look out for you."

Majella and I ended our up-to-then rather prickly exchange on a much warmer note, as we talked about Herschell, and she offered greetings for me to deliver to him the next time I talked to my family in Birmingham. In fact, Majella and I would go on to become dear friends, and she and Herschell would marry a few years hence. But the cheerful tone with which our conversation ended would be of no help to me when I actually went out to pledge AKA, as Majella had graduated by then, along with the nation's future history-making vice president, Kamala Harris.

Soon after, I attended the National Pan-Hellenic Council event, an open forum held by the Divine Nine Black sororities and fraternities to welcome potential pledges and provide information on the rushing process. During the question-and-answer period, I raised my hand. "I was wondering why we are known as Greek organizations when we are Black people?" I said. "Why didn't we name ourselves after African cultural traditions, and ground ourselves in our African cultural heritage?"

I wasn't trying to challenge anyone. I sincerely wanted to know the answer, so I didn't immediately understand why the room suddenly felt tense. Finally, a woman I recognized as an upper-class student in the School of Communications stepped forward. "Well, obviously, if you had read *Stolen Legacy,* you would know," she told me, referring to the George G.M. James book arguing that Greek philosophy had actually originated with the Egyptians.

"But I *did* read *Stolen Legacy*," I assured her. "That's why I know the Greeks built much of their culture and intelligentsia on the traditions and knowledge of North Africa. It just seems like we're giving the Greeks all the credit here."

It was her turn to interrupt me. "Well, Michelle," she said coolly, squinting at my name tag and pronouncing my name with exaggerated emphasis, "I suggest you read the book again. The explanation is in there."

It occurred to me that she might not actually know how to respond to my question, and since all eyes in the room were now trained on the two of us, I backed off. In time, I would piece together my own answer, namely that Black Greek Letter Organizations had based their service agenda on Hellenistic thought, which aimed to elevate the individual within a community through actions that support each person in living wholesomely and well. This Hellenistic philosophy was the foundation of the Divine Nine's approach to the challenges faced by people of African descent, nationally and globally. Their overarching goal was the uplift of our communities through the raising up of individuals who encompassed the health and well-being of the whole.

A couple of weeks after the Pan-Hellenic Council event, even with the chilly response my sincerely posed question had drawn, I was surprised to receive a letter notifying me that I had not been selected by the sorority that my grandmother had pledged in 1913, and my aunt Edna and cousin Lynn in the 1980s. With a pang of regret, I realized that I had taken my acceptance for granted and had failed to observe what should have been glaringly obvious social cues.

I, of all people, should have understood that belonging was earned, not given. For a girl who had spent so much of her life trying to find her way into new school networks, I marveled at my lack of discernment, my unwillingness not just to play the social game, but also to recognize that such a game needed to be played at all. While my journalistic ambitions meant I would always need to ask tough questions, I was learning that such inquiries often came at a cost. If I intended to keep on asking the hard questions—and I did—then I would need to be prepared to pay the price, particularly when the stakes were personal.

At the same time, it wasn't lost on me that as I immersed myself more deeply in life at Howard, the questions about my mother I had spent my life asking no longer felt quite as urgent as they had before. In the midst of everything new that I was experiencing in college, I had become less willing to allow the mysteries of my past to consume my present or my future. The choice to pursue particular questions or to let them rest, I saw now, would always be mine—my engagement with journalism had shown me this quietly empowering truth.

IN THE END, I WOULD NOT FULFILL MY DREAM OF BECOMING AN AKA until fourteen years later, when I was already a broadcast news correspondent. In 2000, I was nominated for honorary membership based, rather ironically, on my work as a journalist. The recognition was humbling, because in being chosen for the sorority's highest accolade—an award given to Black women whose professional contributions have been judged as advancing AKA's ideal of uplifting the Diaspora on a national or global scale—I would be joining the most rarefied of company, a roster that included such achievers as Coretta Scott King, Maya Angelou, Toni Morrison, Debbie Allen, Phylicia Rashad, Alicia Keys, Robin Roberts, Alice Walker, Ursula Burns, Edwidge Danticat, Suzanne Malveaux, among so many others.

On the night of my induction at the Dallas Convention Center, I was euphoric as I stood alongside my fellow honoree Lauren Anderson, the first Black principal dancer of the Houston Ballet, both of us arrayed in white for our welcome to the sisterhood. To be receiving this accolade in the city where my beloved grandmother had been born and raised made the ceremony even more special. I imagined Bigmama smiling down on me, pleased that I had arrived at this moment.

Then, out of nowhere, I recalled a comment I'd made to my roommate, Wendy Robinson, on the day after receiving my rejection letter when I'd gone out to pledge at Howard. "Well, it seems that for me to become an AKA, the national organization is going to have make me an honorary," I had told her ruefully. "I guess that means I'm going to have to go out and do good things in the world." Despite my disappointment at the time, I had not given up hope. Instead, I had put my ardent wish and the intention to be excellent into the universe, and years later it had delivered.

That evening, touching the shimmering strand of pearls at my throat, I was thinking not only of the path I had traveled to get to that stage, but also of the woman who gave me breath, and I found myself wishing she could have been in that room to see the daughter she had forsaken earn her laurels. And then I wondered: *What other heartfelt desires might I yet realize?*

TWELVE

African Spring

I settled into a window seat on the bus as it pulled away from Jomo Kenyatta Airport. I was traveling with fourteen other American students who had flown to Kenya from different parts of the United States in the spring of 1988. Exhausted and sticky from my trans-Atlantic flight, I relished the soft breeze brushing my face through the open window on the one-hour drive to Nairobi. Outside, slender trees arched over the two-lane highway, a gray ribbon narrowing to a pinpoint before disappearing over red-dirt hills in the distance. I thrilled to the brightly painted houses dotting the unfamiliar landscape, the way the rural outskirts gave way to gleaming glass-and-steel skyscrapers in the city center, the adjacent streets bustling with restaurants and nightclubs, thrift markets and shopping plazas. And everywhere I looked there were Black people—vendors selling African wax print fabrics from sidewalk stalls, men playing dominoes on crates outside rum shops, pedestrians dodging the careening cars and minibuses that somehow never collided, groups of schoolchildren heading home in the late afternoon sun. All of it felt so vibrant and inviting to me. I was finally *here*, in the land of my ancestors. I wanted to inhale it all.

Brought together by the Experiment in International Living,

the oldest study abroad program in the world, the students in our group had chosen to embark upon the Kenyan Coastal Studies curriculum that semester. We were there to explore the origins of the WaSwahili people, descendants of the mostly African Muslim traders and merchants who had once been part of the Omani Empire, and whose language and culture were an amalgamation of African, Indian, and Persian-Arab races and traditions.

After centuries of intermarriage, many of the WaSwahili people pictured in the program brochure I had pored over in Howard University's Founders Library, looked as if they could be related to me— the same tawny brown hue, prominent noses, almond-shaped eyes that pointed slightly upward at the outer edges. I thought that physically at least, I'd fit right in—always a powerful lure for me. But this was only one reason I had felt drawn to spending a semester in Kenya. The other was the coastal location of the program. Having grown up on the Pacific coast and attended high school on a campus bordered by the ocean, I was still a beach girl at heart, and the chance to immerse myself in a mixed-race culture on the Kenyan shore was irresistible.

Our group leader, Costas Christ, met us at the youth hostel that would be our home base for the next several weeks. An intrepid traveler who had lived in war zones across the world, he was now domiciled in East Africa with his wife, Sally, a midwife who ran her own study abroad group. Costas's experiences as a White American expat on the African continent had molded him into an insightful cultural translator. This was fortunate, because even though every person in our group had pledged to be open to new experiences, we had brought to Africa inherent biases seeded in us by the racial atmosphere back in the States. These not-always-conscious attitudes quickly sprang to the fore, revealing themselves first in a controversy that developed around the Black women's hair.

Within our group there were three Black women, eleven White women, and one White man. Everything had felt easy and friendly at the outset, so it took the Black women by surprise when racially tinged microaggressions began to creep into some of the women's interactions. Of the three African American women, I was the lightest skinned and wore my hair loose and curly. A second Black woman, Djenne Watkins, was medium brown in complexion and had arrived in Kenya sporting waist-length box braids. The third Black woman, Jen Wynn, had skin the color of strong black coffee, and had traveled with her permed hair pulled back into a bun. Days after we arrived in Kenya, Djenne had convinced Jen to let her braid her hair, too. The process unfolded over the course of an entire week, in between classes and activities, and by the end, with their identical hairstyles, Jen and Djenne looked as alike as sisters. That's when things began to unravel. Some of the White women were confused by the process by which Jen had gone from short pressed hair to a long curtain of braids, and they didn't hold back on the questions. Worse, they would walk right up to Jen and freely touch her hair, holding up individual braids to examine them for clues as to how the style had been achieved.

"Is this your real hair?" one young woman asked with no apparent awareness that she was violating Jen's personal space.

"Is that style hard to keep clean?" another inquired of both Djenne and Jen. "How do you wash it properly when it's all braided up like that?"

They even brought me into their mess. "Michelle, how come your hair is softer than Jen and Djenne's," one group mate wanted to know. She actually plunged her hands in my unruly curls and pronounced, "It feels so fluffy."

None of this was remotely okay, and Jen, Djenne, and I told them so in a polite but firm way. Our group mates protested that they hadn't meant to offend, they were merely curious. I believed them. But that still didn't excuse the freedom they'd felt to touch and invade our persons. We tried to explain this, and when it became clear our effort to be gracious and nuanced wasn't getting through, voices were raised. As the exchange grew more heated, the White girls complained that they were being unfairly attacked, while the Black girls felt defensive and unheard. That's when Costas stepped in. He called us all to a meeting on the wide, breezy verandah of the hostel so that we might talk everything through and constructively air our grievances before they could do lasting damage to the harmony and cohesiveness of our group.

Costas was masterful. He managed to unpack the situation in a way that each person sitting in our circle could accept and understand. Rather than single anyone out, he addressed the White women as a group. "Why do you feel that you have the right to touch a Black woman's hair without asking, or even have an opinion about what style she might choose to wear?" he asked them. "You're not familiar in that way, so what you're really performing is your sense of ownership over your Black peers." The White women gasped, stunned by Costas's assessment of their underlying assumption, but to their credit, they remained receptive as Costas continued. "You may feel as if your questions are innocent, that your curiosity is harmless, but would you walk up to a White person and touch her hairstyle and interrogate her about its care? Would you even ask a White woman, 'Is that a wig?' No, of course you wouldn't. So why do you think it's okay to ask a Black woman if her hair is real? You're basically discounting the sovereignty of another person's being."

Costas then broke down how the history of colonialism and slavery had left White people feeling as though they could have free rein over Black bodies, as if it was their birthright and privilege. "Most of you aren't even aware that you have these attitudes, or that your default is to behave in this way," he insisted. "But you need to *become* aware, because it's a matter of simple human respect for each other's boundaries." A lively discussion of personal space and an exploration of acceptable and nonacceptable ways of being culturally inquisitive followed, and I realized that it was the first time in my life that I had been able to engage so openly with White people on the subject of race.

The White women in our group weren't the only ones that Costas had to school on the subject of entitlement, however. Our leader didn't hesitate to challenge the Black members of our group, too, when he observed us exhibiting our own unconscious behaviors. At the hostel where we were staying, the locals called us *wuzungu,* meaning foreigner, the word always accompanied by a knowing smirk, and they weren't only referring to the White students. Naively, the other two Black women and I had taken for granted that we would blend in easily in an African nation. It was sobering when Costas pointed out that the very manner in which we carried ourselves, and the tone we used when asking for courtesies—as if we felt it was our right to be granted certain considerations—revealed in us the same ingrained sense of American privilege as our White counterparts.

"You all act like, because you're American, you're better than everyone else," he explained, not unkindly. "It's in how you walk, how you talk, how you enter a room. But you all need to check the attitudes, yes, even you Black folks. You're in a different culture now. You're in *their* culture. You are all guests here, so you need to stop acting as if you're owed any favors and learn to be more respectful and appreciative of your hosts."

To a person, we felt indebted to Costas for holding us accountable, and we took his words deeply to heart. I was gratified when, by the end of our first month in Nairobi, local people no longer referred to us as *wuzungu.* Now they greeted us with warm salutations of friendship, and I knew it was because we were becoming more humble, grateful, and aware.

IN EAST AFRICA, THERE WAS ALSO A BOY. A FEW WEEKS INTO THE PRO-gram, our group had traveled to the island of Lamu off the northern coast of Kenya for an immersion course in the Swahili language. On the Saturday we arrived, we had decided to spend the day at Peponi

Beach. That's where I first saw him, walking along the shoreline, the afternoon sun haloing his big, curly light brown Afro and outlining his sculpted shoulders. He was a vision straight out of a resort destination commercial. Indeed, whenever I call back the moment when he crossed my line of sight, my memory reel flickers in fanciful slow motion, the entire scene bathed in cinematic rays of golden light.

He glanced up the beach at our group as he passed us. He must have wondered who we were, a gaggle of young women, three Black, the rest White, with a thirtyish Kenyan man—our teacher and chaperone Bwana O. Next thing I knew, I was on my feet, telling my friends I was going for a stroll. On pure impulse, I followed the bronzed beachcomber some distance down the shore, until he stopped at the patio of a bungalow hotel, where tables were set up next to a kiosk from which guests could order food and drinks. He chose a table on the deck overlooking the foamy ocean. Refusing to overthink what I was doing, I plopped myself down at an adjacent table and ordered a cola. I stirred the fizzy brown liquid with my candy-striped drinking straw and sipped slowly, carefully ignoring the sun-burnished young man at the table next to me.

I'd wagered that he would be curious about me, a young woman his age, probably an American by the looks of my cutoff jean shorts and fluorescent pink bikini top. Even so, my heart did a little somersault when, within five minutes, Dreamboat reached into the pocket of his green cargo swim trunks, retrieved a cigarette, and turned to me.

"Hello," he said, "would you happen to have a light?"

"No, I'm sorry," I replied, looking up and smiling briefly before turning back to my drink. From the corner of my eye, I saw him tuck the cigarette back into his pocket, not bothering to pretend that it was anything but a pretext for conversation, his opening gambit.

"Where are you from?" he asked now.

"Los Angeles," I told him, "but I go to college at Howard University in Washington, D.C. What about you?"

At that point, he rose from his table and moved over to mine, sliding into the chair opposite me, and there we would remain for the next few hours. I learned that his name was Akram, and he had just turned eighteen, which made him two years younger than me. His father was an Omani Swahili Kenyan businessman, his mother a White Englishwoman, and he and a younger brother had been raised in relative privilege in the Lake District in the United Kingdom. That did not absolve him of some hardship, however, as his mother had died after an illness when he was only eight years old.

Having him offer up his story so freely encouraged me to do the same with mine. I told him that I, too, was motherless, that I could recall meeting only once the woman who gave me life. In a matter-of-fact way, I explained that my mother looked White, though she was of Mexican heritage, and she had decided against being saddled with a Black child. This was the crux of what I believed, and I saw no reason to pretend anything different to Akram, with whom I had so quickly fallen into an easy intimacy.

Akram reached across the scuffed little table and placed a hand over mine. "You're not just a lonely mixed-up mutt like me," he said softly. "*You*, Michelle, are pedigree all the way." He delivered the line with all the flirtatious soulfulness he could muster, and I knew then that he was as drawn to me as I was to him.

When he asked why I had come to East Africa, I explained that I was with a study abroad program, and we were there to learn about the WaSwahili culture in Kenya. He let out a short laugh.

"Then you must be studying the Omani Arabs, too," he said, and I nodded. "You know," he continued, "my great-grandfather was the Sultan of Zanzibar." He stated it as fact, with no hint of a boast in his tone. But his eyes were playful, so I thought he was joking, until he outlined his entire family tree, eventually convincing me of his imperial lineage. I laughed then at the absurdity of the stranger I'd met in such an enchanted place as Lamu being an actual African prince.

Sometime later, I looked around and saw that the shadows were lengthening on the beach, the sun already low in the sky. A motherless girl deep in conversation with a motherless boy, I had completely lost track of time. Realizing that my group mates might be waiting for me and worrying whether I was okay, I jumped to my feet.

"I have to go. It's getting dark and I have to meet my friends for dinner."

Akram rose at once and offered to accompany me back to the beach. We slowly retraced our steps down to the shore, the two of us suddenly shy in the fading light. Akram had told me he would be leaving Lamu to stay with his uncle in Mombasa in two days, and now he asked if I would meet him at the beach café at two o'clock the following afternoon. I promised to be there. As we approached the spot where I had left my group, I turned to thank Akram for walking with me. He gazed at me with those gold-flecked eyes, and on impulse, I reached up and hugged him, before stepping back quickly. He grabbed both my hands as I drew away, and pulled me to him with all the tenderness I could have dreamed. When he bent his head and kissed me under a painterly orange sky, it was easily the most intoxicating moment of my young life.

But keen on the heels of this kiss from a prince came a flutter of alarm. Still encircled by Akram's arms, I glanced up the beach to the spot where my friends had been and saw that it was empty. I noticed now that the entire beach was deserted, but for Akram and me at the water's edge. Abruptly, I broke free of Akram's embrace and called out a hasty goodbye as I took off running toward the road, hoping I'd remember the way back to the pension where our group was staying. From the corner of my eye, I glimpsed Akram's frowning confusion as I sprinted away, but I didn't turn back to explain.

I ran along the lonely dirt road through low-lying scrubland, on the verge of panic that I might be going the wrong way. Presently, I heard someone running behind me, and my fear became full blown. I turned my head to see who might be following me, and nearly collapsed with relief when I recognized the manager of the pension, a Swahili Arab with a wild nimbus of curly black hair, whom everyone knew as Bush Baby.

"Oh my gosh, Bush Baby!" I cried. "You scared me."

"I came to find you," he panted, catching up to me. "Everyone is worried. Why are you still out here at this hour? Why did you leave your friends?"

"I'm okay," I assured him, not really answering his question. I thanked him profusely for coming to get me, and slowed my pace to match his.

Bush Baby and I jogged the rest of the way back to the house, a few minutes away from where he had found me. In the living room, everyone was already seated around the rosewood dining table, eating the evening meal. I apologized for being late and causing them concern, only to be met with a flurry of questions about my time away. They wanted the whole story, and pressed for details, so I obliged, spilling everything, including that Akram and I planned to meet up again the next afternoon. I explained that not only had the unknown young man been perfectly chivalrous toward me, but he was also the grandson of the Sultan of Zanzibar, and therefore a prince. I should have guessed this revelation would become fodder for a running joke with my crew.

Hey, Michelle, how is your prince? Is he very charming? Are you excited to see your handsome young sultan again?

I laughed with the rest of them, relishing the innocent joy of my serendipitous encounter. The next afternoon, I dressed carefully for my rendezvous with Akram, with Jen and Djenne consulting eagerly on my choice of a traditionally modest Kanga dress. Jen had even applied mascara, eyeliner, blush, and shell pink lip-gloss to my usually bare face. Feeling beautiful for once, I waited on the beachside patio for almost an hour, my anticipation growing by the minute, but Akram never showed. At last, I made my way back to the pension, dejected but resigned, already burnishing the memory of our one perfect afternoon.

The fairytale wasn't over, however. Several weeks later, our group traveled on to Mombasa on the southern coast for the continuation of our language immersion course. On the second night there, two of our teachers, Bwana O. and Bwana M., agreed to accompany my friends and me to a techno dance club called Toy. The venue had been my suggestion, though no one but Bwana O. was in on my reason for choosing it. Back in Lamu, when I'd shared with Akram that our group would soon be moving on to Mombasa, he had mentioned Toy as one of the places he and his friends frequented.

"How's the crowd?" Bwana O. asked the man taking money at the door.

"Very empty tonight," he said, his response almost drowned out by the electronic beat pulsing from inside. Bwana O. went in ahead of us to investigate the scene. When he returned, he was grinning widely.

"You're going to be very happy, Michelle," he whispered, taking my elbow. "Your prince is here."

"What?" My hands flew to my suddenly hot face. "How do you know?"

"I was on the beach when you first saw him, remember? I know what he looks like, and he's inside."

In the dim, strobe-lit interior, my eyes found him right away, sitting with his friends at the far end of the dance floor. He noticed our group, too, and a moment later was making his way toward me. As he bent to kiss my cheek, he was already apologizing for missing our date in Lamu several weeks before. He wanted to explain what had happened. He had gone out diving with friends that morning, and the boat was late getting back to the dock. Hoping that I might be operating on Africa time, with schedules running at least an hour behind, he'd rushed back to the hotel café in case I was still there. Now he begged me to give him another chance, and laughing at his clear distress, I agreed.

We met up after my classes the next afternoon, at a little dessert place in town. He pulled up on a motorcycle, adding another layer of panache to his story. After sharing a bowl of the most delicious gelato I had ever tasted, I climbed onto the back of his motorcycle and off we went, tooling all around town.

You have to understand, I'd never had a real boyfriend in high school, so this was my first real romance, one that had been deepened by our shared state of being half-orphaned. Before Akram, I was always quietly aware of having missed many of the lessons and insights that mothers impart to their children in ordinary daily discourse, but now I didn't have to worry about such social lapses. From the start, I felt fully accepted exactly as I was. That afternoon, riding with my arms clasped around Akram's torso, and for the next several days, the handsome young prince was attentive in the extreme, even taking me to meet the uncle with whom he was staying in Mombasa. His uncle was gracious to the visiting American student, leaving me with the feeling that I needed to hold my relationship with Akram carefully, so as to preserve his uncle's sense that we were honorable. And so as boy crazy and impulsive as I'd always been, our connection remained as innocent as Bigmama might have wished.

Years later, I would discover that our chaste affair had left a lasting mark on Akram's life. Looking back now, I can see that he was a little bit in awe of me, an American college girl with a firm plan to pursue a career in broadcast journalism in the largest media market in the world. In contrast, ever since graduating from a private boarding school in England one year before, he had been drifting, traveling aimlessly, visiting relatives and friends while waiting for his future to show itself. This was the antithesis of how I understood my own life. Having been raised by my father and Bigmama, I'd been taught to lean into possibilities and to seize experience with both hands, steering my own future with intention.

Sitting with Akram one afternoon, the two of us with fingers laced across a small table in the gelato shop that had become our regular meeting place, I had a brainstorm. "You know, Akram," I said, my tone serious, "I think you should apply to universities in America and Britain."

"I'm not a bold American like you—" he started to say, but I cut him off, placing two fingers against his perfect bow-shaped lips.

"It's not about being bold," I told him. "You don't have to know what you want to study. You just have to try different things until something calls out to you. Besides, what do you have to lose by applying to college?" I winked at him impishly. "You might even end up in America, near me."

He shrugged and smiled, because he was used to my talking his ear off and had fallen into the habit of indulging my stream of chatter. I imagine I must have seemed overly emphatic about almost everything, but he was a generous listener and openly intrigued by my insistence that the world would not fail to open its arms to seekers. This belief was my superpower, really. I refused to let adverse encounters turn me aside, and I had embraced instead a stubborn expectation that *the next time* would turn out more favorably. It was the approach that had bolstered and sustained me through being bused to four new schools in the course of six years, always the new Black girl in a majority White pool, and I had wrapped this resilience around myself like a crusader's cape, with no quit in me at all.

Akram and I became so close during our few days in Mombasa that I had begun to think that our group's return to Nairobi, and then to America, would be a mere inconvenience for us. As we said goodbye to each other late that spring, we vowed to keep in touch, and to travel to see each other again soon. But without the easy global connection afforded by social media platforms today, our lives on opposite continents soon reclaimed us, until our letters and prohibitively expensive phone calls became less frequent, the urgency between us slowly petering out.

Akram did, however, apply to colleges in America, completing his undergraduate degree in economics at the University of Miami before going on to earn a master's in business administration from Columbia University in New York City. We saw each other once or twice during those years, and then not at all for two decades. We wouldn't meet up with each other again until 2011, by which time he had become a successful financier, living and working in London. And so, when I was assigned to cover the wedding of Prince William and Kate Middleton as a news correspondent for CBS, I sent him a message letting him know I would be in his city, and suggested that we get together for afternoon tea. As I was now happily married and the mother of two young children, we both understood that the fairy tale was long over, with not the slightest chance of being rekindled.

We arranged to meet at a corner café not far from Buckingham Palace. Akram, still unmarried, was as handsome and gentle-humored as ever, though he now filled out his clothes, no longer the lean beachcomber in cargo shorts, wrinkled shirts, and sandy flip-flops that he'd worn most of the time when I first met him. I felt a warm, nostalgic affection at the sight of him weaving through the café tables toward me, but he no longer set my heart aflutter. We were now merely old friends who had shared a long-ago African spring, and we quickly fell into an easy repartee.

"I should thank you, Michelle," Akram said at one point, as I was pouring vanilla almond tea from an antique silver tea service.

"What do you mean?" I asked, setting down the pot, frowning at him.

"I never would have applied to college in America if you hadn't encouraged me to try," he explained. "My whole life was changed because I met you."

He said it casually, his voice matter of fact, delivering such a bold and affirming statement in an almost nonchalant way.

"Oh, I don't think I deserve that much credit," I said, smiling. "I'm sure you'd eventually have got there on your own."

"I don't think so," he insisted, his tone more serious now. "Everything I have become is because of you."

I took it in then, the idea that a chance encounter could completely reorient a person's trajectory, and I felt a frisson of something ordained, the sense that our ephemeral African spring had been purposeful after all. Because if I had pointed Akram toward his future, he had given me something of lasting value, too—a sense that our existence could be serendipitous and magical, and the conviction that the ache of growing up half-orphaned that we each carried at our core didn't make us any less worthy of experiencing life's wonder and grace.

Lost in our separate reveries, we were both silent for a while, the only sound the tinkle of silver spoons against porcelain as we stirred our tea. I imagined the sight of us in that café, him in his khaki slacks and navy blue polo shirt, and me in my yellow linen dress, two motherless wayfarers who had found a home in each other an eon ago.

"We were both so young," Akram said finally, breaking the pensive mood.

"So young," I agreed, "but look at us. We wrote a beautiful story."

THIRTEEN

The Rookie

As I took my seat in the interview room during the internship recruitment event on campus, I didn't feel unsure, nervous, or ill prepared. This was new for me. In hindsight, I credit my unusual self-possession to the semesters I had already spent at Howard, where my teachers were like benevolent aunts and uncles who consistently gave the message that I was enough.

During my time at Howard, I would meet lifelong mentors, women and men whom I could call for reasoned advice through the years as I pursued my chosen path. One of them was George Curry, a Tuscaloosa, Alabama, native who had served as past president of the American Society of Magazine Editors and a founding member of the National Association of Black Journalists, and whose illustrious career as a reporter, magazine editor, and columnist had garnered him numerous awards. A tireless champion of the Black press, George often preached about the essential role Black journalists would have to play in making visible the multitude of our lived experiences, challenging the destructive and divisive narratives about us that filled mainstream media. As a national correspondent for the *Chicago Tribune*, George exhorted his students to make sure that our voices, long marginalized, could take their rightful place on media's main stage, correcting and enriching the larger American story by continually centering our truths.

Taking George's impassioned charge to heart, I had applied for an internship for minority students at the Minneapolis *Star Tribune* during the summer before my senior year. I wanted to be a broadcast journalist, but George had convinced me that serving time in the trenches of print journalism could only strengthen my reporting and writing skills. With mentors like George Curry, I felt girded and ready to claim my place in a majority White newsroom.

"Why should we select you?" the man from the *Star Tribune* asked me toward the end of our interview. "You want to be a broadcaster, so why should we invest in someone who isn't in our industry?"

I looked at him, frankly puzzled.

"I'm a journalist in training," I replied. "Aren't you in the journalism business? Don't you want to train the best journalists whether they're writing for print or for broadcast? Besides," I added, "who is to say I won't decide to become a print journalist based on my experience with your newspaper?"

The man nodded at my answer. "Touché," he said, chuckling. "Well, Ms. Michelle Miller, you got the job."

That summer, I lived in a boarding house in St. Paul with another college student and an older woman who worked at the paper. The first morning, decked out in my African Kanga print, my preferred attire ever since my study abroad program in Kenya, I took the bus across the river into Minneapolis for work. With my hair a mass of natural curls, and chunky African cowrie shell bracelets around my wrists, I wasn't the most professional-looking intern, but I was bright eyed and eager to make my mark. Walking into the newsroom, I thrilled to the bustle of rumpled-looking geniuses tapping away at their computer keyboards or working their phones, men and women dressed in the signature working-class garb of newspaper reporters, their shoe leather creased and shabby with wear. Luckily for me, these veteran journalists would have my back, because right out of the gate my racial bona fides would be challenged.

I don't recall the man's name, only that he was an executive at the top of the *Star Tribune* masthead, a classic buttoned-down Master of the Universe archetype. On the first morning, he invited the nine Black college interns to gather in the conference room for a staff meeting. He began by introducing each intern to the rest of the staff and explaining how we would work that summer. We would have opportunities to go out and report our own stories, he promised, but we would also be expected to assist the paper's more seasoned journalists with follow-up phone interviews and research. At the end of his remarks, trying to be helpful I suppose, the executive offered the solemn-faced interns some advice. "You will need to put your Blackness aside," he told us. "You can't be a journalist and Black at the same time. You must be objective."

My jaw fell open. I realized this man had no idea what he was suggesting. Before I even thought about what I was doing, my hand shot up in the air.

"With respect, sir," I said when the executive nodded in my direction, "I wasn't born a nine-pound-nine-ounce journalist. I was born a Black female and I can put neither of those identities aside in the performance of my job. So I'm wondering, has anyone ever asked you to put your Whiteness or your maleness aside? You'll have to forgive me if I happen to think differently from you, but that doesn't mean I can't be fair. It only means my perspective might help me to see something in a story that you might not notice. And I would argue that my perspective is every bit as necessary as your own."

The entire room went silent. Several awkward moments ticked by as the man stared at me, his face suffused with an alarming shade of red, his lips pursed and eyes narrowed. At last, he cleared his throat and offered a cursory, "Very well, then," before abruptly ending the meeting. Though I don't recall another interaction with that executive during the six weeks of my internship, after the staff meeting, almost every one of the paper's reporters, both White and Black, and my fellow interns, came over to thank me for speaking up as I had. More than one of them observed how important it was that a top newspaper executive should hear the view I had expressed. I may not have convinced the paper's reigning Master of the Universe of my perspective, but my lack of a verbal filter had earned me the respect not only of my peers, but also of the paper's old-school reporters, the first real-world journalism colleagues I would ever have.

AMONG MY FELLOW INTERNS WERE TWO WOMEN WHO WERE STUDENTS at Florida A&M University in Tallahassee. Like Howard, FAMU was a historically Black school, and we immediately bonded over our HBCU connection. I met Audra Strong first. I noticed her in the *Star Tribune* newsroom because she was always the first to volunteer for research tasks and stories, determined to excel at everything. She introduced me to Dolly Mosby, whose wicked wit kept us endlessly regaled. Both Audra and Dolly would go on to become stellar journalists, but that summer, we were a footloose trio, rushing headlong into after-hours adventures.

In truth, my friends were the perfect foil to my Kanga-wearing Black bohemian wackiness, helping me rein in my impulsivity in ways I wouldn't fully appreciate for years. Much as I had been since my arrival at Howard, I was running fast on instinct and adrenaline, which helped me avoid getting sucked under by the self-doubt that had long stalked me, ambushing me whenever I became too still. The more I leaned into my life's momentum, the less chance there was that I would stumble over that uneasy internal terrain—and that summer, with Audra and Dolly by my side, I had plenty of momentum.

One night, I was with them outside First Avenue, the club made famous by Prince's breakout 1984 hit film, *Purple Rain*. At twenty years old, I was not yet of legal drinking age, but Audra had decided she would sneak me in. After surveying things inside, however, she returned to say that security was too buttoned-up for our plan to work. The three of us were standing on the sidewalk just outside the entrance trying to figure out where to go next when the club's front doors swung open, and a brilliant slash of yellow light came waltzing out. It was the Purple One, dressed head to toe in resplendent banana yellow—banana Fedora; banana suit; banana shoes. He crossed the sidewalk to where I stood, and paused in front of me. I froze, awestruck, unable to inhale a full breath. Then, overwhelmed by the fact of my idol standing right in front of me, in *that* outfit, I started to chortle, my hands flying up to cover my mouth, my shoulders shaking.

Prince stared at me for a long moment, and in his eyes I could read his thought: *I know you're not making fun of my outfit when you're standing there in your sixties Kanga print.* Nervously, not knowing what else to do, I balled one hand into a fist and thumped Prince's shoulder in a sporty way. Now it was Prince's turn to laugh as he shook his head, turned on his polished high heel, and walked away from me in a streak of banana-colored glory.

"Dang, Michelle," Audra said, "if you'd just had a little more confidence, we could have been hanging with Prince tonight."

"I straight up blew it, didn't I?" I agreed, feeling simultaneously mortified and relieved. Prince hadn't chosen me. He'd taken one look at me and recognized that I didn't have anywhere near the amount of poise and assurance it would take to run with a dynamo like him. And yet, I'd had that moment with my idol, and I would store the memory of it like a rare jewel, a highlight of my six weeks in Minneapolis. I easily accepted that I was not cut out to be a celebrity groupie, even for the Purple One lighting up the night in a banana yellow suit. This realization caused me no distress, however, because that summer I had embraced a far more important trait in myself. At the *Star Tribune*, I had learned that even as a rookie journalist, I wouldn't hesitate to speak my truth and hold my own.

TED KOPPEL, THE VETERAN NEWSMAN, HAS A SMALL CAMEO IN THIS story. I encountered him while standing beside an elevator bank inside ABC's Washington Bureau after an orientation session for the internship I'd managed to secure with ABC News *Nightline* during the fall of my senior year. At the time, I was essentially homeless and bunking with friends, as my campus housing application had never been received. I had been telling my housing woes to Pamela Nears, a fellow Bison who had a part-time job at the ABC studio. Luckily for me, Pamela shared a house near campus with two seniors, and they were looking for a fourth roommate. As she was giving me her phone number and describing the house's decorative pre-war details, the elevator bell dinged. We both turned as the doors slid open, and out walked the venerated *Nightline* host himself.

"Mr. Koppel!" I exclaimed, stepping forward and extending my hand. "I'm one of your new interns. It's such a pleasure to meet you."

Ted Koppel ignored my hand and fixed me with a half-cocked smile. "If you're one of my interns," he said in his famous baritone, "why are you out here gossiping and not inside working?"

Taken aback, my mouth engaged before my brain. "Excuse me, Mr. Koppel, but just because two women are having a conversation does not mean we are gossiping," I retorted archly. "And my first day on the job isn't today, but tomorrow. Rest assured, Mr. Koppel, I will be here at my appointed time of two P.M. tomorrow, ready to work. It was nice meeting you." Without waiting for his response, I turned on my heel, thanked my fellow Bison for the housing lead, and walked away, my back stiff, my chin resolutely in the air.

The next afternoon, unsure whether my rather curt departure might have offended one of my journalism idols, I resolved to perform with extra diligence during my four-month stint with the show. The only Black intern in the newsroom, I had been seated in a cubicle directly across from Ted Koppel's assistant, and assigned to answer phones, work up story pitches, and generally assist the reporters. Though I would have very little actual contact with Mr. Koppel himself, I was conscious of the need to start forging my own connections in the broadcast business. The first week I introduced myself to the two highest-ranking Black journalists on the ABC staff, Carole Simpson, who would later anchor the weekend edition of *World News Tonight*, and George Strait, the future chief medical correspondent for ABC News. I had been nervous to knock on their doors, but they both welcomed me in, offering to help me refine my one-page pitches. I had proposed a segment on the imminent extinction of the African elephant, and another on escalating deforestation of the Amazon in South America, considered the lungs of the planet. Neither story went anywhere (none of the intern pitches ever did), but the experience of writing them up was valuable nonetheless, as it allowed me to get coaching from broadcast veterans on how to make my pitches feel urgent and newsworthy.

Both Carole and George also shared insights about what it took to achieve longevity in the TV news game. They were transparent about the internal pressures of getting stories approved and on air, and how hard they had to struggle to stay relevant every single day. At the time, I was too naïve to grasp what they were trying to tell me. As I saw it, they were on network TV—they'd made it. But years later, their words came back to me, helping me to dig deep when faced with career challenges of my own.

My proactive approach during that internship would pay dividends, because after the internship was over, Ted Koppel would make me look really good when next I saw him in the final semester of my senior year. A group of twelve students from Howard's School of Communications were at the ABC studios for an interview with the *Nightline* host that had been arranged by our dean. We had been invited to interrogate the legendary reporter about his storied career. To my surprise, when I raised my hand to ask a question about how he had developed his piercing moderating style, he called on me by name.

After the session, I was in the back of an elevator packed with the other students in our group when one said to me, "Wow, Michelle, Ted Koppel remembered you."

"I know, I can't believe it," I responded.

Right at that moment the elevator doors opened and the *Nightline* host stepped out. We hadn't noticed him at the front of the crowd, but soon realized he must have overheard our conversation, because he turned to face us, his arms holding the elevator doors ajar. "Michelle Miller, how could I ever forget you?" he said effusively.

"Thank you, Mr. Koppel," I managed, both thrilled and embarrassed by the unexpected attention. He then turned and walked away, and as I watched his retreating blue-suited, carrot-topped figure, another student in our group breathed, "The great Ted Koppel really took pride in you, Michelle."

"I'm shocked," I confessed as the elevator doors slid closed. Yet I knew not to put too much stock in the meaning of the exchange, and just as well, because thirty years later, when Ted Koppel became a contributor to *CBS Sunday Morning*, where I was then working, I reminded him that I had once been his intern at *Nightline*, and he stared at me blankly. "Is that right?" he'd said, unsmiling. I knew by then that you always remember the standout interns, so perhaps in the fall of my senior year, I hadn't yet bloomed.

I GRADUATED IN MAY 1989, FRESH FROM COVERING CAMPUS-WIDE STU-dent protests to stop Republican strategist Lee Atwater, architect of the controversial Willie Horton ad during George H. W. Bush's presidential campaign, from joining the university's board of trustees. The Willie Horton ad had been calculated to portray then vice president Bush's Democratic opponent, former Massachusetts governor Michael Dukakis, as soft on crime, but its more subversive intent was to inflame

White fears by playing on the most disturbing stereotypes held in the White imagination about Black men.

Horton was an African American in jail for murder. Under a program in effect during Dukakis's tenure as governor, he had been granted a weekend pass from prison. While out on furlough, Horton escaped custody, raped a White woman, and stabbed her partner before being recaptured. In the political ad, an ominous voice recounted this horrific episode over mug shots of Horton spliced with pictures of the Democratic nominee. "Dukakis not only opposes the death penalty," the voice intoned, "he allowed first-degree murderers to have weekend passes from prison." As Dukakis's campaign manager Susan Estrich would later observe, the cynical ad had effectively turned Willie Horton into "Dukakis's running mate." It completely devastated the former governor's campaign, ensuring a landslide win for Bush in November of 1988.

Now, not even one year later, Howard's trustees had invited the man who had so crassly exploited racial stereotypes to serve on their board and have a say in the life of a historically Black college. The campus was in an uproar. Student journalists like myself feverishly filed stories on the demonstrations, which culminated in the March 7, 1989, takeover of the main administration building, with hundreds of protestors barricading themselves inside. As I was still in touch with some of the producers at ABC from when I had interned there, I called my contacts to suggest they send a reporter to cover the unfolding events.

My involvement with such a high-profile national story, especially one so critical to the future of a premier Black citadel of learning, felt like the manifestation of what my mentors had been trying to teach—that journalists of color must powerfully use our voices to illuminate the impact of events on our communities. The impassioned on-the-ground stories filed by my fellow student reporters and me, along with network TV news coverage and articles in the national media, ultimately forced Atwater to withdraw from serving as a trustee, with the school's president of two decades, James E. Cheek, also stepping down from his position at the end of the school year.

This story, along with my stints with such respected media organizations as the Minneapolis *Star Tribune* and ABC News, no doubt helped me get my foot in the door for a post-graduation internship with my hometown paper, the *Los Angeles Times*. When I walked into the offices at Times Mirror Square a couple of weeks later, I was overwhelmed by the paper's world-class operation. On a global scale, it was an eventful time to be a hungry young journalist. Alongside my more seasoned colleagues, I was bearing witness to that summer's Chinese Awakening as tens of thousands of students staged mass protests in Beijing's Tiananmen Square, with a million more Chinese joining the growing movement for democracy and calls for an end to the oppressive communist party regime. I felt the tragedy of these activists' trampled dreams when thousands of them were mowed down by security forces firing indiscriminately into the crowd on June 4 of that year. A shocked world denounced the communist party's violence against its own people, with U.S. president Bush imposing economic sanctions against the People's Republic of China in response to the carnage.

My summer with the *L.A. Times* would foster my professional growth in other ways, as well. At Times Mirror Square, I connected with a community of Black journalists who unreservedly welcomed me. Noticing my eagerness to embrace new challenges, they soon voted me in as president of the Southern California Association of Black Journalists. My professional circle was expanding, and with an *L.A. Times* press pass around my neck, so was my access. How else could I have waltzed onto the set of *Harlem Nights* and, with no publicist in sight, be granted an interview with Richard Pryor? It was fortuitous that one of my Howard classmates was working on the film and helped me get behind the scenes. I was learning this was how access in the news business often worked, with reporters navigating the line between following established protocols and tapping into professional networks and personal connections.

But when my *L.A. Times* internship ended in August, I found myself scrambling to figure out my next steps. Through a fellow reporter, I heard about an entry-level position at *Good Morning America* in New York City. I sent in my resume reel, which managed to sufficiently impress the director of casting. She called to let me know she would be flying to L.A. to attend the National Association of Black Journalists convention being held there the next month, and hoped we could set up an interview.

We agreed to meet on the third afternoon of the conference in the grand lobby of the Plaza Hotel in Century City. As the casting director and I settled into comfortable armchairs away from the more heavily trafficked central area, I was a bag of nerves, and it showed. An older woman with a smooth bob of blond hair, my interviewer fired off questions, and I rushed to answer them, hardly pausing to gather my thoughts before responding. The woman smiled kindly as I tripped and stumbled over my words, flustered and babbling, clearly not ready for prime time. At last, she closed the packet with my application and resume reel that had been lying open on the low table between us and leaned toward me.

"You know, Michelle, I see something special in you," she said. "You definitely have *it*." And then her encouraging tone took on a hint of apology, her gentle maternal smile tinged with regret. "I only wish your off-camera confidence was as strong as your on-camera presence," she continued, "because I'm telling you straight, you're a dynamo on screen, but sitting here in front of me, you're a mess. And this job isn't going to put you in front of the camera, not right away. So I'm going to level with you now. You're too transparent, too nakedly vulnerable. You're everything you need to be on camera, but off camera, you need a little more time to grow into your ambitions. But you'll get there. And I'm going to help you."

It took a moment for her words to register, but when they did, her observation sliced deep. *You're a mess.* Her bluntness caught me off guard, especially because what she'd said was true—and I knew it. She had given voice to a reality I'd been fighting for years, namely that I lacked the self-assurance I would need for the life I dreamed of leading. It wasn't a mystery where this lack of confidence came from, but I'd been so wrapped up in my social and academic pursuits at Howard, and so focused on finding my way into a career in journalism afterward, that I'd willfully repressed how my early abandonment was still affecting me.

Ironically, given my natural exuberance, most people failed to notice what the casting director had seen so clearly—that I doubted myself. After all, how could confidence be a problem for the little girl who had forced her way on stage with Big, the young woman who confronted the Minneapolis *Star Tribune* executive and dared to put the great Ted Koppel in his place. But now, hearing the casting director's assessment, I suddenly saw just how hollow, how performative that confidence actually was. Switch things up, turn off the lights, shut down the camera, and I was a different person. I realized that after spending my early years obsessed with unanswered questions about my mother, I had largely silenced them in high school and college. I'd been too busy trying to create the spaces where I could simply belong *as myself.* Yet even though I was now surrounded by loving family and wonderful friends, none of them could compensate for my inability to truly believe in myself.

Though the director of casting wouldn't be offering me the *Good Morning America* job, sitting right there in the lobby of Century City Plaza, she called up a high-powered Los Angeles talent agent and told him she wanted him to rep me. I was beyond grateful, and I hugged her impulsively, promising to keep in touch. I thought I'd found a wise guide, a supportive mother figure who would model for me the bold self-assurance I would need to thrive in our business. But six months later, I got a call from the talent agent letting me know that my would-be mentor had died of a brain aneurysm that week.

Shattered by her loss, with the echo of her words still in my ear, I floundered. I was suddenly devoid of any imagination about where to turn, how to set myself up for the next stage of my career. If I had managed to feign confidence in professional settings before, now I found myself sinking into a morass of doubt and insecurity. Wrestling with the fear that I might be an imposter on the field, I wondered whether Daddy and Big might have been right about me not being tough enough to navigate the television news game after all.

FOURTEEN

Global Citizen

As I fought to stay emotionally afloat during my job search, it didn't help that I was now completely alone in Bigmama's house, where for weeks I did little more than wander the empty rooms and listlessly send out my resume reel to local stations.

After my return from college, I had noticed that Vondela was newly distant and brusque with me, but I couldn't figure out what I had done. I suppose I could have simply asked her what was wrong, yet it somehow never occurred to me to do so. While I could tenaciously pursue the facts as a working reporter, at home I was different. For my entire life in that house, my most urgent questions had gone unanswered, and so I had learned to watch and listen for clues rather than confront hard family conversations in such a direct way. Besides, if I acted as if nothing had changed, I could console myself that I was being oversensitive or imagining things.

In my willful denial, I had been taken completely by surprise when Vondela announced she was moving out. She explained that she'd found a nursing position in Lynwood and had decided to rent a house closer to the job. Cheryl, she informed me, would be going with her. Baffled by her choice to pay rent somewhere when she could have continued living in Bigmama's house rent free, and still oblivious to any transgression on my part, I had only hugged her and offered that she and Cheryl could come back to live at West 80th Street whenever they wanted.

One morning, tired of poring over job notices in the local papers and dreading the empty hours ahead, I decided to drop by the hospital to get breakfast with my dad. As we strolled to the first-floor cafeteria, I was bemoaning my lack of steady employment. That's when Daddy surprised me.

"Look, Michelle, you're going to be working for the rest of your life," he told me. "So why don't you use this interval to travel for a few months, see the world, think about what you really want to do." He went on to suggest that I explore the countries of Europe and North Africa, as he himself had done right after college.

"You mean I should go alone?" I asked incredulously, imagining everything that might befall a young Black American woman backpacking solo across two continents. And yet I was immediately intrigued.

"Yes, alone," Daddy encouraged me. "That's what I did, and I can tell you, there's no better way to find that place inside yourself where you're most brave. I know you can do this, Michelle. You'll grow so much. You'll learn to trust yourself in ways you don't right now. Go and find your life."

I flashed on a memory of the ABC casting director telling me I was a mess, and realized that my father, too, had discerned the core of insecurity she had seen. But Daddy also fully believed in my ability to develop the strength of confidence that would bolster me through life, and I was quietly grateful for his faith. I did not take his belief in me lightly. He had made it clear that I would have to plan my own itinerary and pay my own way, but if I ran short of money, I had his permission to use an emergency credit card he would take out in my name.

Late that September, I flew to England to see my friend Sheila Rule, a *New York Times* correspondent I had met through George

Curry during my time in Nairobi. Sheila and George had previously worked together at the *St. Louis Post-Dispatch*. Now on assignment in London following her stint in Kenya, Sheila showed me the sights of the city for a couple of days, after which I caught a ferry, and then the train to Paris. There, I stayed with an American couple, the parents of my college girlfriend Dawn. Mr. Hightower was in charge of consumer operations for Disney in Europe and the Middle East, and he and Mrs. Hightower had offered to let me use their apartment in the City of Light as a home base for my travels. During the week I spent with them, working out the logistics of my solo excursion, they would become like surrogate parents, giving me kindly advice and sharing their knowledge of the continent. They convinced me to leave most of my bags in Paris, stuffing only a few essentials into a large hiking backpack I had brought with me. I then purchased a Eurail Pass that would allow me to board trains to thirty-three countries across Europe. Paging through my trusty *Let's Go Europe* sightseeing guide, I contemplated where to go next.

One day later I was in Burgundy's wine country, where I wandered alone through cobblestone streets in quaint villages, feeling as if I had gone back in time. In Madrid, I met a young Pakistani woman who was a student at the Sorbonne in Paris. With her and a young man from Boston, I formed a trio and together we drifted through Seville, Cordoba, Cadiz, and Barcelona. I traveled on alone to Nice, where I bunked at a pension with eight other students, and bonded with a woman from Mahwah, New Jersey, named Jen, with whom I have remained friends to this day. Jen and I rode the trains together to Monte Carlo. After she and I separated, I fell in with two Australian girls, Fiona and Sue, and the three of us ended up wandering all over Italy—Florence, Pisa, Rome, Naples, and Brindisi—before boarding the ferry to Greece. In Corfu, we stayed at the famous Pink Palace, part hostel, part frat house, where young, mostly North American travelers shared big family dinners each evening, and played wild games of spin the bottle while drinking ouzo, dancing in a circle, and belting out "Bye, Bye, Miss American Pie."

The entire first month of my sojourn in Europe was like that, marked by random and generally wholesome alliances with fellow wanderers with whom I chased the next interesting entry in my increasingly dog-eared *Let's Go Europe* guide. I began to see that I had inherited enough of my father's gregarious sociability that I easily attracted people of similar temperament, who enriched my experiences a hundredfold. After a while, my trepidation at venturing alone to unknown cities diminished, replaced by an eagerness to discover the new. I even started to believe, almost superstitiously, that the exact right traveling companion would show up at the exact right time, and if one did not, then it only meant that I should trust myself to figure things out on my own. This, of course, was the great lesson that my father had hoped my solo odyssey would impart.

My dawning conviction that I could find my own way in unfamiliar settings would be put to the test in Egypt. I had arranged to visit my friend Suzanne Malveaux, a future CNN White House correspondent who at the time was doing a fellowship at the American University in Cairo. After clearing customs at the airport, I gave a cab driver the address I had for Suzanne, but arrived to discover she didn't live there. Either I had jotted down her information incorrectly, or she had recently moved. There I was in a maze-like North African city with no clue of where I would lay my head that night. But it was early afternoon; I would have several more hours of daylight to solve my dilemma. Besides, I reminded myself, I had chosen a career in journalism, which required knowing how to track people down. I decided the logical first step was to ask my cab driver to take me to the campus of American University. There, I asked around until I found someone who knew my friend and was able to give me an accurate address. As I hadn't been exactly clear about when I would be arriving, Suzanne was stunned to see me standing at her door, a dusty traveler with a khaki backpack almost bigger than I was, grinning with elation that I had been resourceful enough to find her in that old-world city.

During the next several days, as Suzanne showed me Cairo and took me to see the great pyramids at Giza, it was a balm to sink into the comfort of being with a friend from home. A week later, my spirit nourished by our sisterhood, I hugged Suzanne goodbye and went off to see the sights of southern Egypt alone. Thumbing through my copy of *Let's Go Egypt*, which I had packed along with the Europe guide before leaving the U.S., I had become enamored of the idea of submerging my feet in the waters of the Red Sea and walking among the ruins of the Temple at Luxor—goals I would never have imagined for myself before leaving the safety of my Los Angeles hometown. And yet, once the opportunity arose to roam these ancient places, I was determined to experience them, no matter how implausible such odysseys might have seemed to me only months earlier.

AFTER EGYPT, I FLEW BACK TO ATHENS AND CAUGHT THE EURAIL TO Austria, where I spent a day in Vienna before moving on to Salzburg. Though my itinerary had been mostly spontaneous so far, I had decided before leaving Los Angeles that at some point I would make my way to the home of the real Von Trapp family of *The Sound of Music* fame, before their harrowing escape from the Nazis during the Second World War.

The film had been released in 1965, yet I didn't see it in full until my senior year of college. I had borrowed a tape of the movie from a friend, thinking it might provide the perfect break from studying for final exams. I ended up watching that tape again and again, enthralled by the story of Maria, the young governess played by Julie Andrews. In the movie, Maria was a misunderstood loner, a perpetual outsider, which was how I had seen myself through much of my own childhood and adolescence. Maria was also motherless, watched over by caring

but strict older women at the Salzburg Abbey where she was in training to be a nun. The convent's Abbess, whose stern affection reminded
me of Bigmama's, despaired at ever being able to rein in Maria's im-
petuosity, even as she admired her zest for life. By nature, Maria was
as calamitously unfiltered as I was, often creating problems for others
as she bumbled her well-meaning way into situations, making every
mistake possible.

But as much as I identified with Maria, what compelled me even
more was the bittersweet ache that the film's family story provoked in
me. After being sent from the abbey to help care for seven motherless
Von Trapp children in a villa by the lake, Maria becomes their salva-
tion. Despite the children's initial rejection of her, their pranks and
torment, the governess's cheerful and indomitable spirit soon begins to
heal their sense of being orphaned by a mother who died and a father
who is always away on business. Most of us know how the plot un-
folds, with Maria and Captain von Trapp falling in love and marrying.
I never tired of watching the Von Trapp children bloom under the care
of their new mother, within the kind of family unit I had yearned to be
a part of my entire life.

Given such emotional freight, *The Sound of Music* bus tour I joined
in Salzburg held me in thrall. The scenery and grand buildings we visited were magnificent, but the real high point was when I conducted
the entire tour group in singing and dancing in the bus aisle to songs
from the film. On the tour, I also met two young men from Melbourne,
Australia, one of whom looked so much like me he could have been
my twin brother. I journeyed onward with them to see the site of the
Berlin Wall, which had been torn down just a couple of weeks before,
on November 9 while I was Cairo. The historic demolition of the wall
had marked the end of Eastern bloc communism and the beginning
of the reunification of East and West Germany, a nation divided since
World War II.

Our trio found lodging at a hostel in West Berlin. The next day, walking the streets in that part of the city, I was struck by its vibrant atmosphere, its clubs and parks and galleries brimming with art and music and youth culture. In comparison, East Berlin seemed stark and cold, its gray utilitarian buildings shrouded in silence, as if time had stopped when the concrete barrier was erected in the dead of night some years after the war ended.

In this city that had been divided by walls, I found myself lingering on similar divisions within myself—the effervescent, adventurous woman I generally projected to the world, and the more somber terrain within, the wound inside me, frozen by time. It was in Berlin that I decided I didn't have to allow my mother's choice on the day I was born to continue to define me. I could write a larger story for myself, one that cast me as a woman bold enough to meet whatever challenges and opportunities might come my way, as indeed I had already been doing while backpacking across two continents. A part of me might always be "a mess," but somewhere between the solitude and the revelry of my travels, I had located the self-reliance to reconcile both sides of myself, to recreate myself as a whole and confident daughter of the world.

I arrived back in Los Angeles a few days before my twenty-second birthday, exhausted but infinitely surer of myself than when I had left home in September. Before embarking on my solo foray, I had been a provincial California girl from the hood, locked in a not-so-secret battle with imposter syndrome as I attempted to inhabit the role of a dauntless Black American woman journalist. Now, though I might still identify with Maria von Trapp's sticky sense of being a motherless outsider, in my time abroad I had managed to transform not just how I saw myself, but also how I understood my potential. Because just as Maria had recreated herself as the matriarch of a sprawling new family, I had embraced a brand-new sense of my future, too.

FIFTEEN

Orange County News

Back in South Central, no longer doubting my path, I was hustling. I juggled freelance stories for the *Los Angeles Times* and did weekly video segments for South Central Community News, a cable access gig that I'd found through a journalist friend, which had allowed me to report on visits to L.A. by South African freedom fighters Nelson Mandela and Desmond Tutu. But having recently taken over the mortgage on Bigmama's property from my father, financially I was struggling. With Vondela and Cheryl now living elsewhere, I had the bright idea of inviting my older cousin Thomas, now divorced, and his now-grown son, Little Tommy, to move in and split the bills with me. Thomas's girlfriend and their two-year-old Solomon, along with her older son, soon ended up living with us, as well. I loved having everyone around. They accepted me as the de facto warden, the one who assigned chores and went around collecting each housemate's portion of the monthly rent, even as they poked good-natured fun at my bossiness. In bed at night, I imagined Bigmama looking down on her generations of grands and great grands, approving of our sharing the house and garden that she and my grandfather had loved and tended for more than three decades.

A few months after my cousins moved in, I got a call from a recruiter to whom I'd sent my resume reel. The headhunter had shopped my tape to different stations, and had that week received a call from Orange County News (OCN), a twenty-four-hour cable startup that was interested in my joining their team as a reporter, producer, and weekend assignment editor. The pay was modest, the headhunter explained, but since the station was a skeleton operation, the experience I'd gain from wearing so many hats would be invaluable. Was I interested, he wanted to know. He didn't have to ask me twice.

After meeting with executives at OCN, it was agreed that I would come on board at the end of May 1990. That gave me a few weeks to relish the prospect of steady employment while still being deliciously free. The timing was also perfect for me to tag along with Aunt Edna, Uncle Tom, and my cousin Lynn on an upcoming vacation to Hawaii. Since they planned to spend a week in Los Angeles on the other end of the trip, it was arranged that Daddy would pick us up on our return from Honolulu and ferry us home to Bigmama's house. But Daddy never showed.

We stood in the LAX baggage claim area for almost an hour, expecting at any moment to see my tall, distinguished-looking father approaching us through the crowd. Uncle Tom tried to call him at his office, but he reached the answering machine. Starting to worry, I telephoned his home. Maria answered, and told us that Daddy was in emergency surgery. We misunderstood at first, forcing her to clarify that no, he wasn't *performing* the surgery, but was himself under the knife and had been for most of the morning. Reggie was with him at the hospital, she continued, and would call with a status update as soon as Ross was wheeled to the recovery room. She explained that two days before, Daddy had been diagnosed with an advanced form of prostate cancer.

I had long braced for the day I would lose my father. After Bigmama died, and I realized I would eventually have to say goodbye to my father, too, nothing had terrified me more. Who would I even be without the man who had been my rock from day one, clearing a path for me through life's thickets however he could, believing in me unreservedly. Yet as diligently as he had always cared for his family members, his community, his patients, his friends, Daddy had woefully neglected his own health, and now we would all have to reckon with his mortality.

Aunt Edna volunteered to stay on in Los Angeles for a few extra days, assessing that Maria might need some support since, in addition to helping my dad recuperate, she had their two sons, nine-year-old Matt and six-year-old Jon, to care for. Daddy's oncologist had assured us that the prognosis was promising, and indeed my father was back at work on a limited schedule in only a matter of weeks. As Daddy seemed to be rebounding well, I coached myself to stop dwelling in fear that my only known parent had been diagnosed with an illness that could take him from me way too soon.

Trying not to project too far into this future, I started working at OCN, settling into the routine of my forty-mile commute south to Orange County. The station, located in Santa Ana, was a small but state-of-the-art television studio constructed at the back of the building that housed the local newspaper, *The Orange County Register*. The station's general manager was a quiet legend, Ken Tiven, a tech guru who was credited with inventing the live truck set-up used by TV street crews everywhere. But we were still only a handful of staff members, which meant that I had to become involved in almost every aspect of putting together the 24/7 newscasts. My learning curve was exhilaratingly steep.

Officially, I functioned as a news producer three days a week and as an assignment editor on weekends, with Wednesdays and Thursdays off. I had no idea what I was doing at first, but I quickly figured out how to sequence stories in a line-up, choose the day's lead, and craft news copy on a short timeline for the anchors to read on air. One day, I wrote a late-breaking story about the United Arab Emirates joining the Persian Gulf War on the U.S. side, shortly after Iraq had invaded and annexed Kuwait. A coalition of nations led by the U.S. would soon begin bombarding the region from air and sea to force the withdrawal of Iraqi troops.

I'd handed the story to the evening news anchor with minutes to spare. Just before she went live, she called me over. Pointing to my copy she said, "Don't you mean United Arab *Immigrants?*" Taken aback by her question, I was trying to stammer out an answer when the station's executive editor, Ed Kasacia, chimed in, "It's United Arab *Emirates*. Michelle got it right. It's a country." *What a guy,* I thought with relief. *Ed Kasacia saves the day.*

Fortunately, the news anchor chose not to hold that embarrassing moment against me, perhaps because I'd developed a reputation for being a workhorse, regularly churning out three or four field segments a day. I was able to take ownership of many high-profile pieces of national and global interest that would never have been assigned to me as a young reporter at a more established station. In my two-and-a-half years with OCN, I would interview political doyennes Margaret Thatcher and Lady Bird Johnson, follow the maverick campaign of Independent presidential candidate Ross Perot, and cover soon-to-be First Lady Hillary Rodham Clinton when she made her West Coast stops.

But by far the most significant story during those years exploded on April 29, 1992, when four LAPD officers who had been caught on videotape beating unarmed motorist Rodney King during a traffic stop were acquitted of using excessive force. The court ruled that Rodney King's attempt to evade arrest had justified the police officers stomping, kicking, tasing, and pummeling him with batons for fifteen brutal minutes as he writhed on the ground. My own neighborhood of South Central, now 70 percent African American, erupted. Within hours of the verdict, the four main avenues surrounding my home became a war zone. Outraged and grieving at what felt to them like one more miscarriage of justice that devalued Black lives, rioters rampaged through the streets, overturning vehicles, smashing shop fronts, looting stores, and setting fire to everything that could burn.

I was at home on my day off when the uprising started, but I immediately called the station to request that my executive producer send a camera crew north to meet me, so that we could cover the riots in real time. This would have been any news reporter's professional imperative, and so I was shocked when my producer refused me. "It's too dangerous," he said. "We'll pick up video from other stations."

"But I'm already on the ground here," I insisted, hardly believing that he was asking me to sit out such a consequential story. "All I need is a camera crew. I *live* here. This is *my* neighborhood. I *know* these people. The story that I will be able to tell no other station will get."

"I don't care," the producer said. "I want you to stay inside. People are getting killed out there."

"But that's exactly why we need to cover it," I cried, my frustration boiling over. "You send crews across the world to report on the Persian Gulf War, but we can't send a camera just down the road to where people are dying in our own backyard?"

No matter what arguments I came up with, my producer would not be moved. At last I put down the phone, feeling utterly betrayed and crushed at the realization that the station to which I gave my all each workday, simply didn't find the anger and anguish of my community to be a story worth covering.

Sixty-five people would lose their lives over four days of rioting in the aftermath of the cops being acquitted in the Rodney King case. By the time the rage and the looting finally burned themselves out, more than one billion dollars' worth of property had been damaged or destroyed, a citywide dusk-to-dawn curfew had been imposed by L.A. Mayor Tom Bradley, and thousands of National Guard troops, marines, and other military personnel had been deployed to Compton and other hot spots. Watching everything unfold as a citizen on the sidelines rather than as a journalist in the thick of the story, I had resolved that I needed to move on from OCN sooner rather than later.

But I didn't feel as if I could pull up stakes just yet. My dad was due to undergo follow-up surgery as part of his cancer treatment, and I wanted to be there to help him recover. And, despite my producer's refusal to allow me to properly report on the tragedy that had unfolded in my hometown, I still appreciated most of my colleagues at OCN, even him, and had developed warm friendships with several of them. But perhaps what most sustained me as I weighed the timing of my next career move was a scene I'd happened upon in my own neighborhood as I was driving home from church on the fourth day of the curfew.

I had turned a corner only to be confronted by four White police officers chasing half a dozen little Black boys in the middle of the street. Concerned, I pulled my car over to the curb to assess what was happening. But as I observed the action, I realized that the officers and the boys were playing a game of pick-up basketball, the V-shaped branch of a sidewalk tree serving as the hoop. And then I noticed a lone Black officer refereeing the game from on top of his squad car. I felt a stirring of faith in our besieged city as I watched the players for a while, before restarting my car and continuing toward home. I was thinking that if my father hadn't borrowed my camera the week before, I would surely have won a Pulitzer Prize for immortalizing that unexpectedly hopeful scene.

DADDY CONTINUED TO INSIST THAT HIS FORM OF CANCER WAS HIGHLY treatable, even as the chemo rounds began to hollow him out by degrees. His hair was now starkly white against the deep brown of his skin, his cheeks more gaunt, his elegant carriage slightly more stooped though he was still an imposing figure at sixty-three. On the day I went to the hospital to see him after his second surgery, he appeared weaker

than ever. But what really made my heart clutch was the brittle urgency
with which he greeted me.

"Michelle, thank God, at last," he whispered hoarsely as soon as
I appeared at his door. With some effort, he lifted his head from the
pillow so as to fix me more squarely in his gaze. "I need you to do something for me," he said, his eyes glassy, his breathing labored. He was
clearly still groggy from the anesthesia, and his shrunken legs under
the white hospital sheets were agonizing to see. Disturbed by his new
frailness, I wasn't prepared for what came next.

"I want you to find your mother," he rasped out. "I'll give you her
married name, her birthdate, previous addresses, everything I know
that might help you track her down."

Bone tired, he let his head fall back onto the pillow, and closed his
eyes, so he didn't see my expression of astonishment or notice that I
couldn't in that moment find my voice. All I could do was stare at him
with my mouth hanging open, wondering if perhaps he might be the
slightest bit delirious from whatever medication they had given him.
Now you want me to find her, I thought incredulously, *despite more than
a decade of the two of us literally never mentioning her name?*

After what felt like an interminable silence, Daddy opened his eyes
again and, staring into space now, he explained that he wanted me to
learn my medical history on my mother's side.

"It's your genetic inheritance," he told me, "and you have every right
to know it." He paused and released a breath of deep and utter resig-
nation. "You need to know your mother," he added, almost as an after-
thought, and then he murmured so softly that I wondered if he knew he
was still speaking out loud, "and she needs to know you."

SIXTEEN

My Mother, Reprise

After a lifetime of longing—years haunted by tides of self-doubt at the ambiguity of having a mother while having no mother—it turned out to be absurdly easy to trace the whereabouts of Laura Hernandez. I found her within a week, helped by a college friend who was now a police officer with the LAPD. I had told him my story back when we were at Howard, and when he heard I was now searching for the woman who had left me behind at birth, he offered to run her maiden and married names and birthdate through the Department of Motor Vehicles database.

Almost as soon as he entered her identifying details, she popped up on his screen, apparently living with her attorney husband a couple of hours south in San Diego. It was pure serendipity, because if Laura Hernandez had registered her car anywhere but in the state of California, my search for her would surely have been more protracted. Though she now went by her married identity, I continued to think of her by the name she had carried when I was born, as it made the idea of this stranger being my mother feel less remote. I was, I reminded myself, half a Hernandez, too.

The day I got the call letting me know she had been located, I was at work in the studio. I'd scribbled her phone number on a scrap of paper and tucked it into the pocket of my new red blazer, which I'd purchased on impulse earlier that morning thinking it would pop nicely on camera. I quickly decided that I would hold off telling my father or anyone else in the family that my mother had been found. Their certain flurry of anticipation about what came next felt like too much weight to have to carry as I figured out how I wanted to proceed. It was enough that I transported that scrap of paper with Laura Hernandez's number scrawled on it back and forth between work and home for an entire week, safe in the pocket of the red blazer I grabbed every morning, without ever making the call. Terrified that my mother would not welcome my voice on the other end of her phone line, I even contemplated just letting her be, allowing us both to continue on with our lives as we had before.

If I was keeping my family in the dark, some of my colleagues at OCN were aware that I was trying to screw up my nerve to speak with a woman I had last seen for a few brief minutes when I was nine. One afternoon, the station's sports producer took me by the hand and led me to the old black rotary phone sitting on a desk in the edit bay.

"Call your mother," he commanded. "You know you're dying to talk to her." As I settled myself in a chair and picked up the receiver from its cradle with one hand, my coworker and friend enfolded my other hand in his, and pledged to stay in the room with me as I dialed the number on my crumpled slip of paper. "You can do this," he said simply.

I made the call—and hung up frantically at the first ring. My coworker stood next to me like a sentinel, not judging my fear, only smiling his encouragement to try again. This time, a woman picked up. I fielded a wild urge to slam down the receiver again, but I felt my colleague clasp my hand more tightly, urging me on.

"Hello, may I please speak with Laura Hernandez?"

"This is she," the woman said.

I felt lightheaded, the world swimming away from me. My coworker gave my hand one last squeeze and then bowed out of the edit bay, leaving me to conduct my phone call in face-saving privacy. Once I was alone, the words tumbled out of me.

"My name is Michelle Miller, and I was born in December of 1967," I began, reciting my lines the way I had practiced them every time I had imagined this call. "Do you know who I am?"

There was a thick silence on the line. I resisted the urge to cover the discomfort with benign chatter. Instead, I let the pause hang there between us, our memories careening through a black hole of years. More seconds ticked by, and I sensed that the woman on the other end of the call had fully grasped the enormity of my question.

"Yes," she said finally. "Yes, I do."

"I don't mean to startle you," I continued, "but my father is ill, and he wanted me to get in touch with you in case anything happens to him, in case . . . in case . . . well, he thought I might have questions. And I was just hoping"—I begin improvising now—"I was just hoping that you might be able to meet with me because I have to be in Southern California next week for my job, and I wonder if we might find a time to talk."

"When will you be down this way?" she asked me.

"Next Wednesday," I replied.

It would be my next day off, which meant that no late-breaking news stories would interfere with my catching a one-hour flight south to San Diego for the day. The truth was, I had no work commitments in or around the city where Laura Hernandez lived, but I hadn't wanted her to feel unduly pressured by the idea that I would be coming to town just to see her. She was quiet for a few moments, and I was sure she could hear the drumbeat of my heart. I barely allowed myself to breathe as she asked for my call back number and promised to telephone the next day with a time and a place for us to meet. Relief, excitement, and trepidation spun wildly inside me.

"Thank you so much," I said, trying, and failing, to steady my voice. But she couldn't hear me emotionally collapsing. She had already ended the call.

As a young mother in Boston in 1930, Beatrice Burson Miller posed with her children, Edna, then four, and Ross Jr., who had just turned one. Later that year, the family relocated to East St. Louis, Illinois, where my grandfather, the first Ross Matthew Miller, had accepted a position as principal of a local school.

In 1951, my father, Ross (*left*), had recently completed medical school at Howard University and was doing his general surgery internship at a hospital in Newark, New Jersey. His sister, Edna, had followed in her parents' footsteps, becoming an educator at Lawson State College in Birmingham, Alabama.

My father headed west to Los Angeles for his surgical residency in the late 1950s. He soon persuaded his parents to join him in the shining City of Angels, where a decade later I would be born to a White Chicana hospital administrator, with whom my then married father had had a clandestine affair.

Hours after I was born, my mother handed me to my father and walked out of my life. As a child I had no memory of her except for this photograph, taken in secret when I was a year old. As far as I know, it is the only image that exists of me with my both my parents.

Dr. Ross Miller was the first to attend Democratic presidential candidate Robert F. Kennedy on the night he was shot at L.A.'s Ambassador Hotel, following his June 4, 1968, victory in the California primary. Years later, I would discover this CBS News video of my father being interviewed about the condition of the New York senator, who would die of his injuries the following day.

My dad and his first wife had adopted my older sister, Cheryl, before I was born. Daddy posed with us in 1975, when Cheryl (*right*) was nine and I was seven.

On the same day that Senator Kennedy died, my grandmother, Bigmama, brought me to live with her in South Central. Four years later, she enrolled me in kindergarten at Marie Fegan School, where this class photo was taken. My dad, now divorced, lived apart from us but visited regularly.

I was in second grade at Loren Miller Elementary in 1974 when four classmates labeled me a racial imposter because I had "White girl hair." Shattered by the confrontation, I grew to resent the mother who had abandoned me in a world where I was too brown to be White and too light-skinned to be embraced by some as a Black girl.

I was a chubby Girl Scout in the mid-1970s as I stood with my dad and Bigmama in the garden of the storybook house on West 80th Street, where I grew up.

As the new girl in Hamlin Elementary's gifted program in fifth grade, I became part of the first wave of students to be bused from communities of color to wealthy White schools in the San Fernando Valley. I would end up being bused to four different schools in five years as part of the city's school desegregation effort.

By my tenth year, Bigmama's health was growing frail. With no mother in my life, I tried not to think about who would take care of me if anything happened to her.

At Palisades High in 1985, I was part of a crew called Slap ("pals" spelled backward). *Clockwise from left:* Karen, Gayle, Dana, Shelli, Chris, and I partied together on weekends while protecting our places on the school honor roll.

The family gathered in 1975 to celebrate Bigmama's eightieth birthday. From left are my cousin Reggie, Uncle Tom, cousins Lynn and Paul, Bigmama, cousin Eric, Aunt Edna, cousin Tommy, and my dad.

After Bigmama passed away in March of 1982, Vondela Pilot moved into the house on West 80th Street to care for me as my guardian. At my cotillion in my senior year of high school, I was secretly relieved that my formal picture would look like every other debutante's, with both a mother figure and a father figure beside me.

As a college sophomore at Howard University in 1986, I was already dreaming of becoming a journalist. I hosted a talk show for the campus radio station and wrote for the college newspaper, *The Hilltop*.

During my time at Howard, I was able to check off an item on my bucket list, becoming a model for the homecoming weekend fashion show one year.

While studying abroad in Kenya in the spring of 1988, I met the great-grandson of the Sultan of Zanzibar. Having both come of age without our mothers, Akram and I bonded over our half-orphaned state and helped each other feel more at home in ourselves.

A year after his cancer diagnosis, Daddy was once again in stable health as he huddled with his second wife, Maria, my brothers Jonathan (*second from left*) and Matt (*right*), and me in the family condo in Long Beach.

After a post-college summer internship with the *L.A. Times*, I spent the fall of 1989 backpacking alone through Europe and North Africa. Meeting fellow travelers and visiting ancient sites such as the ruined city of Pompeii helped build my core of resilience.

On returning from my solo travels, I embarked in earnest on a career in broadcast news. After stints with two other stations, in 1994 I landed in New Orleans as a reporter and weekend anchor for WWL-TV.

The Crescent City had elected its first Black mayor, Ernest Nathan "Dutch" Morial, in 1977. This political firebrand and his elegant First Lady, Sybil Morial, were the parents of New Orleans's third Black mayor, Marc Morial, who had been elected to office only months before I moved to the city.

My future husband, Marc Morial, as a twelve-year-old Catholic schoolboy.

Though concerned that my job as a news correspondent made dating the mayor a conflict of interest, we could not deny our chemistry. We let down our guard at the 1995 wedding of one of my cousins in New York. A year later, Marc flew to Los Angeles to ask for my father's blessing on our intention to marry. Daddy passed away four months later.

I earned my master's degree in urban studies from the University of New Orleans in 1997. My beloved Aunt Edna and cousins Lynn and Reggie (*on my right*), along with Marc and Reggie's wife, Terry (*left*), attended my graduation.

Local newspapers hailed our nuptials on September 11, 1999, as the city's "wedding of the decade." Guests packed the sanctuary of the historic St. Louis Cathedral and spilled out onto Jackson Square. The Rev. Dr. Andrew Young, the Civil Rights leader who had grown up with Marc's mom and attended medical school with my dad, and Father Harry Thompson, Marc's former Jesuit High School headmaster, performed the interfaith ceremony.

Xernona Clayton, whom I called Big, was among the guests at Aunt Edna's eightieth birthday party in 2005. The first Black woman to host her own television talk show in the South, Big had been a dazzling role model for me from the time I was a small child.

In July 2005, the Miller and Gardner cousins gathered in Birmingham, Alabama, for a family photo with Aunt Edna on the occasion of her eightieth birthday.

I joined my brother Matt (*standing next to me*) and my stepmom, Maria, at my youngest brother Jon's graduation from UC Santa Cruz in 2008.

Marc's older daughter, Kemah, who grew up in Cote d'Ivoire with her mother, Rose Dennis, spent summers and holidays with her dad in New Orleans.

Our son, Mason, was born in 2002, and our daughter, Margeaux, in 2005. The love I felt for my children when I became a mother gave me a wrenching new understanding of just how much my own mother had given up when she chose to walk away from me on the day of my birth.

In February 2012, our family, now living in New Jersey, traveled back to New Orleans for Mardi Gras, where Marc and I served as Grand Marshals of the Zulu Social Aid and Pleasure Club, along with Ambassador Andrew Young.

As a news correspondent, I have covered my share of weather disasters, including the Merrimack River flood in Pacific, Missouri, in 2017. But no storm would ever be more personally devastating to me than Hurricane Katrina, which ravaged my adopted hometown of New Orleans in 2005. *(Photograph by Jake Barlow)*

In this picture with my then three-year-old daughter, I see all the maternal tenderness I had wished for from my own mother. Being able to give that care to my children was the beginning of my deepest healing.

At the launch of her 2015 memoir, *Witness to Change: From Jim Crow to Political Empowerment,* Sybil Morial, aka my mother-in-law Miz Mo, was introduced to the audience inside the New Orleans Museum of Art.

After two terms as mayor of New Orleans, Marc took over as president of the National Urban League in 2003. Here, with Miz Mo at my side, I settled Mason and Margeaux during a stump speech by then Democratic presidential candidate Barack Obama at the organization's annual conference in Orlando in 2008.

One of Marc and my fondest memories was attending President Barack Obama's last White House Correspondents' Dinner in 2016.

I was overjoyed to be named cohost of
CBS Saturday Morning in July 2018.

My co-anchors Dana
Jacobson and Jeff Glor
and I posed for an official
portrait on the set of our
Saturday-morning show.
(*Photograph by Michelle
Crowe*)

To mark the fiftieth
anniversary of the death of
Dr. Martin Luther King Jr. in
2018, *CBS This Morning* sat
down with his children Martin
Luther King III, Bernice King,
and Dexter King at Ebenezer
Baptist Church in Atlanta. It
was the King children's first
joint interview in more than a
decade.

Mason (with me in 2018) challenged me to prove that my father had indeed been the first doctor to attend to Senator Robert Kennedy on the night he was shot. His questions led me to undertake a cross-country reporting odyssey to restore his late grandfather's name to the historical record of that fateful night.

Margeaux and I attended Kemah's wedding to Julius West in 2019. As a child, Margeaux would often ask me about my absent mother, her young mind trying to understand why she hadn't stayed around to raise me.

Marc and I could not have navigated the constant travel required by our high-octane careers had it not been for our family housekeeper, Hope Zapata, who took impeccable care not just of our children, but of their parents, too. I have often observed that Hope was perfectly named.

Our family returned to New Orleans in 2018 to attend the Essence Festival, held annually on the July Fourth weekend. While there, we reunited with Mason's former nanny, Judy Lopez Whitt, who had also watched over Marc when he was a young boy.

I was honored to witness Georgia congressman John Lewis's flag-draped casket making its memorial crossing of the Edmund Pettus Bridge in Selma, Alabama, in July 2020. Sixty-five years earlier, Lewis had been among six hundred souls who walked from Selma to Montgomery to protest Black Americans' disenfranchisement. Lewis would become an enduring example of courage under fire and a distinguished icon of the Civil Rights movement. *(Photograph by Dwaine Scott)*

Only two months after John Lewis died, Aunt Edna also closed her eyes for the last time. Despite a chaotic and intensely busy news cycle—with the Black Lives Matter protests of 2020, the Covid-19 pandemic, and a polarizing presidential campaign—I was thankful to have been with my beloved aunt for her ninety-fifth birthday in July of that year.

On the morning of George Floyd's memorial service in June 2020, I talked with the Floyd family's attorney Lee Merritt, who also represented the families of Ahmaud Arbery and Breonna Taylor. We discussed the toll of police and vigilante violence against Black bodies, as well the families' hopes for what would come next.

The extended Miller-Morial-Gardner clan gathered for a long-overdue reunion in Gulf Shores, Alabama, during the 2021 holiday season.

On July 3, 2022, Kemah and her husband, Julius, became the parents of our beautiful granddaughter, Audrey.

With my older sister, Cheryl (*at left*), now living near to us on the East Coast, our family attended Christmas services together at Newark's Cathedral Basilica of the Sacred Heart.

The people who make me feel most grounded posed all in white on a beach in Martha's Vineyard. Despite my fractured childhood, this is the whole and intact family Marc and I made, for whom I am forever grateful. *(Photograph by Randi Baird)*

I am the picture of pure joy standing in the middle of Central Park South in New York City. *(Photograph by Paul Undersinger)*

AS I PUSHED OPEN THE DOOR OF THE FAMILY-STYLE RESTAURANT IN San Diego the following Wednesday afternoon, I harbored a single fervent wish: I wanted Laura Hernandez to gaze upon the daughter she had given away twenty-four years before, and in that moment regret not keeping me. Never mind that a mother who might have had that response would likely have stayed to raise her own child.

I saw her as soon as I entered, a woman in her fifties sitting by the window, draped in a stylish red kaftan piped with lines of blue. Her dark hair waved softly around her face, kissing the white column of her neck, threads of silver catching the light as she turned toward the sound of the door opening, then closing behind me. She looked like a White woman, the undertone of some ethnic other that I had once detected no longer visible in her skin. Fifteen years older than when I last saw her, she had obviously taken care of herself, or perhaps it was merely good genes, and I hoped in passing that I might inherit them as I aged. Her complexion was near flawless, the creases around her eyes and lips deepening gently as she rose from her seat, smiling at the sight of me in my unfussy white suit and blush pink polka-dot blouse. Approaching her, I felt suddenly plain, almost frumpy, and fretted that she would be disappointed in me.

"Laura?" I asked when I got to the table, though I knew it was she.

"Oh, you're so beautiful," she exclaimed. "You look just like your father."

She held open her arms, and I stepped in for a brief embrace before taking the banquet seat across from her. We chatted about the dry summer heat and other benign topics for a while, like where I'd gone to college, why I'd decided to pursue journalism, the ideological disconnect I felt at my current job. She shared that she worked for her husband, managing his law practice. She asked me about my father's cancer, when he had been diagnosed, his prognosis, how he was holding up through treatment. Her tone was polite and measured, as if she were inquiring after the health of a person she hardly knew. I reminded myself that the woman before me was someone else's wife, and but for the fact of me sitting there, my father had ceased to matter in her life the moment she had handed me to him in the hospital nursery. I would soon discover how mistaken I was in this assessment.

We waded cautiously into deeper waters. Laura asked what it had been like to be raised by my grandmother. I told her about growing up in South Central, about feeling conspicuous and wrong in almost every school I attended, not only because people routinely interrogated my mixed-race appearance, but also because I had noted that other kids had mothers in the home who saw them off each morning and, I imagined, tucked them into bed each night. As a child, I had been absolutely convinced this was true, though of course I now knew there had been many more family configurations among my classmates than I had allowed myself to see, including households just like mine, presided over by no-nonsense grandmothers. Not that I had ever been uncared for, I hastened to clarify. I had been attentively watched over by my father and Bigmama, both of whom had been devoted to me.

Laura listened, her perfectly penciled brows bunching together. "Your grandmother and your father did an incredible job with you," she said when I was done. I didn't respond, just pushed the food I had ordered around on my plate. I had no appetite, no attention for anything but the fact that I was actually *here*, in the presence of *my mother*. Indeed, when I recounted our lunch to my father later, I could not for the life of me recall such details as the name of the restaurant where we met, the dishes we had ordered, how the meal tasted. But I recalled the way the light from the window illuminated the tiniest hairs along the line of my mother's powdered cheek as she reflected, "If I had raised you, Michelle, you wouldn't be the woman you are today. You were much better off with your father and grandmother."

"Why would you say that?" I asked, feeling saddened by her words.

"I'm sure you would have been a great mother." I wasn't sure I actually believed this, but it seemed like the right thing to say.

"I was weak," she said softly. "I wasn't strong enough to defy my family. I'm so sorry I wasn't there for you, Michelle. I know I should have been."

Looking back, I think this was the moment when I decided to forgive her, or at least the moment when I understood that I wanted very badly to forgive her.

"Did you ever have other children?" I asked her then.

"No," she said. Her beautiful brown eyes were pools of regret. "That was my punishment—to never have another child from my own body, but to raise another woman's children."

"I knew you got married," I said. "My father told me. That was why he brought me to see you that day. He thought you were moving away and we'd never again know where you were. He was almost right," I added dryly.

"That was such a hard day," she nodded. "I had no idea you were coming, and I was terrified my husband—my fiancé back then—would come by and find you and Ross in my apartment." She paused. "I never told him about you," she said finally. "We were moving to another country with his kids, and I just thought it would be better for all of us if I just made a clean break."

Better for you, I thought bitterly.

"Given the way your family felt about my father being African American, I'm assuming the man you married was of European descent?" I said.

"He is," Laura admitted, looking somewhat uncomfortable. She went on to tell me that before opening his law practice in San Diego, her husband had served many tours as a diplomat with the U.S. Foreign Service. She had accompanied him on those overseas assignments in South America, along with some of his six children from a previous marriage, whom she had stepped in to mother. I felt a stab of jealousy when she spoke of her stepchildren, but I swallowed hard and just listened. All of them older than I had been when she wed their father, they were grown now, and some had children of their own. In fact, Laura shared, she was now raising one of those grandchildren, a thirteen-year-old girl whose mother had struggled to care for her alone. The tenderness in her tone, the naked love on her face as she spoke about this particular child almost annihilated me.

Reminding myself that Bigmama had felt much the same about me, I forced a smile, told myself every girl needed a mother figure to love her, blood related or not, and I held on.

At last, I dared the question that had most plagued me as a little girl growing up without her mother. "What about us?" I asked. "My father really loved you. Didn't you love him enough? Is that why you left us?"

Laura looked stricken. "What?" she said, as if struggling to comprehend what I was saying. "Oh, my dear, my dear, your father. Oh, Michelle, you must understand, at the time you were born and for years after, Ross was the love of my life."

ROSS WAS THE LOVE OF MY LIFE.

That one sentence reverberated in my brain, along with three other words—*for years after*. My mother had continued to be in love with my father *for years after* I was born. This I had not suspected.

The way my mother told it to me that afternoon, she and my father had shared a great love story, even with all the inconvenient details, like Ross being married to someone else, and the fact that her Mexican immigrant parents, who had counted on their daughter being able to enjoy the privileges of looking White, were incensed to discover she was dating a Black man, even if he was a respected surgeon at the hospital where Laura worked as an administrator.

Her family had demanded that she end the relationship—this I already knew. Now, I incorporated the new details Laura was sharing into the narrative of my parents that I had been contriving for the entirety of my life. A caveat: Memory is notoriously convenient and even fickle in its need to defend the psyche. Mired in this protective subjectivity, and perhaps also in a wishful romanticism, I would inevitably marry my mother's description of the events that led to my birth with the scraps of information I had painstakingly collected from my father through the years. In my reconciled version of Ross and Laura's accounts, the story went something like this:

In 1965, when Ross Miller, a thirty-six-year-old trauma surgeon, first locked eyes with twenty-six-year-old Laura Hernandez making her way through gurneys haphazardly lined up in a corridor at Dominguez Hills Hospital, they stole each other's breath away. A stylishly attired Chicana with lively brown eyes, dramatic matte pink lipstick, and a shiny bouffant of black hair, Laura seemed to have light coming off her as she glided by, which made Ross want to say something to her, anything that would make her stop and turn back toward him. Instead, he merely gave a polite nod as she passed him, because he already had a wife at home, and they were in the process of adopting two infant daughters.

Since my father never indulged my questions about what had attracted him to my mother, I am left to infer that she had simply commandeered his imagination with her dazzling smile, sparkling eyes, and voluminous halo of black hair. Still, Laura said, for almost a year, when they ran into each other at the hospital, they would only nod, say hello, and keep moving. Then one day, Laura's big bouffant was gone, and in its place was a short pixie cut. "You chopped off all your hair?" Ross remarked, leaning against the nurses' station as the woman who was not yet my mother walked toward him. Laura laughed. I imagine the sound in my father's ear was like a musical chime. "It's a wig," she said, her eyes coy. "I'm trying out a different look. What do you think?"

That was the day Ross invited Laura to get coffee with him in the hospital cafeteria. No doubt he convinced himself that it was innocent enough. But the air around the two of them felt charged, their potent attraction obvious to everyone. Again, I might be making up this part. You see, I've conjured this scene so many times, with only the detail of a handsome young doctor noticing a gorgeous woman's change of hairstyle to build on. But since my mother would continue to insist that theirs was a love story, the electricity they must have felt when their eyes locked and their two hearts raced without knowledge of the child they would bear isn't so hard to imagine.

IRONICALLY, GIVEN HER FAMILY'S RESPONSE TO THE NEWS SHE WAS IN-volved with a Black man, Laura shared that it was Ross's passionate Civil Rights activism that had so powerfully attracted her. She had recently undergone an awakening of her own, after making a pilgrim-age to the rural farming community in Mexico where her family had eked out a meager subsistence before leaving to seek a better life in Los Angeles. And with undocumented migrant workers in California organizing themselves into labor unions to agitate for better living and working conditions, and the emergence of Chicano leaders like Cesar Chavez and Dolores Huerta, Laura had felt the stir of renewed pride in her own heritage and Mexican American identity.

My mother's parents had no idea when they insisted she stop seeing my father that she was already pregnant with me. I had been completely unplanned. With Ross having convinced Iris to adopt little Cheryl and Adrienne one year before, neither he nor Laura had intended to con-ceive an out-of-wedlock child. Laura had already pledged to her parents that she would end the relationship but did not clarify this would only happen after she had delivered me into the world. In the mid-1960s, it took courage to make such a decision, even for a good Catholic girl. Laura thought at first that she would put me up for adoption, but my father vehemently opposed that idea, assuring her that he would keep and raise me on his own.

In San Diego that afternoon, Laura shared that when she and Ross had first learned I was on the way, my father had proposed asking Iris for a divorce so that he might make a life with my mother, but he came to understand they would never have a future together. It had apparently broken him that Laura could not withstand her family's condemnation of their love. As they had no idea he was married, their opposition had been based on nothing more than the color of his skin. He had tried to argue that her parents would come around, especially when she presented them with a grandchild.

But, Laura admitted now, she had been afraid. She saw how people of color were treated in America. She herself had grown up with the mainstream media's ubiquitous depiction of us as second-class citizens denied basic rights. She had seen how the culture scorned Black people in particular, stereotyping us as lazy and shiftless, believing us to be of inferior intellect and culture, brutalizing our bodies with impunity. Though she herself did not hold with these attitudes, without her family's support she'd had no heart for the hardships she might face if she chained her life to a Black man—and their Black child.

Disheartened by my mother's lack of faith in their union, Ross nevertheless resolved to support her however he could in carrying me to term. This required that he help Laura hide her condition from her family for the entire nine months. The two of them came up with a plan: With her pregnancy not yet showing, Laura told her parents she would be moving to Chicago for several months to complete a certificate course in hospital administration. To make the ruse believable, she went so far as to write letters to family members throughout the following year. Ross would tuck these missives into a manila envelope and mail them to a friend from his Howard Medical School days, who now lived in the Windy City. The friend would then mail Laura's letters back to Los Angeles in envelopes bearing a Chicago postmark.

Ross and Laura kept up this deception throughout the summer and fall of 1967, with me growing inside my mother's belly as she hid from her family in a small studio near to the hospital that my dad had rented. As autumn turned to winter that year, she went into labor early one morning and pushed me into the world. That afternoon, after holding me in her arms for hours, tears pooling in the cups of her collarbones, Laura discharged herself from the maternity floor and went home to her family.

Imagine my surprise in that San Diego restaurant when Laura went on to reveal that her relationship with my father had lasted for seven years, five of them after I was born. In shock, I learned that during my first year of life, my father would bring me to her apartment on weekends, where the two of them would care for me until he returned me to Bigmama's house on Sunday evenings. I recalled the only photo I had ever seen of Laura, my father, and me, my face stained with tears, and I realized it must have been taken during that brief window of time.

"Why did my father stop bringing me to see you?" I asked her. "Why couldn't I have grown up knowing you?"

"It was too hard," she told me. "It was so painful every time I had to tell you goodbye, knowing that I could never tell my family about you, that I could only ever see you in secret. And how you cried every time you left me. My God, you cried."

Laura reflected that I had seemed to be fully aware that the raven-haired woman I saw on weekends was my mother, which accounted for my inconsolable weeping every time Ross took me from her arms to bring me home to Bigmama. Though my unconscious mind must have recorded the misery of being ripped from my mother again and again during that year—how else to explain the loneliness I had felt through-out my childhood for a woman I didn't remember meeting—perhaps it was a mercy that I had retained no conscious recollection of those visits, because I felt no bitterness as she recounted them now. I didn't even blame my father for never having told me; no doubt he had judged that the knowledge of those visits would have made Laura's subsequent dis-appearance even harder for me to understand, certainly harder to bear.

But I was no longer a child trying to unravel the mystery of her absent mother, and all I wanted in the present moment was to discover what kind of relationship my Caucasian-appearing mother might yet desire with her Black daughter.

"Would it be okay if I called you sometime?" I asked after she was done telling her story. She didn't answer right away. Instead, she signaled for the waiter to clear away our plates and bring the bill, which she insisted on paying. Only after the waiter walked away with her platinum credit card did she look at me.

"You know, Michelle, I have to be careful," she said. "I hope you understand that I can never tell my husband about you, nor my children"—*stepchildren,* I mentally corrected her—"but I would still welcome hearing how you're doing now and then."

I heard her loud and clear: *Just don't make the calls a habit, okay? That would be inconvenient and could possibly blow up the bunker I've spent decades building to house the incendiary secret of your existence.*

"What about your parents?" I inquired. "Did they ever find out about me?"

"No," Laura said, her eyes downcast. "I hope you can understand this, Michelle. My mother and brother would disown me, even now. I can't acknowledge you publicly as my daughter—that's just how it has to be. But we can still have something, don't you think?"

Perhaps because I would shortly be taking leave of my mother, having only just found her, I reached across the table to cover her pale ringed hands with my own. I wanted to ease what I now understood to be her burden of shame, borne in silence for all these years. She didn't flinch when I touched her, as I had expected she might. Instead, we just gazed down at our hands, two contrasting skin tones resting on the table between us, a story of America. I found myself wanting to tell my mother that for me, the years without her had been a lonely walk of faith, despite the succession of formidable mother figures who had stepped in to care for me. I wanted to say that the two of us might yet rise above everything that had come between us, including her long-held secret and especially her shame.

But on that warm San Diego afternoon, I said none of this, because as I sat across from the woman who had not stayed to raise me, I was still trying to figure out if I did in fact belong to her, and she to me. Not knowing the answer, I had found it safer to protect the tender flesh, to guard at all costs the foundational wound of having been sent into the world a motherless child.

PART THREE
The Way Home

"After a while, whoever you are, you just have to
let go, and the river brings you home."

—Joanne Harris, *Five Quarters of the Orange*

SEVENTEEN

Crashing

I think it's time you stop fussing over me," my father announced one afternoon. With his health once again stabilized, he had grown increasingly weary of my hovering concern. Then, echoing a familiar refrain, he added, "You need to go out and claim your place in the world, Michelle. Find out where you belong."

He could not have guessed how much I had needed him to push me out of the nest, to release me from the comfort and safety of being at his side, especially as the months rolled by with no further word from my mother.

When I'd initially recounted our lunch conversation to my father afterward, he had listened attentively from behind the desk in his office on the second floor of St. Francis Hospital, nodding at intervals but saying very little.

"Did you ask her everything you wanted?" he queried me at one point.

"I think so," I replied, though I wasn't sure that one afternoon could erase a lifetime of questions.

"And how do you feel?" he asked, watching me closely.

"I'm okay," I said slowly and realized it was true. Indeed, in the days after meeting my mother, I had felt elated, almost euphoric, though my buoyant mood had been threaded with uncertainty about what came next. As more time passed, and our single shared afternoon grew more fragile in memory, I understood clearly that if I wanted to talk to my mother again, I would have to be the one to make the call.

"She said you were the love of her life," I'd told my father as I sat in his office. "That surprised me, given that she's married to someone else."

"We were in love," my father allowed, "but it wasn't enough in the end."

"She said she was still in love with you *for years* after I was born. I didn't know that. I mean I saw the picture of the three of us, so I knew you'd taken me to see her at least that one time. But I never really thought that you and she still saw each other without me."

Daddy shrugged. "What was the point in telling you that I knew where your mother was but she had chosen not to be with you?" he said. "It would have been cruel. Besides, our seeing each other was an occasional thing. When she moved on from you, I moved on from her. As I told you, I only took you to visit her that evening when you were nine because she was moving to another country. I wanted her to see you, and you to see her, one last time."

"So what do you think now?" I asked him.

I had risen from the chair opposite his desk and was pacing back and forth beside a wall of windows in his long, narrow office. Daddy rose, too, and came to stand at my shoulder, the two of us looking out at the hospital's manicured lawn.

"I'm glad you found her," he said simply. "And that she was receptive."

"But do you want to talk to her, too," I pressed, "now that we know how to reach her again? Don't you need some closure?"

"No," he said. "I really don't. Why complicate things? Laura and I have been over for a very long time. But it's different for you, Michelle.

She's still your mother. You have no idea what the future might hold, so try to keep that channel open, okay?"

As much as I wanted to do as he suggested, I remained loath to reach out to Laura again, remembering the awkwardness when I'd asked if I might call her. Not wanting to cause her any trouble, I had instead found distraction by immersing myself in what was more immediate, and apart from Daddy's health, nothing felt quite as immediate that year as finding a new job.

I began working with my agent, Rob Jordan, to apply for positions in other cities. I ended up with offers from two stations, KMOV in San Antonio, Texas, a Top 40 media market, and WIS-TV in Columbia, South Carolina, which ranked forty points lower on the market scale. But I'd done my research, and had noted that the team at WIS-TV had forged strong relationships within the African American community through an alliance with the city's Urban League and its CEO J. T. McLawhorn. I ultimately went with my gut, judging that Columbia, being home to the University of South Carolina, might translate into a more progressive news environment. Granted, I would be heading to the Deep South, where a Confederate flag still flew above the State House, but the station itself seemed to be well managed and politically neutral. Wagering that I'd find my stride more quickly in a smaller market, I signed an eighteen-month contract with WIS-TV, daring to believe I was finally stepping onto the fast track.

All that was left was for me to say a round of farewells to family and friends. The weekend before I was to leave for South Carolina, Maria offered to drive me out to Lynwood to bid goodbye to Vondela and Cheryl, as the new car I had purchased for myself the week before hadn't yet been delivered. Perhaps because my heart was newly open after so recently meeting with my mother, I was overcome with gratitude at Maria's thoughtfulness, which set me thinking about all the ways in which my stepmother had been unfailingly kind to both my sister and me through the years, even when I was a surly teenager, barely disguising how much I had initially resented her. Now, sitting next to her in the passenger seat of her car on the drive out to Lynwood, I felt the need to offer some sort of apology for my past behavior, and to express my appreciation for the unstinting way she had cared for my dad after his cancer diagnosis.

"Maria," I started, "I just want to tell you that I'm really sorry about the way I treated you when you and Daddy first got together. It wasn't fair to you, you didn't deserve what I was dishing out."

"Oh, darling girl," she said, "I knew you were hurting. All I ever wanted was for you and Cheryl to be okay. I had no desire to ever come between you and your dad. And besides, I knew you were trying to stay loyal to Dodye. She'd been in your life for ages."

"You knew that?" I said wonderingly, belatedly discovering just how much Maria had understood. "I was so mad at Daddy," I confessed then. "I hated that he was cheating on you both."

"I didn't know about Dodye at first," Maria told me, confirming what I had suspected at the time.

"That must have been awful for both of you," I said, shaking my head at my dad's serial faithlessness with women he professed to so love. "I'm shocked Dodye was able to stay friends with him after they broke up."

"Oh, you know your father," Maria said, chuckling as she steered her car onto the street in Lynwood where Vondela and Cheryl were living. "The man is nothing if not charming."

"Oh, he is," I agreed ruefully. "It's crazy what he gets away with because of it."

Vondela was alone at home when we arrived. She explained that Cheryl had left for the mall earlier and hadn't yet returned. That afternoon, as I hugged my former guardian, I was remembering my suspicion that she, too, had been in love with my dad, and that she had agreed to finish raising Cheryl and me as much to be in his life and win his favor as to safeguard his daughters. I pulled Vondela closer, trying to imagine what it must have felt like to harbor unrequited feelings for a man like my father, who belonged to everyone and no one. *Oh Daddy,* I thought, trying to reconcile my father's undeniable charisma and social idealism with his now fully apparent feet of clay. From the day of my birth, and indeed before it, he had left such heartache in his wake, yet he acted as if he didn't even see it. And because he always showed up for family, friends, and community in other important ways, everyone forgave him in the end.

Sure enough, a week later, Daddy was right there helping me pack my worldly possessions into the trunk and back seat of my brand-new lipstick-red Saturn sports coupe. Though he was still relatively weak from his cancer treatments, he would not have missed being there to wave me off on my new adventure, watching as I backed out of the driveway of Bigmama's house and headed for the open road. I knew he would miss me as much as I was already missing him, and yet he had never hesitated to push me toward my future, and to let me know that in his estimation, I was equal to everything.

Now, as I passed through prairie heartland towns in the middle of the country, I was feeling as brave and adventurous as my father had always thought me to be. Prince's *Purple Rain* album was the soundtrack on my car CD player, and I belted out every song, sunlight pouring through my open sunroof, my voice rising into the wind as I crossed the miles to a new life on the other coast.

I SOON FOUND MY WAY INTO COLUMBIA'S FLOURISHING AFRICAN AMER-ican community, thanks to the Dargans. An old medical school class-mate of my father, Dr. Everett Dargan, and his wife, Carol, knew just about everyone in town. My father had prevailed on me to make myself known to them. I obeyed and was immediately folded into their leg-endary dinner parties and famous Thanksgiving gatherings, the latter held at their home in Hilton Head and attended by a retinue of guests at least five hundred strong. Black folks traveled from all over the country to eat collards and turkey and sweet potato pie with the Dargans every year. At these events, I met people like National Urban League president Vernon Jordan, the parents of Senator Cory Booker, former Health and Human Services secretary Dr. Louis Sullivan and his wife, Ginger, and a slew of other well-connected friends and associates, many of whom also vacationed with the Dargans each summer on Martha's Vineyard, playground of the Black intelligentsia.

But if I was thriving socially, at work I didn't seem to be cutting it. I had been assigned to cover the evening shift, filing lead stories for both the seven o'clock and ten o'clock newscasts. It was a tough gig for a newbie, as most of the personnel we relied on ended their workday in the middle of my shift. A couple of months in, my boss Randy Covington decided he wasn't happy with how I handled the deadline pressures of the night shift, and he demoted me to weekends. Randy was demanding in an old-school way. Yet I never felt as if he was picking on me, only that he had no intention of giving me a pass simply because I was relatively inexperienced. I considered that completely fair, as he was equally rough on everyone.

Still, I could see the writing on the wall. Randy had lost confidence in me, and it was looking less and less likely that my contract would be renewed. I struggled not to lose confidence in myself, even as I quietly began sending out feelers for jobs in other markets. In the end, I sealed my own fate. About a month before my tenure was up, my team and I committed an unforgivable error on a story, one that would not only get the station sued, but would also cause untold trauma to a mother and child who were already in turmoil.

The unfortunate situation had unfolded one Saturday when I was on duty with my executive producer and our camera operator, who also covered the role of story editor on our three-person team. A woman had called the station to say her daughter was being molested, and the police had declined to intervene to protect her child. Hoping to pressure law enforcement to investigate her claim, she entreated us to do a story. I should have known better than to pursue such a potentially volatile piece while the station was running a skeleton shift, but she sounded desperate. And so, despite the fact that there were no managers around to vet ideas, and lawyers were off the clock, our crew decided to move forward. Aware that we would need to safeguard the child's identity, which meant also keeping the mother's identity hidden, I directed our cameraperson to shoot an extreme tight crop of the woman's lips as I interviewed her, a privacy technique that I'd seen used on *60 Minutes*.

The problem was, the mother had a recognizable mole near her mouth, which I completely failed to consider. We might have weathered that oversight, however, had it not been for the teaser that ran at the top of the show. For the headline, our story editor had used a shot of the little girl on her bicycle with her back to the camera. But a split second before he ended the tape, the child turned around, and for an instant her whole face was visible—an egregious error that exacerbated everything else.

As the reporter, I had nothing to do with creating headline teasers. It was a completely separate responsibility from editing the story footage, writing the script, and recording the voice-over narration. So I didn't really think much about it when I ran to the bathroom, only to discover on my return that the editor had sent in the headline teaser without me seeing it. Too late, I would grasp that on such a sensitive story, I should have insisted on previewing every part of the completed set before it aired. Had I done that, I would certainly have seen that the little girl's face had been revealed in the teaser. I can only hope that I would also have noticed the mother's identifying mole in the main story.

Distraught over our negligence, the girl's mother sued the station. With absolutely no possibility of correcting my error, I struggled with the shame and remorse of having betrayed my subjects, my bosses, my audience, and myself. I now fully expected to be fired. But before that

outcome could be decided, I received a call from the news director of a
CBS affiliate station in New Orleans, to which I had sent my resume
reel. The caller, who gave his name as Joe Duke, was inviting me to fly
down to the Crescent City for two days to interview with the station's
hiring executives.

Joe Duke was a compact man, barely five-foot-five, with merry
blue eyes in a ruddy face, and a blond handlebar mustache. What he
lacked in stature he more than made up for in his crackling energy and
ebullient wit. He greeted me with a megawatt smile, the kind a father
gives when you've been gone too long and he's welcoming you home. It
steadied me at once, and encouraged me to think, *Okay, Michelle, you've
got this.* I would soon learn that Joe, a shrewd journalist, had a way of
making people feel safe enough to let down their guard, only to have
him zero in on salient details like the veteran newshound he was. This
approach had propelled the Louisiana native up through the ranks and
into a leadership role at WWL-TV. His expansive warmth and astute
sense of people would work its magic on me, too.

My round of interviews went well on the first day. On day two, Joe
Duke pronounced himself pleased with the feedback he had received
about me, and suggested that to celebrate my success, we should grab
lunch before I headed to the airport for my flight back to South Carolina. He chose Mr. B's Bistro in the French Quarter, a fine dining
establishment famous for its mouthwatering Creole cuisine.

"Order anything you want," Joe declared, snapping open his white
linen napkin and smoothing it across his lap. I understood he was trying to impress me with a taste of the best his city had to offer, and he
looked crestfallen when I ordered potato and leek soup and a humble
green salad.

"This is on the station," he assured me. "You can go bigger than that."

I hated to break it to him. "I'm a vegan," I said with an apologetic
smile. Then, noticing the sommelier standing at his shoulder holding
out a list of fine wines, I added, "I don't drink either."

"You do know you're trying out for a job in the City That Care Forgot?" he said, his laughter booming. I laughed, too, and expressed the hope that despite being a teetotaler, I might still have a shot.

"Well, I already think you'll be a really good fit for the job—" he began, but stopped. He must have caught the grimace that flitted across my face before I could snatch it back. "What's wrong?" he asked.

All morning I had been fighting the desire to come clean about the situation at my station back in South Carolina. Now, since Joe Duke missed nothing, he had given me the perfect opening.

"Mr. Duke, Joe," I said, "is it okay to call you Joe?"

"Why not?" he guffawed. "We've known each other for two whole days!"

I managed a smile, my heart picking up speed as I realized I was about to spill some very damning details that might ruin my chance of being hired.

"Joe, may I ask you something? Have you ever made a really big mistake on the job, one that affected people's lives in a very painful way?"

His puckish cheer disappeared, and he studied me thoughtfully. "Yes," he said at last. "I have. Maybe one day I'll tell you the story, or maybe not, because honestly, Michelle, it would make me cry. But why do you ask?"

Giving only the broad strokes, I explained how I had dropped the ball on a highly sensitive weekend segment and deeply hurt the subjects of my story. I took complete ownership of my failure to go the extra mile by previewing the finished set, including the headline teaser, before it aired. "The buck stopped with me," I summed up, searching Joe's face for some clue as to how he might receive this new information. "I failed to protect my subjects."

Joe sighed, nodded his head slowly, and let a small silence sit between us. His acknowledgement of the seriousness of what I had just revealed was oddly comforting; it told me I had done the right thing in not withholding or glossing over my blunder.

"Well, I appreciate your honesty and transparency," he said finally. Then, declining to question me further, he turned our conversation back to lighter fare. Though I was now quite sure I had forfeited the anchor-reporter job, I was relieved that Joe had the full picture. I could stop worrying about tripping over my secret.

Back in Columbia the next day, my boss called me to his office for a meeting. On entering, I noted that the Human Resources manager was already there. She was swiping at her eyes as I took a seat beside her, so I knew what was about to happen. My boss explained that the mother of the child whose identity we had revealed had demanded that the entire crew on the story—the executive producer, the story editor/cameraperson, and the reporter—be fired, and the station had agreed. I assured him that I understood the difficulties my team had created for everyone, apologized again for our inexcusable lapse, and thanked my boss and the HR manager for the opportunities extended to me during the past year. I then left to clear out my desk, as I had been asked to kindly vacate the premises that very afternoon.

Now I was unemployed again—and unlikely to get the job I had interviewed for in New Orleans. Joe Duke had actually called WIS-TV the following Monday and asked to speak with me, only to be told I no longer worked there. When I discovered from my agent that he had tried to reach me, I called him back to explain that my leaving the station had to do with the mistake I'd previously shared with him. On the other end of the line, Joe seemed busy and distracted, but before hanging up he asked me to reach out to him again in a few days—I assumed so that he could officially reject me. Instead, to my shock and elation, on our follow-up call Joe offered me the position as news correspondent and weekend anchor at WWL-TV in New Orleans, laying out salary, benefits, expected start date in November, and other terms. I accepted the job at once, expressing my appreciation profusely.

"You should know that we're asking you to come on board for two reasons other than your obvious ability to do the job," Joe shared before signing off the call. "One, I like that you were completely straight with me about what was happening *before* you were fired. And two, I know you will never make that same mistake again."

A couple of days later, I was once again cruising down a highway, this time bound for New Orleans, a ten-hour drive from Columbia. All I knew as I headed south was that Joe Duke had decided to take a chance on me, for which I would be forever grateful. I had no idea then of just how profoundly my move to the Crescent City would determine everything that came after.

EIGHTEEN

Boy Wonder

I first laid eyes on Mayor Marc Morial at City Hall, where I had been assigned to cover his press conference on public safety. Elected in early 1994, he had been in office for only six months when I came on board at WWL-TV. At thirty-six years old, he was the youngest mayor ever elected in New Orleans history, and only the third Black mayor to hold office. The first had been his father, Ernest Nathan "Dutch" Morial, who had crashed the establishment guardrails of that segregated southern city to serve in state government and on the juvenile court bench, before being elected in 1977 to run the whole town. With his light skin and straight black hair, Dutch could easily have passed for White, but he was a race man to his core, and New Orleans's majority Black population knew he would fight for them. By a coalition that included 95 percent of the African American vote and 20 percent of the progressive White vote, he was swept into office with an emphatic mandate for social reform.

Famous for his gloves-off approach to municipal governing—he had no choice given the flat-out animosity he encountered from many local White politicians—Dutch Morial's first term was rocked by legendary clashes with the city's police force. After his election, cops had taken to riding around in gorilla suits and throwing eggs at Dutch's house to protest having to work with a Black mayor. Indeed, the town's establishment elite was so notoriously racist that one of its more famous restaurants was rumored to give away free hams every time a police officer killed a Black person.

When the NOPD's contract came up for renegotiation in 1979, Dutch played hardball, demanding independent oversight of cops to rein in corruption and protect Black and Brown communities against rampant police violence. In response, the police union called a strike in the weeks leading up to Mardi Gras, confident this would force the mayor to cave to the NOPD's salary increase and other demands without holding out for corresponding reforms. Everyone was stunned when Dutch called the cops' bluff, canceling Mardi Gras for the first time since the Second World War, and ultimately winning the public safety initiatives he'd deemed non-negotiable. Despite, or perhaps because of such epic confrontations, three years later Dutch was elected to a second term, retaining his near-total share of the Black vote and earning an even larger portion of White progressive support than he had in his first mayoral run.

This was the firebrand from whom Marc Morial had learned political craft, sitting at his father's knee through his many campaigns for public office, accompanying him to civic ceremonies and listening in on meetings with the city's power brokers when he was still a young boy. Marc later took off the first semester of his sophomore year at the University of Pennsylvania to return home and run his dad's lawn sign operation during his mayoral election bid in 1977. And, just eight years after the Crescent City's first Black mayor was term limited out of office in 1986, and five years after his death from an asthma attack, his eldest son and the second of Dutch and Sybil Morial's five children, would be elected mayor by a coalition of popular support similar to the one that had twice elected his father.

Right out the gate, Mayor Morial the younger had instituted daily press conferences, aware that an agreeable working relationship with local reporters would go a long way to helping him get his message out. He had even designated a permanent pressroom on the second floor of City Hall, with a handsome wooden podium bearing the seal of the city and outlets for media microphones. Before his tenure, press conferences had been more ad hoc, held in the lobby or the hallway of City Hall whenever the mayor had an announcement. Marc wanted to be a more accessible chief executive, especially with regard to the continuing problems of police corruption and public safety, which had been the central issues of his campaign. With up to four hundred murders a year, crime in New Orleans was at epidemic levels. Complicating matters, the young mayor was forced to engage in a pitched conflict with a police union that still remembered the hard-knuckle tactics of his father. Marc was generally poised and charming in public while playing hardball behind closed doors, but when necessary, he could be a street brawler, too. Some of my colleagues had observed that he combined the best of both his parents—Dutch's grit and toughness with Sybil's social diplomacy and finesse—and that he would employ his full arsenal of political skills to shore up the city's fortunes.

In those early days, I was seduced by the city—its diverse communities and world-class offerings in music, art, and cuisine, so much of it rooted in Black American history and culture. Similar to when I'd first arrived at college, I found myself consumed by an exciting new Afrocentric reality, and I set about discovering all the places in it where I could belong—as a journalist and a citizen.

New Orleans became the town where I would challenge jazz royalty Wynton Marsalis to a game of pick-up basketball—and win, wearing heels, no less—and where I would attend a vampire costume party in the company of the enigmatic author of *The Vampire Chronicles*, Anne Rice. I was already eagerly anticipating my first Mardi Gras, as well as the debut July Fourth festival marking the twenty-fifth anniversary of *Essence* magazine. I had heard that when the young mayor learned that the iconic Black women's magazine was looking for a location to hold its quarter-century celebration, he had wooed its leadership to bring their "party with a purpose" to the Crescent City. He envisioned the proposed music festival advancing his goal of making New Orleans a multicultural tourist destination, especially during the sweltering months of summer when most hotels stood empty. Indeed, the runaway success of that first four-day event in 1995 would launch an annual Essence Fest tradition that continues to this day, with African American women from across the country descending on downtown for concerts by the Black music vanguard, as well as free empowerment seminars led by experts in African American health and wellness, fashion and beauty, and politics and social activism.

Taken as I was with the city's charms, at first I didn't fully grasp the systemic racism that hummed through practically every interface in my new town. Despite its progressive enclaves and cultural wealth, this was also the place where former KKK grand wizard David Duke had been voted into the Louisiana House of Representatives in 1988, and where a low-wage economy combined to keep a vast majority of Black residents, as well as poor Whites, in desperate straits. Beyond the grand antebellum estates and lovely Garden District homes, beyond the music and laughter spilling out of downtown restaurants and bars, beyond the haunting moss-hung trees and picturesque bayous, there was also the entrenched disenfranchisement of people of color alongside the blatant neglect of other poor communities. As I would come to understand, race and caste infiltrated every aspect of life in the City That Care Forgot.

However, on the day I first met the new young mayor—"Boy Wonder," as some people wryly referred to him—I was still prone to romanticizing the brightly colored shotgun houses in Tremé, the vibrant art scene in the Warehouse District, and the French Quarter's intricate wooden gables, wrought-iron balconies, and faded Victorian appeal. As the new girl on the scene, I was a bit of a curiosity in the City Hall pressroom, with colleagues coming over to introduce themselves and take my measure. My back was to the podium when some forty-five minutes after the event had been scheduled to begin, a deep baritone cleared his throat over the microphone.

The sound seemed to be thrown toward me, and as I whipped my head around to confront its source, I'm almost certain I was rolling my neck with quintessential Black girl attitude, as if to say, "I *know* you're not talking to me." Casting my eyes to the podium, I found myself in an unblinking stare-down with the mayor.

"I believe we're ready to get started," he said, addressing me.

Despite his professional tone, I could see the amusement in his crinkled eyes. That he had the nerve to be enjoying the moment only added insult to injury, because his implied rebuke had embarrassed me, and right as I was trying to make a good impression on my colleagues. He had been almost an hour late, so what right did he have to call me out? I instantly went on the offensive, lobbing question after question at him without bothering to disguise my pique.

In years to come, Marc would never tire of recalling that press conference. "You were madder than an alligator in a net," he would say, chortling every time. Invariably he would add that he had found my rapid-fire volley of questions entertaining, and that he had found himself looking forward to sparring with me again. I was less impressed. That night, when I mentioned to my father that I had covered the mayor's press conference, Daddy commented, "I think I played poker with his dad at an Alpha Phi Alpha Convention." No doubt he had, because Dutch Morial had pledged the same college fraternity as my father, with Dutch also serving a term as the organization's national president. "What is the son like?" my father asked me.

"Smart," I said dryly, "and full of himself."

Marc was indeed clever and supremely confident, with the calculating edge of a born tactician, a man practiced at keeping all angles in view. I had to admit that he was also handsome, and that as I had peppered him with questions during that first press event, there had been a spark of something between us, which I hoped had gone unnoticed by everyone else in the room.

A few days later I received a letter on the mayor's official stationery, mailed to me at the station. In formal black type, he welcomed me to New Orleans and wished me well in my new position with WWL-TV. He also advised me on the phonetically correct way to say New Orleans, noting that nothing revealed a newcomer more than pronouncing the city's name incorrectly. "It's New Or-*lee-ans*," Marc instructed me, "not New Or-*leans*." However, he added, if referring to Orleans parish rather than the city as a whole, then it should be pronounced Or-*leans*. I didn't know quite how to feel about his letter. Did the mayor welcome all newly hired reporters in this way, or had he singled me out? And was he mocking me in telling me the correct way to pronounce his city's name or was he sincerely looking to help me save face and ensure my success?

I didn't see the mayor again until a few weeks later, at an event for Senator Carol Moseley Braun. Earlier that day, I had interviewed Congress's lone Black woman senator for a story I'd had to fight to get approved. When I'd first proposed covering her visit to the city for a NAACP luncheon at which she was being honored, my assignment editor had objected. "Why are you aligning yourself with this politician," she complained, forcing me to explain that it wasn't about aligning myself with anyone, but Carol Moseley Braun was a pioneer in a political body that had long been off-limits to women, and women of color in particular. "She's made history as a Black woman, which makes her an important story for our African American viewers," I'd argued, finally winning approval to cover the luncheon and do a news piece on the senator.

Marc had spoken at the luncheon, and when he was done, his director of communications, Michele Moore, walked over to me. After identifying herself as the daughter of the best friend of Mrs. Holmes,

my neighbor on West 80th Street back in South Central, she shared
that Mrs. Holmes had told her I would be moving to New Orleans
and had asked her to look out for me. She then invited me to a reception for Senator Moseley Braun that had been organized for that
evening at the Pontalba, a landmarked block of apartments and shops
located on Jackson Square, with historic features that had been painstakingly maintained.

I knew the history of the Pontalba, which dated back to 1850 and
was said to be the oldest apartment building in the country, but the
event for Senator Moseley Braun would be my first time venturing inside. As I circled the reception room, taking in its architectural details,
I also noted that every demographic in town was represented among
the guests, from local politicos and state Supreme Court justices, to
activists, business leaders, academics, and a cross-section of regular folk
representing the diverse communities of the city. I would learn that this
mix of people was a signature feature of any event that the young mayor
had a hand in. He always took pains to ensure that all his constituencies
felt included in the political life of their town.

I was talking with a man I'd recently met at another event when
the mayor's brother, Jacques Morial, approached me and introduced
himself.

"Michelle Miller from WWL-TV?" he said before I could respond
with my own name. "What are you doing here? Aren't political fundraisers off limits for news people?"

"This is a fundraiser?" I asked him, taken aback.

"Sure is," he nodded.

"Oh my God," I said, "I gotta go!"

I hastily bid Jacques and the man I'd been talking to a good evening and was rushing down the stairs, thinking to catch a cab back to
the station before anyone else noticed my professional transgression.
Rounding onto the last flight of stairs down to the street, I literally
bumped into Marc, who had just arrived for the reception.

"Hello there," he greeted me, both hands instinctively grabbing my upper arms to steady me. "Where are you hurrying off to? The event just started."

"I have to leave," I said. "I didn't realize it was a fundraiser."

"Oh," he said. "Well, hold on then. Just give me five minutes. I'll give you a ride. You'll never catch a cab at this hour, and it could be a little sketchy for you to walk to wherever you're headed at night, alone." I saw his lips twitch as he glanced down at my strappy stilettos. "And in those heels."

Watching him disappear up the stairs, I realized that I didn't actually have enough cash in my wallet to afford a cab anyway and would indeed have been forced to walk back to the station in my cocktail party shoes. I appreciated the brash young mayor then, whose chivalry was about to rescue my evening. He reappeared very shortly and with great courtliness ushered me down the rest of the stairs to the sidewalk, where a black Lincoln towncar was waiting at the curb, the suited police officer assigned to his security detail behind the wheel.

"Wow," I breathed, "I didn't know we would be all official like this."

"This is how I roll," Marc said lightly, holding open the back door for me. I thought he would slide in beside me, but taking nothing for granted, he instead closed my door in gentlemanly fashion and slipped into the front passenger seat.

"This is Larry Taplin," he said, nodding toward the driver. "We call him Tap."

"Thanks for the ride, Tap," I said, suddenly feeling a bit like the little girl sitting in the middle of the back seat of my neighbor's great boat of a car on the morning that my grandmother fell on the stairs. The flash of memory left me feeling vulnerable and unsure of myself, even as Marc shot perfectly innocent questions at me from the front seat: Where had I gone to college? What had I studied there? What made me decide to come to New Orleans?

I had asked to be driven back to the studio, as I was scheduled to anchor the 10 P.M. newscast. As we approached the station's back entrance on Burgundy Street, I prepared to jump out of the conspicuous towncar quickly, a rolling stop, so no one would know that the mayor himself had transported me back to work. My heart leapt into my throat when the car made a sudden sharp left through the gate that led to the parking lot at the back of the building. I realized then that the mayor probably knew better than I did all the ways into and out of the studio, including this more private Burgundy Street entrance. However, since most of my colleagues also came and went using this entrance, I was mortified that someone would notice me getting out of the mayor's official vehicle.

"Stop! Stop!" I cried as the car turned into the gate. "Let me out here!" But it was too late. Marc's driver was already inside the lot and pulling to a stop right in front of the double glass doors. "Oh my God," I moaned, unable to stop the ripple of nervous laughter that broke from me as I recognized the 10 P.M. director and one of the station photographers leaving the building right at that moment.

'What's the matter?" Marc asked, concerned by my apparent angst.

"This really won't look good, for you or for me," I explained. "People are going to make some assumptions."

"Let them," Marc said, relaxing visibly. "Why should it matter? You and I know the truth, and besides, I am free, single, and disengaged. It's not like either of us is doing anything wrong."

"But I'm a journalist," I chided him. "The last thing I need is people thinking that I can't be objective when I'm covering you."

Even so, what else could I do at that point but thank Marc and Tap for seeing me safely back to the studio, and exit the back seat with my shoulders squared and head held high. As it happened, my concerns about propriety would prove to have been completely valid when I learned later that a rumor that I was dating the mayor had begun circulating among my colleagues that very evening.

IN FACT, MARC AND I WOULD NOT START SEEING EACH OTHER IN A romantic sense for several more months, though we had begun that night to establish a camaraderie outside the bounds of our professional relationship as journalist and newsmaker. We took the next step forward at another public gathering we both attended. A friend from my Howard University days, who now worked for the New Orleans Sports Foundation, had invited me to a press junket, a jazz dinner cruise up the Mississippi River aboard the Natchez steamboat. A few minutes after I boarded, I saw Marc strolling up the gangway. This wasn't a surprise; the invitation had noted that he was scheduled to give a few remarks to kick things off before the boat departed. He noticed me at once and walked right over, greeting me with his usual gallantry.

The two of us chatted for a bit about Joe Duke's imminent departure from WWL to take over the leadership of a station in Houston. We both agreed we would miss the man. Soon, a wiry little guy in a gray suit tapped Marc on the shoulder to indicate it was time for him to offer his remarks. He nodded at me politely and went to where the microphone had been set up. He didn't speak for very long, and when he was done, he did the rounds, conversing with several people on board before waving goodbye to his hosts and jogging briskly down the gangway. Watching him leave, I surmised that he probably had other official commitments scheduled for that evening. Just then the same wiry little guy appeared beside me.

"Excuse me, ma'am, but Mayor Morial would like a word with you," he said.

"Okay," I replied, looking around. "But he already left the boat."

"Yes, ma'am, you'll have to get off the boat to speak with him."

"But the cruise is about to leave," I pointed out.

The aide tried to hide a smile. "The boat won't leave before you've had your conversation with the mayor," he said, regaining his sober demeanor.

Not quite convinced, I followed him to the gangplank but stopped halfway down. From there I called out to Marc, who was standing on the dock talking to another of his aides, his back turned to me.

"Mayor Morial, you wanted to say something to me?"

He turned and looked up at me. "I was wondering if you might like to have dinner with me," he said. I don't know what I had been expecting, but it surely wasn't a dinner invitation.

"Tonight?" I asked, scrunching up my face, stalling for time as I digested the fact that the mayor had just asked me out on a date.

"Yes, tonight," he confirmed, "if you're willing to forgo the cruise."

"I can't," I told him. "I came with someone."

"Who is it?" he wanted to know. "Is it a date-date?"

"None of your beeswax," I said, feigning shock at his impertinence in asking.

"Are you seeing this person?"

"He's a friend," I allowed. "But I'm still here with him. And you know what they say—you always leave with the one who brung you."

"Fair enough." Marc laughed and started to take his leave, but then paused and turned back to look at me from the foot of the gangplank, his hands folded in front of him, as if he was considering saying something more. After a few moments he took a few steps up the wooden gangway toward me, and said more quietly, so that no one else could hear, "Well, I still would like to take you out to dinner. Are you okay with that in principle?"

"Maybe a rain check," I replied.

"Well then, I'm going to need your number."

"Aren't you the mayor? Can't you just get my number yourself?"

"It doesn't work like that," he said, obviously enjoying our jousting. "I'm going to need you to give it to me."

And so I gave him my number.

He called me that very night to ask if I might be free to dine with him in the coming week. As I'd just started dating a young business school graduate who was trying to ignite a relationship, I said I'd have to think about it.

The next time I saw Marc was at the opening of the local Planet Hollywood restaurant. "Hey, Mayor Morial," I greeted him breezily.

"Marc," he said. "You've *got* to start calling me Marc."

"Okay, Marc," I conceded with a laugh, not quite clear if he was flirting with me or just turning on the same charm that he showed to everyone.

"So how about that dinner," he reminded me then. The flutter of excitement I felt at his question told me that I was becoming altogether too intrigued by the young mayor, and I decided that I needed to clarify things.

"You know, Marc," I responded, "you're a public figure and I'm a journalist, so while we can be friends, it can't be more than that, otherwise it could affect my career."

"I understand," Marc said sincerely. "And I totally respect that."

After that, Marc was hesitant to do anything that would make me feel uncomfortable. Our friendship deepened nevertheless, because Marc happened to walk some mornings in City Park at the same early hour that I did, and we often ran into each other there. We'd invariably fall in step with one another, talking and circling the track together. We developed an easy familiarity, punctuated by moments of overt flirtation that we would both pull back from as soon as we caught ourselves going there.

I realized that my feelings for the mayor were quite a bit more than friendly on the day I interviewed him about an education initiative in the studio. Marc and I could barely contain the attraction sizzling between us. A few minutes in, as we slipped into our usual back-and-forth banter, I had a devil of a time holding back the coy glances and nervous body language that threatened to reveal my feelings for this man to the entire city. I refused to even look at him as I asked my questions, sure I would betray myself, as if the mischief in his eyes weren't enough of a giveaway. Afterward, I tore off my mic and gave a panicked exhale. "Oh my God," I exclaimed, "we are *never* doing that again!" Marc only chuckled, as if rather appreciating the now undeniable fact of our chemistry.

It had taken a ridiculously long time for it to occur to me that when people saw us walking together in City Park in the early morning, certain assumptions could be made. When at last this thought presented itself after our studio interview, I was alarmed that I had allowed myself to be so careless with my professional reputation.

"Look, Marc, I can't walk with you in the mornings anymore," I told him on the phone soon after. "People will think we spent the night together. And if my boss gets wind of people thinking that, even though it's not true, I'm worried she'll fire me."

Marc was quiet for a few moments, possibly remembering the insecurity I'd confessed to feeling when it came to my new boss, who had taken over as News Director after the departure of Joe Duke. Though I admired her accomplishment in winning the job, I had never felt that she saw my value. It didn't help that I shared a desk with her husband, also a reporter at the station, and the awkwardness of it all mortified me.

"Okay, Michelle, I have an idea," Marc said, interrupting my fretful train of thought. "Maybe it's time to get ahead of this thing."

"What do you mean?"

"I think you should go and talk to the big man himself, the president and general manager, Mr. Early. If anyone will understand the situation, he will."

J. Michael Early was a legend in the news business. A deeply respected leader, he had run WWL since the 1970s, and his innovative programming, ability to retain talent, and commitment to broadcasting excellence had been instrumental in building the CBS affiliate into a top-ranked national market leader in the country and a local cable news powerhouse. Mr. Early also had eleven children of his own, Marc reminded me, so a young person's dating conundrums weren't likely to rattle him. Rather, he would have the wisdom and perspective bestowed by his years not just as a station manager, but also as a father and grandfather.

Moreover, Marc added, Mr. Early knew his character. Not only was he an alumnus of Jesuit High School, which Marc had also attended, but he had also interacted with the mayor during years of professional association, and would understand Marc's intentions toward me to be honorable. Perhaps another factor in our favor was that one of Mr. Early's daughters-in-law worked for Marc as a city attorney. And Mr. Early had family members who had run for and held elected office—a son who was a former city councilman and a brother who was a judge—which meant he would have a more pragmatic sense of where to draw the line if one of his reporters was interested in dating a newsmaker. After all, New Orleans was a town where everybody knew everybody, and relationships developed along all sorts of lines. If anyone would be sympathetic to that, Marc was convinced it would be Mr. Early. As the station's longtime assistant station manager, Phil Johnson, would later reflect, "Mr. Early likely heard more confessions at the Rampart Street studios than the Jesuits did in their church on Baronne Street."

I decided to make an appointment to speak with the revered president and station manager. My hands were shaking as I took the chair opposite his wooden battleship of a desk. "Mr. Early," I began, my voice as unsteady as my hands, "I wanted to speak with you because I have a problem, and I hoped you'd be able to help me figure out how to address it in the right way."

"What's the problem?" he asked, his blue eyes genial in a round, rosy Irish Catholic face.

I decided there was no other way but to stomp right to the indelicate heart of the matter. "There's this guy that I'm interested in," I said, "but he's a public figure. And I understand that to date him would be a conflict of interest given my position here at the station, so I thought it was important to come to you and get your advice."

"Would this young man happen to be the mayor of New Orleans?" Mr. Early said, choosing to be equally direct.

"Yes," I said, my face suddenly hot. "How did you know?"

Mr. Early smiled. "I make it my business to know these things," he said. "So how about this," he continued. "If your relationship with the mayor ever becomes a problem, we will let you know."

His response was heartening, but there was one more thing that I thought needed to be put on the table. "Mr. Early, I want you to know that I've already removed myself from covering City Hall and anything else the mayor is involved in," I said. "I just want to quietly see where a relationship between us might lead, but the last thing I want is a scandal."

"I do think it's smart for you to step away from those stories," Mr. Early nodded, "but don't worry too much about a scandal. I will promise that what you've shared with me won't leave these doors, though I'm sure you have probably guessed that a certain rumor is already making the rounds. But so what?" He shrugged kindly, and then half rose from his chair to signal our meeting was over. "You go and live your life, young lady."

Relief flooded me as I thanked him and took my leave of his office. I had particularly appreciated his closing sentiment, which echoed words my father had previously spoken to me.

Even with Mr. Early's blessing, however, Marc and I kept our dating life extremely low key. But at the end of September 1995, we decided to travel together to Washington, D.C., to attend the Congressional

Black Caucus Foundation awards weekend. My mistake was visiting my friend Suzanne Malveaux at her station, accompanied by Marc. I had completely forgotten that a former colleague from WWL-TV was now working with Suzanne at the station in D.C. The moment he saw Marc and me together, I knew the gig was up. He must have gone straight back to his desk and phoned his contacts back in New Orleans, because the news apparently spread through the North Rampart Street studio like wildfire.

As soon as I got back to work on Monday, I was called in by my news director. She was a smart and sensible woman whose news acumen served her well, though I had continued to suspect that she was not a fan of mine. Much as I told myself I was a grown woman and had done nothing wrong, I felt like a guilty schoolgirl being summoned to the principal's office.

"Are you friends with the mayor?" she asked me without preamble.

"Yes," I replied.

"Well," she said, "didn't you feel that it was important to tell us that?"

She used the word *us*—"tell *us* that" rather than "tell *me* that"— giving me the perfect out. "Of course, I did," I said, feeling calmer.

The news director looked puzzled.

"Whom did you tell?" she wanted to know.

"I told Mr. Early a few months ago, to make sure it wouldn't be a problem," I responded.

"And what did he say?" she asked.

"He said"—I took pains to quote him exactly—"'If your relationship with the mayor ever becomes a problem, we will let you know,'" I responded.

I could see confusion and surprise on the news director's face. If she had intended to confront me about the conflict created by my relationship, Mr. Early's name caused her to retreat. When she spoke again, she seemed less hostile, respectful even.

"Well, I guess you really did tell *us* if you told Mr. Early," she said. "But why didn't you just come to me?"

Her conciliatory tone suggested she was trying to build a bridge between us, and that made me feel warmer toward her. And so, in my most reasonable manner, I explained that while I hadn't intended to hide anything from her, I had not thought it appropriate to ask her to keep my secret given how closely we worked together day to day in the studio and the fact that I sat right across from her husband, who covered City Hall. Mr. Early, on the other hand, I hardly ever saw, and besides, he was always going to be the final word on the sensitivities of the matter at hand anyway. And, of course, I reminded her, I'd also stepped away from the high-profile City Hall stories months ago.

She appeared to accept my words. But as I walked back to my desk, I knew that our conversation that morning would not be the end of the matter, and that I would likely suffer a change in status because of my personal affiliation with the mayor.

SURE ENOUGH, I WAS MOVED OFF THE PRESTIGIOUS WEEKEND NEWS anchor desk, and assigned to the *Early Edition* show that aired at 5:30 A.M. during the week. I saw it as a demotion of sorts, under the guise of removing me from having to cover stories that might prove to be a conflict of interest. However, it didn't take me long to see that the morning show was actually an opportunity for me. The half-hour program had been launched by a promising young reporter, Karen Swensen, an unfailingly kind and supportive colleague, who understood my initial disappointment and helped to make my transition to the show as smooth as possible.

Fortuitously, my new role also put me in daily contact with two of the top journalists in New Orleans, Sally Ann Roberts and Eric Paulsen, from whom I would learn the rudiments of the morning news game. Soon, our half hour show was expanded to a full hour each morning, with me substitute anchoring for the lead and delivering breaking news for our show as well as for the station's noon newscast. I had managed to take the lemons I'd been handed and make the best damn lemonade I could.

I mixed up a particularly sweet batch one morning when our photographer Jimmie Brown was called to cover a man hanging from a tree—not *that* kind of hanging fortunately, although this being the Old South one could be forgiven for fearing the worst. But no, this hanging involved a man holding onto the limb of a giant oak that brushed the side of his Orleans Avenue balcony. How he ended up there had more to do with his being a diabetic and his sugar levels being high than with any street drugs he may have taken.

I had arrived on the scene at just past 7 A.M., as the man was being strapped onto a gurney to be wheeled to a waiting ambulance. A fire truck was also at the scene, its telescoping metal ladder still raised and resting against the oak branch from which the man had been rescued. My eyes roamed over the throng of onlookers gathered around the base of the tree, and came to rest on two boys, neither one older than ten years old. *Why weren't they in school?* I walked over to introduce myself and ask this question.

Breathlessly, they spilled their story. They had been on their way to school when they heard someone crying out for help. Looking for the source of the call, they discovered the man hanging from the tree, terrified he would fall two stories to earth and badly injure himself. The boys ran to several houses on the street, banging on doors and shouting for someone to call 911. In that high-crime neighborhood, the fact that one person actually opened the front door to the frantically yelling boys was a miracle in itself. The occupant of that house did indeed call for emergency rescue, while the boys ran back to tell the man that help was on the way.

"What did you say to him?" I asked them.

"We said 'Just hang on!'" the boys shared in unison.

The irony of those particular words given as assurance to a man hanging from a tree made me laugh so hard that it became the punch line in a story that could have ended in tragedy, but which became instead an uplifting piece about concerned citizenship.

The story would earn me my very first journalistic prize— a National Association of Black Journalists Salute to Excellence Award for social interest reporting. I had won recognition for telling a little story with a big meaning, and learned several lessons from the experience: First, anyone can be a hero. Second, pay attention to the less obvious stories that run alongside the main one. And third, look for human greatness in every situation. Best of all, I had called the boys' school to let them know about the quick thinking of these young students. As a result, they were not only recognized by their teachers and the city for their initiative in helping an endangered neighbor, but they also became local role models, showing how a small yet critical action can make all the difference in the life of another person.

NINETEEN

True North

Walking with Marc along the track in City Park one morning, I found myself opening up in a way I hadn't before about how much I had missed being raised by my own mother. Marc already knew that I had met the woman who birthed me only twice that I could recall, but this was the first time I was sharing how lonely I had been without her, how deeply her absence had shaped my sense of myself, and my place in the world.

"I'm so sorry you had to go through that," Marc said simply, reaching out to touch my arm. He reflected then that he had experienced something similar, but from the other side of the equation. He revealed that he had fathered a daughter with a Liberian woman named Rose Dennis, who had been two years ahead of him in law school. Their daughter, Kemah, now lived in Côte d'Ivoire with her mother. Kemah's situation was in some ways similar to mine, Marc said, because she had seen her father only a handful of times in her thirteen years.

Noticing the way his shoulders drooped as he spoke of missing his daughter, and hearing how his voice became tender, almost reverential, as he described her, I immediately assessed that Kemah's story and mine weren't the same at all. The difference, I pointed out to Marc, was that he *was aching* for more time with his child, but circumstances of geography had precluded his being able to forge a more continuous relationship with her.

I was struck by how this situation was showing up yet again in my life—a child for whom one parent wasn't fully in the picture—and the fact that it was connected to a man I was dating made me all the more intrigued. Remembering how acutely I had identified with my friend Chrystal back in the days of Saturday afternoon pool parties at Little and Tony's house, I understood that it was my longing for my own mother that provoked such visceral grief in me at this particular story of parental absence. Even though I had now sat with Laura Hernandez long enough to ask the questions that had haunted me, since our lunch in San Diego there had continued to be no further contact between us. The mystery of my mother's whereabouts had been solved, and yet she was still absent from my life. As she poured herself into raising children she had not birthed from her own body, I was still her abandoned child.

In Marc and Kemah's case, there was some good news: Since 1993, Kemah had been spending a part of each summer in New Orleans with Marc, a continent away from her maternal family. In anticipation of her visit in the summer of 1995, I spent weeks helping her dad to redecorate her room, choosing pretty curtains and bedding I imagined that a teen girl might like, and coming up with an itinerary of activities that I thought she might enjoy. An out-of-wedlock child myself, I probably understood more intensely than Marc the questions Kemah might hold about where she belonged in her father's life, and I resolved to do whatever I could to help her feel assured of her primacy in her father's affections.

That summer, with Marc juggling the relentless demands of running the city, Kemah and I explored the Big Easy together, eating beignets at Café du Monde, attending local concerts, and hanging out with the numerous nieces and nephews of Marc's best friend, Winston Burns. Kemah was shy and polite at first, brilliant and piercing in her opinions later on. I adored her at once, and couldn't help but recall the women my own father had dated when I was her age—the ones I had loved and wished he would marry, and the ones I had quietly endured. I knew by then that I was in love with Marc, and so I sent up a silent prayer that my deepening friendship with his daughter might be a sign that for Kemah, I might fall into the first category.

Even before Kemah had arrived for her visit, Marc had shared that he had fallen for me, too. I refrained from telling him that I sometimes fantasized about a future together, because at twenty-seven, I wasn't remotely ready to get married. However, at the end of the summer, after seeing Kemah off on her flight back to Cote d'Ivoire to be reunited with her mom, Marc was driving me back to work when he mentioned, casual as you please, that we made a good team, and perhaps we should make it permanent. There was no warning, no fanfare, just a musing out loud that he thought we were perfect for each other. I looked at him, a bit stunned by the suddenness of his declaration, but since he hadn't mentioned the M-word, I said nothing.

"So what do you think?" he pressed. "Can you see it? The two of us together?"

"Yes," I said. "I can see it. But I hope you know this conversation right here doesn't count as any kind of a proposal."

"Duly noted!" Marc laughed. "Oh, I'm taking notes. Definitely no half-stepping allowed if I hope to win the hand of Ms. Michelle Miller!"

"You got that right," I agreed, wagging my forefinger with mock severity that put me in the mind of Bigmama. I imagined she would have approved of Marc and me, and that made everything feel more right somehow. Not unrelated, I recalled how, during freshman orientation week at Howard, boys and girls relishing their first taste of freedom had hung out for hours each day "on the wall," the famous meet-up spot on campus. My roommate, Wendy Raquel Robinson, who had become a well-known actress after college, wanted to know how come she'd never seen me over by the wall.

"I don't need to meet any riffraff," I'd replied archly. We were walking across the main quad after a new students information session with the school's president. "Besides," I had added, "I have my five-point rule."

"Five-point rule?" Wendy frowned. "What are you talking about?"

"I'm looking for my Big Five," I explained. "My grandmother always told me to hold out for a partner who is smart, funny, attractive, ambitious, and conscientious—like my dad, she used to say. You know I'm not going to find all that in someone hanging out on the wall and hoping for a quick hookup."

"You do you, Michelle," Wendy had said as she swanned away from me in the direction of the wall. "But girl, you're missing out on some fun."

I smiled now, remembering our exchange, because in Marc, I had found every one of the qualities on my Big Five wish list. As we turned off the highway and headed toward the studio, I realized I was feeling as bright as the sunbeams flooding into the car. I barely recognized myself in that moment, a woman basking in a new and unfamiliar state of being, in which I felt perhaps for the first time in my life, that it was wholly within my power to fill the well of loneliness that secretly plagued me, with hope, possibility, and Big Five love.

THAT OCTOBER, MARIA CALLED TO SAY THAT DADDY HAD TAKEN A turn for the worse and had been rushed to the hospital that morning. Scans had shown that the cancer had recently flared and was now marching throughout his body, uncontained.

"It's serious," she told me. "I think you need to come and see your father soon."

I put down the phone and went to find Marc, who was in my living room waiting for me to finish getting ready for a dinner engagement with friends. Seeing my solemn expression, he looked at me questioningly. "It's my dad," I said. "I'm not sure how much longer he'll be with us. You know, Marc, if you have a notion to ask my father for my hand in marriage, I think you're going to have to do that very soon."

We flew to L.A. a few days later, going straight from the airport to see Daddy at the hospital. As always, he hated our fussing over him, but he was now so debilitated, even he had to admit that he needed help getting out of bed. And yet his spirit remained as robust as ever. He had taken one look at Marc and me when we'd first walked into his hospital room, and discerned Marc's reason for accompanying me on this trip. He'd winked at me and patted my hand in an all-knowing way.

On the second night of our visit, after Maria and my brothers had left the hospital for the evening, a nurse helped Daddy sit upright in the bed. As soon as she left the room, Marc asked my father if they might have a word. Fully aware of what was coming, Daddy nodded and smiled at the two of us, a sphinxlike expression on his face. Standing across from Marc at Daddy's bedside, I gave silent thanks that the man I loved was the sort who would choose a moment when my father was sitting, rather than lying down, to ask his question man to man. That small unspoken act of consideration had allowed the good doctor his dignity.

"Dr. Miller, sir, I love your daughter," Marc said, wasting no time in getting to the main reason for his presence in that room, "and I would like to ask for your blessing to marry her."

Daddy thanked Marc for granting him the honor of asking for my hand, and then he continued, "I think you're a fine young man, but I want to tell you one thing. If ever you don't want her anymore, send her home. Don't beat her!"

I was *aghast*!

"Daddy, why would you say such a thing?" I demanded. "Don't *beat* her? What on *earth* are you thinking?"

My father was unrepentant. "And you," he said, jabbing an index finger toward me, "Don't you fuck it up!"

I was dumbfounded, because Daddy had never cursed like that in front of me.

"I'm calling Aunt Edna right now to tell her what you said," I scolded him, unable to fathom what had gotten into my normally egalitarian and unchauvinistic father.

"Go right ahead," he said pleasantly.

I was starting to catch on that there might be some backstory to all this that I was clearly missing, an inkling that became a certainty when Aunt Edna's immediate response to my complaint about what Daddy had told Marc was to dissolve into peals of laughter. I demanded to know why she found the whole thing so uproariously funny.

"Oh Michelle, that's exactly what my father told your Uncle Tom when he asked for my hand," she explained, still trying to catch her breath. "Your dad was sixteen years old, and he was eavesdropping outside the door. He was so excited by what he heard that he ran back to tell Mama and me the whole thing. He's been waiting forty years to say those very same words!"

A little while later, when Marc went to the floor lounge to make a work call, Daddy did soften my chagrin somewhat. As I rearranged his pillows and tucked the covers around him, he said, "Marc is a good man, and it's clear to me that he loves you very much. I have to say, it eases my mind to know you've chosen a partner as smart and steady as that young man. Because I'm going to die soon," he went on. "I probably have one more Christmas, and then you'll be on your own. But at least where the life partner you've chosen is concerned, I can die in peace."

WHEN I SPOKE WITH DADDY FROM THE WHITE HOUSE IN EARLY FEBRU-ary 1996, I didn't know it would be the last time. Maria had told us he was "sinking." But Daddy had rallied so many times that I refused to entertain the thought that he could not do so one more time. I was in Washington, D.C., with Marc, attending an official state dinner for French president Jacques Chirac. In the midst of the event, I had looked around the room and taken in the elegance of the occasion, with President Bill Clinton and First Lady Hillary Rodham Clinton doing the rounds of all the VIP tables, and I suddenly wanted nothing more than to call my dad and share the moment with him.

The first time I had been inside the White House had been with him, back when I was nine years old and he had brought me along to a National Medical Association convention in Washington, D.C. That week, Daddy had taken a day away from the programmed events to show me his old stomping ground from the days when he was a student at Howard. As I listened to his endless stories, we had stopped at the Reflecting Pool on the National Mall, and climbed the steps of the Lincoln Memorial where Dr. King gave his famous "I Have a Dream" speech on August 28, 1963. The next morning, Daddy had taken me on a tour of the White House, and the simple contentment I had felt, spending uninterrupted stretches of time with my usually busy father, made me want to now share my grown-up sequel to that day—a full circle moment in which I was an invited guest at a White House state dinner, in the distinguished company of the young mayor of New Orleans, who just three months before had asked for my hand.

This was in the days before every pocket held a cell phone, and so I whispered to Marc that I'd be right back and went to find a pay phone. I found none, but I did notice a red landline sitting on a table just inside the front doors, which were guarded by two statue-still marines in full dress uniform. Standing next to the phone was a man wearing dark glasses and a black suit, with the tell-tale Secret Service walkie-talkie cord snaking from his earpiece to under his suit collar. I approached him, resplendent in my ruby red strapless dinner gown, clearly an escapee from the state dinner.

"Excuse me, but may I use that phone?" I asked. "I have my own calling card number so it won't get charged to the White House."

"No need to use your card," the man replied with a smile. "You can place the phone call on us."

I thanked him and dialed the number to my father's hospital room. My brother Matt answered and handed Daddy the phone. I could hear his breathy weariness across the line as I described the scene inside the state dinner, and regaled him with stories of everyone I'd recognized whom he might possibly know. "Hot dog," he said, punctuating each new detail I shared with his scratchy whisper. "Hot dog." He was so weak he couldn't even speak a full sentence, yet somehow I failed to recognize, or perhaps admit, how close he was to the end.

Daddy released his final breath less than two weeks later, on February 17, 1996, two days shy of his sixty-seventh birthday. It was late in the evening when Aunt Edna called to say he was gone. Alone at home, I dared not allow myself to take in the full impact of the news, because I knew that if I shattered then, I'd never be able to fit myself back together. And so I reached for numbness as if it were a life raft, allowing me to keep breathing in a world where my father no longer was.

I called Marc first, but got his voice mail. I left a message.

"Daddy just died," I said.

Next, I called Chris Thomas, one of my best girlfriends and the person in town who had known me the longest. Chris had been part of my crew back in high school, and had met my dad on several occasions. After high school, she and I had attended Howard together, and now here we were once again in the same city to which Chris had moved sometime after college. I remembered that Chris and three others of our friends had planned to meet up that night at a speakeasy in the Tremé, the oldest African American neighborhood in the country and the acknowledged birthplace of jazz. I had initially declined to join them, but after Aunt Edna's call, I didn't want to be alone. I left Marc another message telling him where I was headed, and drove myself to the Tremé.

As soon as I walked into the club and Chris saw my face, she knew something was wrong. When I told her what had happened, she wrapped me in a hug and held me close. Our other friends, Phillipa Bowers, Renee Gusman, and Justin Woods, seeing her comforting me, came over, too, and all arms encircled me, holding me upright. I sank into their embrace gratefully, feeling as dry as the desert, too parched even to cry. The rest of that night is a blur. I know that at some point, Marc appeared and drove me home. He must also have put me to bed, but I have no memory of it. The next morning, I awoke to a world in which Dr. Ross Matthew Miller, my life's true north, would never again be.

I RETURNED TO LOS ANGELES TO HELP MARIA AND AUNT EDNA PLAN Daddy's memorial service. Marc traveled with me, and we decided to stay in a hotel. The house in which I had come of age didn't feel like home to me anymore. Vondela and Cheryl had returned to live there a couple of years before, around the time that my older cousin Thomas and his family moved away. I had been heartsick on my last visit to the house, noticing how badly it had fallen into disrepair, with cracked walls, paint peeling from the ceilings, floorboards coming up, windows unwashed, light bulbs expired and unchanged, and corners as gloomy and unattended as if a ghost had come in and haunted the place.

The dilapidation was all the more painful because when I'd moved home after college, I had sunk every dollar I could spare and more that I couldn't into bringing my Bigmama's house and garden back to tip-top shape. But on my last visit, I'd realized with a pang that even with Cheryl's inheritance from her late mother, Iris, who had been taken by cancer several years before, she and Vondela could ill afford the physical upkeep of the property. I had no choice but to continue straining under its monthly mortgage payments, even though I was earning more than a livable wage.

I could not have guessed what lay in store for me on this trip home

to bury my father, however. Turning into the West 80th Street driveway after getting settled in our hotel, I noticed at once that my grandfather's beloved garden—the fruit trees he had carefully tended, the
exotic flowers he had loved, all the luxuriant foliage he had planted—
had been utterly demolished. I stared at the scrubby overgrown grass
where the garden had been, wondering what could have possessed anyone to destroy that exquisitely beautiful plot of land. I marched into the
house, demanding to know who and when and why, my voice trembling
with shock and turmoil, my eyes leaking tears. In response, Vondela
looked over at Cheryl, who refused to speak. I kept pressing, desperate
to know what had led to the obliteration of the garden that had been
the setting for so many of my childhood games and dreams. But no
matter how ardently I pursued answers, Vondela remained resolutely
silent, while Cheryl only stared at me blankly before walking away.

Though I would never gain insight on who exactly had been responsible for the desecration of my grandfather's garden, or their reasons
why, what no one seemed to grasp was that the dark, brooding house
and razed yard had become a mirror for how the whole world felt to me
in the weeks after Daddy died. Dimly at first, and then with searing
clarity, I understood that my father's death together with the ruined
state of Bigmama's house marked the irrevocable end of my life *before*. I
had no heart to continue paying a mortgage that I couldn't really afford,
and no emotional resources left to take on restoring the house to a condition that would prevent my late grandmother turning in her grave.

"I've decided to put the house on the market," I told Vondela and
Cheryl a few weeks later. "No one is paying rent or covering the upkeep,
and I can't manage the mortgage note any longer. I'm going to have to
sell the property, so I'm asking you to help me get it ready to show."
Neither of the house's two remaining tenants was exactly pleased with
my announcement, and they both dragged their feet on the cleanup,
leaving it to me to arrange with the assistance of other family members
and some of my friends who lived locally.

By the time I had a buyer, Vondela and Cheryl had relocated to an affordable apartment building in Gardenia. But our relationship had become so frayed that every time I called the number for the place where they were now living, the phone rang and rang. With me several states away in New Orleans, and cell phones not yet a thing, I couldn't seem to connect with my former guardian or get news of my sister. I was aware they were still feeling betrayed by the way I had handled the dispossession of my grandmother's property, but I was hurt and disappointed, too, not just by their neglect of the house and garden I had so loved, but also by their unwillingness to grasp the untenable financial position I was in. They refused to understand that I simply couldn't afford to continue underwriting the two of them living rent-free in Bigmama's house as I had done for the better part of the last decade.

As grateful as I would always be to Vondela for stepping in to mother Cheryl and me during the five years between my grandmother's death and my leaving for college, I knew that I would never again live in the house I had held on to almost as a shrine to Bigmama. I needed to turn my attention to the work of building a future rather than trying to reclaim a broken past. And so, despite our three lives having been domestically entwined for so long, for the next several years Vondela, Cheryl, and I would fall out of contact, each side feeling wronged by the other, our little household no more.

SEVERAL MONTHS AFTER MY FATHER'S FUNERAL, ON A DAY WHEN I had dialed Vondela's number yet another time with no answer, I decided to call Laura Hernandez and let her know that Daddy had died. *Ross was the love of my life*, my mother had said of my father—those words had never stopped echoing in my mind. The death of that love now seemed a sufficiently valid reason to initiate contact between us for the first time since our lunch in San Diego five years before. Perhaps I was hoping I might yet be able to foster a closer relationship with my only remaining parent, especially now that Vondela had removed herself from the picture. I held my breath as the phone rang, praying that Laura and not her husband would pick up. When a woman answered, I exhaled, but quickly realized it wasn't my mother's voice.

"Hello, may I please speak to Laura Hernandez?"

"Who may I say is calling?"

The voice sounded young, bright, and sunny. I thought perhaps it might belong to the step-granddaughter Laura had told me about, though it could also have been any one of her several stepdaughters.

"Michelle Miller," I said, realizing too late that perhaps I should not have given my name. "I'm a friend," I added. "Is Laura home?"

"Hold on, I'll get her," the voice said.

Laura came on the line. "Hello, Michelle, how can I help you?"

I could hear the controlled tension in her superficially pleasant tone. I imagined her husband eavesdropping in the background.

"I was just calling to give you some sad news," I said. "I wanted to let you know that my father died last February."

"Oh no," Laura said softly. I heard a rustling sound through the phone line, and realized she must be taking herself to a more private location in her home. When she spoke again, her emotion was undisguised. "Oh Michelle, I am so very sorry for your loss," she told me. "Your father was a great man, and I never stopped loving him. I only wish everything could have worked out differently for us."

"Me too," I admitted, feeling increasingly unmoored. I covered my sense of being adrift in our conversation by sharing that my father had been in a lot of pain during his final months, and so perhaps his death had been merciful. "He was so weak at the end," I told her. "You can probably guess how much it frustrated him to have to depend on other people."

"Oh, I know," my mother said fervently, as if she really did know.

An awkward silence fell, and as talkative as I was by nature, I couldn't for the life of me think how to fill the yawning space between us.

"Well, thank you for calling to let me know," Laura said finally, and I could hear in her renewed formality that it was time to end the call.

"Okay," I said, my voice small and uncertain. "I'll stay in touch, I guess."

"Please do," she responded politely. "And do take care of yourself."

I held the phone to my ear for a long time after she hung up, listening to the dial tone's tinny whine and feeling like the orphan I now truly was.

TWENTY

Love and Politics

Marc suggested that we not wait to get married, that we do it before the end of the year. "I'm not ready," I told him. I was still reeling, a dry husk of myself, going through the motions of my everyday life but not truly engaged by anything outside the dark country of my grief. During that first year after Daddy left this earth, I remained numb for months, until slowly the muted grays of my world began to turn back to color.

"I think I'm ready to get married now," I announced to Marc in the fall of 1997.

"That's great," he said, somewhat distractedly. We were at his house, and he was standing next to his desk, scowling at an official-looking document on the top of a pile of many more official-looking folders and documents. "Uh, we just have to figure out the right time."

In truth, my timing could not have been worse, because Marc was now in the heat of his re-election campaign. We quickly agreed that it would be madness to plan a wedding in the midst of his race for a second term as mayor—there would be way too many moving pieces, not to mention local right-wing factions that would jump at the chance to portray Marc as a frivolous bridegroom who was woefully unfocused on city governance. Even though there was no other candidate in the race who could truly challenge him for the popular vote, Marc was keenly aware that nothing short of a landslide victory would silence his detractors.

Though I fully grasped these realities, I didn't see any reason why Marc couldn't still tie a ribbon on our intention to marry by getting down on one knee and putting a ring on it. We had grown comfortable together, perhaps too much so, I reflected now, and I wondered if Marc might be having second thoughts about taking our union to the next level. Granted, we were both usually so busy with work that our private time was scarce, and yet when we did see each other, our relationship felt almost effortless. We laughed constantly and could debate social issues with a conviction that stretched each of us to see the world in a more nuanced way.

Marc would be handily re-elected in early 1998, posting an even greater share of the Black, Hispanic, and White progressive vote. But the demands on his time only increased at the start of his second term, with the usual forces mounting every outrageous incursion they could think of to see him fail. Marc, never one to shrink from trench warfare, went toe to toe with his detractors, while making sure that loyal constituents were kept apprised of all the ways in which he was fighting to make their lives safer and better. He was far too inundated with the endless speaking appearances and demands of public office to notice that I was growing antsy. My contract with the station was coming up for renewal, and I had begun to weigh whether to stick around and wait for Marc to make good on the declaration he had made to my father—or just cut and run.

At last, I decided to consult his mother, Sybil Morial, the former First Lady and beloved doyenne of New Orleans society. Miz Mo, as I called her, had always been warm and maternal toward me, and I felt I could share my heart with her. When I called and told her I needed to discuss a personal matter, she had invited me to stop by her home.

Sitting in her exquisitely appointed living room later that afternoon, I wasn't sure how to begin. As I tried to gather my thoughts, I studied the large gilt-framed black-and-white portrait of Sybil and the late Dutch Morial, taken shortly after they were married. Oh, she was a stunner, petite and stylish, with dark curls, shining eyes, and Kewpie doll lips, all of it countered by the determined set of her chin. Beside her, Marc's father rested his cheek against her hair, his expression calm and assured, as if he knew that with a quiet warrior like Sybil Morial at his side, innocent as she might appear, he would always be fully armored. Miz Mo, who held the distinction of becoming the Crescent City's first Black First Lady when Dutch was elected in the mid-seventies, had only grown more beautiful with age, her salon-streaked hair impeccably coiffed, her lipstick flawless, her eyes alight with the intelligence of a woman who had seen just about everything in life and politics, yet was far too wise to ever grow jaded.

"So, my dear, what did you want to talk to me about?" she asked me, direct as always, her manicured hands resting on the lap of her green silk dress. I resolved that there was no other way to do this but to wade right in.

"Miz Mo, my contract with WWL-TV is coming up for renegotiation soon, but I'm not really sure if I should renew. I seem to have limited upward mobility at the station, so I don't know if I should stay where I am or look for a position somewhere else. The thing is I would stay if I thought Marc was still serious about me. But he hasn't formally proposed, hasn't even thought about a ring, and the truth is, I wonder if he's getting cold feet. Maybe he's changed his mind about marrying me, but if so, I need to know that, so that I can go on and live my life."

"I see," Miz Mo said thoughtfully. "Well, Michelle, I do know this: my son loves you very much, but sometimes men need a little nudging. Why don't you go ahead and apply for jobs in other cities and see if that moves the needle? A woman always needs to have choices, right? You're not making a decision by looking into your options; you're just giving yourself some choices. So you do what you need to do, and I think then we'll have our answer."

Miz Mo's advice was the kind that a mother would give her daughter, and I was grateful for it. And so, with this wise woman squarely in my corner, I began investigating open positions in other media markets. Over the next month I flew to Atlanta, Washington, D.C., Minneapolis, and Cleveland to be interviewed for anchor positions in each of those cities. I discovered that I had met the general manager at WEWS in Cleveland once before. He had interviewed me for a job at his former station in Minneapolis back when I was looking to move on from the station in South Carolina, but I had decided to try out New Orleans instead.

Now, running a new station in a new city, he was once again interested in me. He joked that this time he would make the hiring package so appealing that I would not turn him down. *This just might work out,* I thought on my flight back to New Orleans early the next morning. If Marc had changed his mind about marrying me, at least I could set myself up to land well elsewhere. As soon as I got to my desk at the station, I called Marc to suggest that we get together for dinner that evening, as I had something exciting to tell him. We decided to meet at Peristyle, a new eatery in the French Quarter that had garnered good reviews. We hadn't been seated for five minutes when, with my typical lack of impulse control, I blurted out my news.

"Guess what? I just got offered a great job with WEWS-TV in Cleveland."

Marc stared at me for several seconds, dumbfounded. And then he began to rearrange the table settings, moving the salt and pepper grinders around as if they were chess pieces, and obsessively realigning each piece of cutlery. He was clearly discombobulated, and for the first time since I had known him, at a loss for words. *Has he not noticed that I've been on a whirlwind of out-of-town interviews?* I wondered as he struggled to regain command of himself. Watching him, I felt affectionate sympathy for the distress I had provoked, as well as some amusement.

"What do you mean you got a job in Cleveland?" he said at last. "When were you going to tell me this?"

"I'm telling you now," I pointed out. "I only got the final offer this morning."

"Honestly, Michelle, I can't believe you would do something like this without talking to me first," he said, his eyes like angry darts.

"But honey," I said in my most soothing tone, "you've been so busy. I didn't want to bother you."

Abruptly, Marc pushed back from the table. "I'm taking you home," he said, his words clipped. "Let's go. I really can't believe this."

I saw now that the possibility of my moving on had never even pinged his radar. Marc was a strategist, a man who prided himself on seeing all the angles, yet in this case, he had been totally blindsided. I had never seen him so agitated, which told me that he was hardly indifferent to the possibility of my leaving town. If he hadn't cared and was looking for an easy out, he would have simply said, "Wow, that's great! I sure hate to see you go, but it's much too good an opportunity for you to pass up." Instead, the man had lost composure in a way that the poised, charming, and often steely young mayor never did. You simply didn't freak out the way Marc was freaking out unless you had some skin in the game.

Miz Mo laughed delightedly when I called her later to share how her son had taken the news. Her response tickled me. We were like two gossipy schoolgirls dissecting every nuance of the interrupted dinner at Peristyle, and plotting the next move. "Well, my dear, I think you have your answer," Miz Mo said before we hung up the phone. "You just need to bide your time. I believe he'll come around."

Two whole days went by. Then, bright and early the following Sunday morning, Marc called to invite me to join him for a jazz brunch in the warehouse district. I could tell he was missing my company, and I missed his, too, so I readily agreed. He was as loving as could be all morning, holding my hand and being his most captivating, wry humored self. Afterward, we went back to my house so I could pick up some clothes for work the next morning, as we'd agreed that I would spend the rest of the day at his house. My room was as messy as always, with clothes piled high on my bed and spilling onto the floor. Later, I would tease Marc, who was famously neat, that it was the visual chaos that had made him finally break down.

"Michelle," he said as I was stuffing garments into an overnight bag. "I can't lose you. I know I messed up bad, and I hope it's not too late. I love you so much."

It used to drive Bigmama to distraction when I would giggle uncontrollably in situations that did not call for laughter. I did that now, a wave of laughter breaking from me. As much as I tried to hold it back, I couldn't help myself. The moment was just so surreal, and to be honest, exhilarating, too. Here was this man whom I loved completely, who wielded so much power in the world, yet in this moment, he had dared to be emotionally naked with me. And even though I was feeling rather giddy and excited about it, I didn't take his declaration lightly. He had made it clear that he really did want to make me his wife, and I wanted nothing more right then than to take all that he was offering, all his brilliance, love, strength, humor, and startling vulnerability, and hold it sacred for a lifetime.

"You haven't lost me, Marc," I said when I finally caught my breath. "I'm still right here. I don't *have* to take the job in Cleveland. I can renew my contract here."

Marc crossed the room, took my hands in his, and got down on one knee in front of me. And then he said the damn words.

"Michelle, will you marry me?"

I pulled Marc to his feet and put my arms around him as I replied, "Yes, I will marry you." And then I stepped back from him and added, "But I don't see any ring accompanying this proposal, so I don't really consider this is all the way official. I'm just going to say it, boo—don't keep me waiting too long. I love you."

It would be another eight months before Marc actually closed the deal. On Christmas Eve 1998 he once again took a knee and presented me with a beautiful diamond ring. The next morning, we boarded a flight to Birmingham to tell Aunt Edna that it was official—Marc and I were to be married.

We said our vows September 11, 1999, in a ceremony that local newspapers declared to be the Crescent City's "wedding of the decade." As a Baptist, I was one of the few non-Catholics ever to be married in the oldest standing Catholic Church in the South, the vaunted St. Louis Cathedral—and with bare shoulders, no less. My wedding gown had been designed by the sought-after Jamaican-born couturier Harold Clarke, whose Front Street atelier was famous for its high-end creations. In the dress Harold and his wife Iona had conceived for my wedding day, I felt like royalty, exquisitely gowned in white silk adorned with colorful embroidered floral appliqués, and pearlesque sequins that caught the light and scattered it everywhere.

The Rev. Dr. Andrew Young and Father Harry Thompson performed the interfaith ceremony. Rev. Young, the prominent Civil Rights leader, former United Nations ambassador, and previous mayor of Atlanta, had grown up with Marc's mother and had even squired her to her high school prom. As he had later attended Howard University with my father, he was a perfect officiant to unite our two families, along with Father Thompson, who had been a mentor and advisor to Marc ever since serving as headmaster of Jesuit High School when Marc had been a student there.

Some thirteen hundred guests packed the sanctuary, standing two and three deep along the sides and spilling out onto Jackson Square, and three thousand more would join us for the reception afterward at the Morial Convention Center. I was on a tight budget, and would have opted for an intimate affair, but I was marrying one of the Crescent City's favorite sons, and so there was no question of our holding a small, exclusive ceremony. I knew that on any occasion he hosted, Marc preferred to throw the doors open to everyone, from the Sisters of the Holy Family to the street people who greeted him on his morning walks—"Nuns and pimps, bluebloods and gangsters," he liked to say—all of them shoulder to shoulder with family members, longtime friends, grass roots constituents, national celebrities, and the city's social and political elites.

The service itself was glorious, with the Greater St. Stephen Church Choir becoming the first Baptist chorus to sing in the storied Roman Catholic cathedral. As my cousin Reggie walked me down the aisle to the sound of their voices raised in song, I imagined my father and Bigmama on either side of us, guiding me as they always had when they were alive. Afterward, Marc and I jumped the broom, as our enslaved ancestors had done for centuries to mark the joining of two lives in matrimony. The entire day felt like something out of a movie, yet this was no fantasy. This was the rest of our lives.

APART FROM VONDELA AND CHERYL, WITH WHOM I STILL HAD NOT spoken, there was one other person I had wished to be at my wedding, who did not attend—my mother, Laura. I had sent her an invitation, even though I fully expected that she would decline it. For her to show up would have raised too many difficult questions, none of which she felt ready to answer. I didn't agonize over her absence. I had had my Aunt Edna, Miz Mo, and Maria with me in the church, in whose love I had felt completely enfolded.

I did call Laura a few days afterward, however. With Daddy gone, I was intensely aware that she would be my future children's only maternal grandparent by blood, and now that I was a married woman, I had revived the secret hope that she might one day acknowledge me and mine as her own. I was surprised when she told me that she had seen part of the ceremony on television. Apparently, since I was a California girl and a journalist who had started out in L.A., my wedding had made the local news. Laura said I had looked stunning in my Harold Clarke gown, and that I had been a beautiful bride. She also reflected that my new husband seemed to her to be as much a man of the people as my father had been, and she sincerely wished Marc and me all the happiness in the world. As I hung up the phone, I decided that, from a woman who barely knew me, it was enough. I'd never truly belonged to her, and perhaps I never would. But I also knew without question that I belonged where I had landed, with Marc beside me.

Even so, like my mother-in-law Sybil Morial, I would never be a traditional First Lady. Throughout her husband's two terms as mayor, Miz Mo had been employed as a dean at Xavier University. I, too, would continue to work. But this meant that merely standing beside my husband as he toasted the King of Mardi Gras, much less accompanying him to political events, would undermine my credibility as a newscaster. Forced to decide between my career and my ceremonial role as Mayor Morial's wife, I chose to retain my livelihood, and with it my independent identity as a working journalist. Still, I couldn't help but wonder if the roles had been reversed, if I had been the chief executive and Marc had been a local news anchor, would he have been similarly obliged to stand aside?

From my professional remove, I offered what support I could, bearing witness to the battles Marc routinely faced in trying to reform law enforcement, in shoring up the city's economy and crumbling infrastructure, most of all in navigating the racial bias that permeated every facet of life in the city that had become my heart's home. By the time Marc's second term ended in 2002, he had managed to post many successes, including reducing violent crime in New Orleans by more than 60 percent overall, and building a police force that increasingly functioned as a support to communities of color rather than as racial antagonists.

As it happened, we would leave the Crescent City just one year later, when Marc accepted the position as president and CEO of the National Urban League, a job that required him to relocate to New York. It was a natural progression from the work he had done first as a state senator, and then as mayor of New Orleans, when he had fought so hard to secure economic and social justice for Black folks, who comprised some 60 percent of his town. Now, in leading the historic Civil Rights organization, he would be able to take that fight national, working to dismantle the systemic racism that blocked opportunities for people of color across the country.

But Marc and I would not be moving to the Northeast as a couple. With Marc's oldest, Kemah, now a sophomore at Tufts University in Massachusetts, we would be traveling north with our son, Mason, whom we had welcomed with great jubilation in the spring of 2002. We both doted on our perfect little boy, and relished being his parents, but for me, a whole new understanding of my own birth story was slowly rising into view. Now that I had become a mother myself, everything I thought I knew about my beginnings in this world was about to change.

TWENTY-ONE

Motherhood

Laura and I had remained in intermittent contact after my wedding, mostly through phone calls I initiated and the occasional greeting card sent by me. I had acquired a curious desire to keep her apprised of developments in my personal and professional life, wagering that a day would come when I had become so familiar and known to her that she would stop hiding my existence. And so in April 2002, when Mason was born, I had included her on the list of family and friends to whom I sent birth announcements. I anticipated that she would call me on receiving the news to share in my joy. Mason was, after all, the direct extension of her bloodline, which would only ever be achieved through me. But several weeks went by with not a word from my mother. With each passing day, as I held my baby boy in my arms and felt an incandescent love for him flood my being, a new pain assaulted me.

This, I realized, was the feeling that Laura Hernandez had walked away from when she had left me behind in the hospital nursery—this overwhelming devotion and desire to cherish and care for another human being, which now took precedence over every concern or thought I had ever had for myself. Suddenly, my mother's decades-old abandonment of me felt as near and as raw as if it had happened yesterday. In becoming a mother, I had stumbled upon a vast reservoir of hurt that I hadn't even realized I was still carrying, one that might have been forever drained of its poison with one simple act—a phone call or a card from my mother hailing the arrival of our beloved boy.

I tried to hold grace for the fact that when she left me, my mother had reasonably judged her relationship with my father to be untenable, and not just because she had no will to confront America's ancient racial story, but also because Daddy had been married at the time. I had long accepted how complicated everything had been, leading to her decision to walk away from their relationship. But now I realized that I had never quite absolved her for also forsaking *me*. I thought I had forgiven her after we met for lunch a decade before in San Diego, when I had glimpsed her self-imposed prison of shame, and decided that my mother had punished herself enough for both of us. Yet as I pressed Mason's squirming little body against mine, I realized that the reprieve I had silently granted that afternoon had not been unconditional. I saw that it had been a fragile truce, and entirely revocable.

Maybe I had subconsciously known that starting a family might lead me to scrutinize my own childhood anew. Now, nuzzling Mason's head, inhaling the newborn smell of him, I felt the rush of questions come flooding back, as though I was suddenly nine years old again, trying to parse my father's evasiveness. It was true that I now had more context from both my parents than I'd had back then, and yet with Mason in my arms, Laura's apparent indifference to his birth seemed entirely indefensible.

Laura was in her sixties now—surely old enough to come to terms with the past and welcome her grandson. I wasn't even asking her to publicly declare his arrival. I didn't mind that she might still want to keep our relationship a secret from her husband and the rest of her family. I only wanted her to acknowledge Mason as her blood, because my child deserved even the covert regard of his maternal grandmother. I could not help the bitterness that rose in me at the thought that she did not care enough to pick up the phone and welcome my son to the world, as indeed she had not welcomed me.

After a few months, I swallowed my hurt and called to let Laura know that I was now a mother. I told myself it was possible that Mason's mailed birth announcement could have gone astray. In fact, it had not. Laura readily shared that she had received it, though she seemed amiably indifferent to the news. On our call, she spoke mostly about her step-granddaughter, whom she had recently visited in New York City, where the young woman was now living. I tried to fight off the resentment I felt that she so clearly regarded this young woman, unrelated to her by blood, as more fully her grandchild than my son. We exchanged a few hollow pleasantries and soon ended the call.

Our conversations grew more sporadic after that, though I continued to reach out periodically. I still felt somehow compelled to keep Laura apprised of where I was and what I was doing, as if her awareness of these details allowed me to assure myself that my mother and I had a relationship. And so I would update Laura on my life—our family relocating to Brooklyn from New Orleans in October 2003, so that Marc could assume the leadership of the National Urban League; my freelancing for CBS Newspath, which assigned me to its partner Black Entertainment Television (BET) thanks to an introduction brokered by my old boss, Joe Duke; how the *BET Nightly News* gig had led to a plum job as a news correspondent with CBS in 2005, where I'd had the unexpected joy of finding my junior high school friend Otis Livingston now working for the same network as me.

Laura always took my calls, but she greeted me with a politeness that always left me feeling someone might be listening over her shoulder. We had never again approached the depth of feeling that had been present during our in-person meeting in San Diego, and again when I had called to let her know that my father had passed away. Now, no matter when I called or what I chose to report, I was met with the same civil but shallow interest, as if what I might or might not be doing with my life mattered to her hardly at all. It began to seem that our already tenuous relationship was becoming increasingly one sided, as if only one of us cared enough to keep the connection going. After a while, without my consciously choosing it, our calls became less frequent.

AS LONGER PERIODS ELAPSED BETWEEN MY CALLS TO LAURA, I FOUND myself missing Vondela more intensely, and appreciating in a new light her constancy and care for me after Bigmama died. We had gone many years without speaking by the time Mason was born, but now, just as I had wanted to share with Laura that I had become a mother, I found myself wanting to tell Vondela, as well. Despite our estrangement, I still dearly loved her, perhaps even more than I had understood before I was charged with mothering another human myself. Vondela had no blood tie to me, and yet she had unobtrusively provided everything I had needed in the years when I might have lost my way without her quietly watching over me.

As I grasped more fully just how much Vondela had done for me, I could no longer sit with the knowledge that she was feeling hurt and betrayed by the actions I had taken in selling Bigmama's house. It didn't feel right that I had become a mother and she didn't even know. I needed to make amends, to heal the rift that had opened up between us. But when I rang the only number I had for her, there was still no answer. I decided to call her sister, to see if she could offer some insight on how I could begin to mend the relationship with my former guardian.

But I had waited too long to reach out.

"Oh, Michelle, Vondela passed away two years ago," her sister said when I asked her how she was. "I can't believe no one told you."

I was stunned.

"What? How—?" I stammered.

"She died from diabetic complications," her sister said. "She went to sleep and just didn't wake up the next morning."

As devastated as I was by this news, and the realization that I would now never be able to reconcile with my former guardian, or place my son in her capable arms, further crushing revelations lay in store.

In offering condolences to her sister, I mentioned how deeply I regretted the unraveling of my once-close bond with Vondela, and I reflected that she had seemed to pull away from me the summer after I returned home from college, finally shutting me out completely after I sold the house in South Central. That's when I discovered that the reasons for our estrangement had run much deeper than my insisting that Vondela and Cheryl find other accommodations after Daddy died. My original transgression, I now learned, had been committed a decade before.

"You know, Michelle," Vondela's sister said, "you didn't really ever call Von while you were away at college. You all but ignored her for four years, and then you didn't even invite her to your graduation. She felt as if you'd abandoned her."

Her words landed like a fist to the solar plexus. "What! Whoa! Hold on!" I protested. "I didn't invite *anyone* to my graduation. I didn't even invite my dad or Aunt Edna. I didn't know I was supposed to. I just assumed everyone knew they were welcome and whoever wanted to be there would come."

On the other end of the line, Vondela's sister sighed. "That might have been okay for your father and your aunt," she said gently, "but not for Von. You needed to let her know explicitly that you wanted her there. She took care of you for years, so the least you could have done was to extend a personal invitation. Don't get me wrong, Michelle. I'm not blaming you. I know you weren't thinking about any of that back then, and maybe somebody should have said something, made you aware. But I didn't think about it myself until afterward, when I heard Von say that you no longer needed her. That's when I knew you had hurt her feelings."

"My God, I swear I didn't know," I croaked, my breath constricted by remorse and shame. "But you know, nobody was making long distance calls like that from the dorm. The phone on the floor hardly ever worked anyway. And Vondela didn't ever call me while I was away at college either, so shouldn't I have felt hurt, too?"

"I don't know," her sister responded. "*Did* you feel hurt?"

"No!" I exclaimed. "I had no idea there was a problem!" But even as I tried to justify myself, I knew I needed to own that I hadn't made any particular effort to stay in contact with my former guardian and friend. "I'm so sorry," I finally said. "I should have thought to call her, and I should have invited her to graduation."

The truth was, I'd never guessed Vondela would read anything into my long silences other than the fact that I must be distracted. I'd thought she understood me well enough to mark it down to my propensity to get so caught up in what was happening around me that I seldom kept in proper touch with *anyone*. I hadn't calculated that Vondela might doubt how much she mattered to me, how very thankful I was to her for moving in and caring for me after Bigmama died. Sadly, the realization of how I had failed her came when heartfelt apologies and restorative action were no longer possible. All that was left was for me to receive rather than resist the lesson, and do better.

And what a painful lesson it was—full of bitter ironies. For one thing, I had spent years obsessing over the mother who did not stay, and fixating on the maternal surrogates who had been there for me while their relationships with my father ran their course. Yet I had hardly noted that it was Vondela who had truly stepped up to care for me. She had been more of a mother to me than anyone else, save Bigmama. Though she had never been romantically involved with my dad, she had never left me on my own. Indeed, I was the one who had left her. I had taken all her love and commitment for granted, assuming my appreciation of her constancy was understood, and never bothering to expressly thank her for all she had done for my sister and me. And now it was too late.

"What about Cheryl?" I asked, suddenly seared by the realization that I'd assumed Vondela had been looking out for her all this time, when in fact she'd been on her own. "Is she still living at the apartment?"

"No, we have no idea where she is," Vondela's sister said heavily. "She moved out soon after Von passed away. She didn't even come to the funeral."

I got off the phone and immediately dialed Maria's number, a rising panic over the welfare of my sister making it hard to breathe.

"Maria, Vondela died and no one's seen Cheryl since."

Maria was astonishingly calm. "I know about Vondela," she told me. "We found out a few weeks ago. The boys and I had been trying to reach your sister for a while, but the number we had for her has been disconnected. Matt went by the apartment in Gardena to look for her and that's when the landlord told him that Von had died and that Cheryl couldn't pay the rent and was evicted soon after."

"Maria, why didn't you tell me?" I moaned.

"You've had so much going on, you were traveling all the time for work, and I just didn't want to upset you till we had more definitive news. Matt's been combing his online sources to see if we can locate your sister. I promise to call you as soon as we know anything."

I hung up the phone, terrified by the possibility that Cheryl, too, had died without any of us knowing it. My relief was immense when just two days later Maria called to say that Matt had found an updated cell number for our sister, and that when he dialed it, Cheryl herself had picked up the phone. She told Matt that she was living in Inglewood with a friend, an older veteran who had allowed her to move in with him after she left the apartment building in Gardenia. Cheryl insisted that she was okay and promised to keep in touch.

She didn't of course, but now that we knew how to reach her, we all took turns calling her weekly, and Matt stopped by to visit her periodically, to make sure that she didn't once again fall through the cracks of our sorely fractured little family.

Then, about a year after Matt first located her, Cheryl called Maria one day and asked her to come and get her from an Inglewood strip mall. Maria found my sister sitting on a bench, looking disheveled and disoriented. Concerned that her stepdaughter might possibly be homeless, Maria brought Cheryl back to the condo in Long Beach that very afternoon. Over the next few days, she managed to piece together what had happened.

The man with whom Cheryl had been living had died of a heart attack in the middle of the night. Knowing she wouldn't be able to take over paying rent on the apartment, and having nowhere to go, Cheryl had reached out to her stepmother, hoping there would be room for her at the condo where she had once been welcomed. With my brothers now grown and out the house—Matt working in computer technology in L.A. and Jon at college in Santa Cruz—Maria decided that Cheryl should move in and live permanently in the family home. She could see no other way to properly secure the troubled eldest daughter of the man who had been her great love.

Sad to say, once I knew that my sister was safe in Maria's care, I exhaled and allowed myself to become once more caught up in my own endlessly eventful life as a wife, mother, and CBS-TV news correspondent who, apart from time spent with my husband and young son, relished nothing more than being sent into the field to cover fast-breaking investigative and human-interest stories.

TWENTY-TWO

What Care Forgot

I was five months pregnant with my second child when Hurricane Katrina hit New Orleans on August 29, 2005. Few events would be as significant in my career as covering the plight of those forced to evacuate their homes after the killer storm breached the city's levees, rampaging through overwhelmingly Black and poor low-lying neighborhoods. Entire blocks had been flattened by gale-force winds or washed away by the flood, with an unbearable number of people never making it out alive.

Katrina made landfall on a Monday. Marc had traveled to New Orleans the Friday before to deliver the eulogy at the funeral of one of his Urban League associates. When in the middle of the service it became clear that Katrina was approaching as a monster hurricane, his communications director had urged that they get to the airport as soon as possible, as all flights out of the city would soon be grounded. Marc delivered the eulogy as planned, but before heading to the airport with his team, he stopped by his mother's home to make sure she had arranged to get to safety ahead of the storm. Discovering that Sybil Morial intended to defy the citywide evacuation order that had just been issued, and ride out the hurricane at home, Marc decided he dare not leave town until he had convinced his mother to drive north to his sister Cheri's home in Baton Rouge. He sent his communications team on ahead, hoping he'd be able to catch a later flight. It took him until 4 A.M. Sunday morning to finally persuade Miz Mo to leave town. After packing her car and seeing her safely on her way, he barely made the last flight out, arriving back in New York City around noon.

Only days before, Marc and I had gone to contract on our new home across the Hudson River in Maplewood, New Jersey, but our seller had unexpectedly pushed back her date to vacate the premises. Since we had already given up our apartment in Brooklyn in anticipation of moving, Marc and I spent the rest of that Sunday afternoon transporting the contents of our household to storage units. As Katrina came ashore on the Gulf Coast on Monday, Marc and his very pregnant wife were hauling our two-year-old son and the last of our possessions to a room at the Marriott Hotel in downtown Manhattan. When we finally collapsed from our labor and turned on the news that evening, it was to reports of tens of thousands of people crammed into the stifling hot Louisiana Superdome and the Convention Center, frantic for food, water, soap, and medical supplies. Residents who had been unable to leave town had been told to seek refuge at these two city-designated shelters, but it was now apparent that the provisions made for them there had been woefully inadequate.

With no medical personnel stationed in or around the downtown arenas, some people had already succumbed to dehydration and other health emergencies. They were left unattended where they lay, the living having no choice but to step over the dead. Nor had adequate security measures been put in place, and with the entire city's power grid down, the displaced became prey to prowling thieves and other predators in the cavernous auditoriums. There were reports of gunshots flying in the dark, as parents covered their children's bodies with their own.

Amid the general mayhem inside the Superdome, where the bathrooms quickly overflowed, the stench was overwhelming, and terror and misery were rampant.

Watching the horror, my eyes stung, as much from anger as from sorrow at what the people of New Orleans were being forced to endure. Marc and I felt so helpless, wondering why news reporters could get to the downtown shelters on the day after the storm, yet local government agencies had not found a way to provision the many thousands of people huddled there. Why was emergency assistance taking so long to arrive? All that day and the next, Marc's cell phone didn't stop ringing. As no one seemed able to reach the current mayor, Ray Nagin, who had allegedly sequestered himself on the twenty-sixth floor of the Hyatt Hotel across from the Superdome, officials like Secretary of State Condoleezza Rice were reaching out to my husband for insights on how best to help the people of New Orleans, and former colleagues were using their last bit of cell phone charge to plead with Marc to intercede with federal authorities to mount an organized response to the humanitarian crisis unfolding in their hometown.

Marc did all he could from afar, but for three whole days, the poor and displaced in New Orleans were left to wallow in heat and filth. Finally, on September 9, Lt. General Russel Honoré arrived to coordinate military relief efforts and mass evacuations to neighboring cities. By then the Coast Guard had performed heroic rescues of thousands of residents who had been stranded inside their flooded homes, many of whom had been forced to scramble onto rooftops to avoid drowning in the rising floodwaters.

More than anything, I wanted to be in New Orleans reporting on the relief efforts, but since I was five months pregnant and conditions in my former city continued to be dangerous, my doctor advised against my traveling there. Instead, my producers at CBS News sent me to cover the plight of evacuees in Houston, to which a quarter of a million of the Crescent City's population had fled. I interviewed volunteers from Houston's churches, businesses, and nonprofit charities, which had mobilized within days to accommodate those displaced by Katrina. Inside the Houston Astrodome, where many of the Superdome evacuees were sent, I remember thinking that the difference between here and what I had seen on TV was no less than the difference between heaven and hell. Some twenty-three thousand beds had been set up almost overnight, with faith-based groups cooking meals and handing out water and snacks around the clock, and local citizens moving among the desperate, offering space in their own homes to families with young children.

As I reported on Houston's outpouring of generosity, and talked to evacuees who had been among the last to leave the Crescent City, people recognized me from my nine years with WWL-TV. They surrounded me and called me by name, cried that I had cared enough to be there to share with the world their stories of loss and despair. I was deeply moved that the city of Houston had seen these New Orleanians, so desperately poor and now also homeless, as brothers and sisters worth saving.

Marc had also traveled to Houston, where he worked with the local Urban League to help find temporary housing for the displaced and provide families with other services they might need, such as emergency health care and placements for their children in local schools. He came to the Astrodome one afternoon while I was reporting on the relief effort there, and when he walked in, everyone started clapping and cheering. "All this wouldn't have got so bad on his watch," one woman commented to me, and I did not doubt that what she said was true.

On September 11, our sixth wedding anniversary, Marc and I flew back to New York, where Mason had been cared for during our absence by Judy Lopez Whitt, a saint of a woman who had babysat for Marc when he was a boy, and who had reached out to us with an offer to be a nanny to Mason after he was born. Judy had traveled with us when we moved to Brooklyn, and had been invaluable as we set ourselves up in that bustling metropolis. But when we returned from Houston that Sunday, she broke the news that her family in New Orleans had lost everything in the flood, and she needed to return home and help them rebuild.

The whole time I had been filing stories on the evacuees in Houston, I had been focused on channeling their plight and perspectives, while checking my own emotions at the door. But now, pregnant with my second child and having to say goodbye to Mason's beloved nanny in a midtown hotel room, the nightmarish stories I'd heard during the past couple of weeks finally breached my defenses. I hugged Judy close, thanking her for the warmth and security she had brought to Mason, and we wept for the City That Care Forgot together.

Though we were between homes ourselves, I understood how fortunate our family was compared to the thousands of newly homeless people of New Orleans. By the time our daughter Margeaux arrived four months later, we had settled into our new house in Maplewood, where neighbors introduced themselves at block parties, gathered for backyard barbecues or potlucks in each other's homes, took early morning walks together, carpooled their kids to the same schools, and covered childcare for one another in a pinch. The atmosphere reminded me of nothing so much as those long-ago weekends at Little and Tony's house with my dad, and I was grateful for the unexpected blessing of now being able to offer my own children a similarly welcoming community.

Our blessings were multiplied a hundredfold when God sent us Hope Zapanta. Referred by the woman who had sold us our home, Hope seemed a bit shy when I first met her, but as the months and then years passed, she would prove to be the most organized, assertive, and loving addition to our household that any of us could have dreamed. Hope was truly well named, because without her, my career as a newscaster could not have blossomed. A warm caregiver to our children and capable household manager for my husband, for me Hope was also what every incredibly busy and hardworking woman truly needs by her side—a wife.

I DID CALL LAURA TO LET HER KNOW THAT SHE HAD A NEW GRAND-daughter, though by now I knew not to expect any maternal warmth from her at the news. I offered to send her a photo of my beautiful little girl, and she said, "I would like that." After that, our intermittent calls dwindled, with my mother and I speaking once, perhaps twice, in the course of a year.

Then came the day in July 2010 that I called Laura after years of not speaking, and she shared that her husband had recently passed away. I already knew that her father had died in the mid-nineties, and her mother had followed eight years later, ending a long battle with dementia. I felt a shiver of possibility as I quickly processed the fact that everyone whom Laura had most feared finding out about me was gone from this earth.

"So can you acknowledge me now?" I heard myself say.

The words were out of my mouth before I knew they were queued up in my tongue. To my own ear, my voice sounded like that of a plaintive child. "The people you were most worried about hurting are no longer here," I added, trying to offer an argument that would sound more adult and rational. "So now you can acknowledge that I exist."

"Oh no, no, I can't," Laura responded. "I can't tell my family about you."

"But why not?" I pressed her. "What harm can it do after all this time?"

"Everyone will think that I'm a liar," she said quietly.

"But you are!" I burst out.

And then I caught myself, belatedly registering the remorse and self-loathing in her tone. I realized that I hadn't yet expressed sympathy for the loss of her husband, one of the men in her life whom she had loved enough to protect from all knowledge of my birth. "Please accept my condolences," I said then, trying for the millionth time to put myself in her shoes. But it was too late. I had gone too far, something I only comprehended when Laura spoke again.

"You are being cruel," she said bitterly. "I'm so disappointed in you, Michelle. How can you not understand that I can't ever tell anyone that I had a daughter forty-three years ago? Why can you not see that it's impossible?"

I was so used to giving my mother a pass for behavior that wounded me that I was tempted to let her remonstration go without a response, unfair as her choice felt to me. But I had never been very good at holding my tongue, especially when the thing I wanted to say felt so urgent.

"I don't think I'm being cruel," I said with more firmness than Laura had ever heard from me. "I'm just telling you the reality of what you're doing. You've got to own up to the fact that you have held onto this secret for my entire life, yet this truth is part of you. *I am part of you.* That is why you seem to carry such shame, why you seem so anxious all the time, so frightened of being found out. But I am nothing to be ashamed of. You should be proud of what I've managed to become despite never having my mother there to show me which way I should go. I'm only being honest with you, because you aren't ever going to be free until you release this secret, until you stop hiding and find the courage to tell people the truth."

Laura didn't say a word. I heard her sniffle on the other end of the line, and realized she was crying. I understood then that the emotion between us was already too heightened for us to endure any more. Sore of heart, I forced myself not to apologize for my sudden burst of truth telling as I bid my mother an uncomfortable goodbye. I knew that it would be a long time before I heard her voice again.

TWENTY-THREE

American History

As the silence between Laura and me stretched into months, and then approached a year, I began to contemplate reaching out to her step-granddaughter, the one she had talked so much about. I knew that Miranda—not her real name—was now living in New York, because Laura had waxed on about visiting her there during the spring that Mason was born. Hearing my mother speak so adoringly about a child who did not share her blood, I had wondered what the experience of being raised by Laura Hernandez might have been. I wasn't jealous of Miranda exactly, and I certainly didn't begrudge her the devotion of a loving grandmother, in which I myself had basked and been formatively secured. I think I was just nostalgic for the life I might have had, if one can be nostalgic for a reality only yearned for, but never known.

My justification for considering such a controversial action came from, of all places, my ruminations during Barack Obama's first inauguration two years before. Marc and I, with six-year-old Mason in tow, had been in VIP seating at the Capitol on January 21, 2009, thrilled to be among the almost two million Americans who had shown up in person on that frigid cold day to witness the historic swearing in of our nation's first African American president. The hum of the crowd was stilled as President-elect Barack Obama recited his solemn oath, and I imagined that my own wonder that our country had achieved this milestone, despite our racial history, must have been shared by everyone who watched his inauguration—on the steps of the Capitol, on giant screens set up on the packed Washington Mall, on televisions in homes and offices across the country, and throughout the world.

All morning, I had been thinking about how Barack Obama's personal history mirrored my own missing-parent story, and how, as a young man, he had pursued the facts of his paternity, filling in the narrative of his Kenyan father, who had been absent for much of his upbringing. Obama had met his father for the first time that he could recall when he was ten years old, almost the same age I was when my father took me to visit my mother out of the blue one Sunday evening. After that year, our new president never again saw his father, who died in a car accident in 1982. I completely understood his subsequent drive to reconstruct the paternal side of his story. I knew as well as anyone how great tracts of the self could feel unfinished and unrealized when aspects of your origin story remained murky.

As a child, I'd had no choice but to accept the scraps of information given to me, but that was no longer the case. Now, if I wanted to know more about my maternal family than Ross or Laura had told me, I could do what our new president had done: track down the details on my own. This was what I did for a living, after all—I investigated the facts and connected the dots to bring the larger picture into view. Perhaps this sudden impulse to more actively pursue what I didn't yet know had something to do with the fact of Barack Obama becoming our first Black commander in chief, an occasion that few of us had conceived could happen in our lifetimes. But now, watching our new president and his First Lady, my namesake, step into their full power, I felt inspired to bring my whole self into the light, too.

And so, while scrolling through Facebook one evening in the summer of 2011, looking up old friends from high school, I had veered without warning, and the next thing I knew I had entered Miranda's name in the search field. Her profile popped up at once, with personal details that established I had found the right Miranda. I stopped for a long time at a photo of her laughing with my mother, their heads thrown back and throats exposed in an attitude of joy. I had never seen Laura look so carefree. With me, she always seemed so damaged, so tightly wound and riddled with self-loathing, so much so that she often asserted, and seemed to sincerely believe, that I had been better off without her. I did not dispute this. I had come to see that it might be true. And yet it had both saddened and angered me that after my son was born, she never so much as inquired about him, never once seemed curious about how he was doing, who he resembled, what his budding personality might be.

Three years later, she behaved in much the same way when I told her about my daughter. She acted as if my children's presence in this world was completely incidental to hers. I suppose I should not have been surprised, because even now, the woman whose body pushed me into the world still could not bring herself to tell her family—the stepchildren and grandchildren by marriage whom she obviously considered to be her *true* family—of my existence.

Impulsively I tapped out a message to the attractive, chestnut-haired young woman laughing with Laura in the picture.

"Are you the granddaughter of Laura Hernandez?" I inquired.

"Why yes, I am," she wrote back at once. "Who are you?"

"Our families are old friends," I texted. "From back in L.A."

"Oh, nice to meet you," she responded, and from there we introduced ourselves and began chatting, very benign texts about our respective jobs—she worked in the nonprofit world and was curious about my job in network TV—and favorite places to eat and things to do as West Coast transplants in New York.

As we texted back and forth, I knew that I was breaking an unspoken rule between Laura and me. I did not underestimate how bold it was to insert myself into her life in this way, to create another layer of secrets within a family that already had its share. Even when I'd cold-called Laura all those years ago, that action hadn't felt as audacious as this. I realized it was because in reaching out to Miranda, I was bringing an unwitting innocent into our story.

And yet I felt wholly justified in my decision to contact Laura's step-granddaughter. I didn't have a plan or an endgame in mind, though I had no intention of embarrassing Laura by suddenly revealing my identity. Still, my whole life I had been looking to be recognized by my mother, to be brought into her circle, and it hadn't happened. Now I played with the idea that the next best thing might be for me to engage with someone from her world. Perhaps if someone she loved from the family she had made without me could know me as myself, it would be like entering the forbidden circle—like becoming even for a brief moment a part of my mother's life.

When Miranda suggested a few days later that we meet for drinks at a restaurant in Greenwich Village, I readily agreed. I was nervous as we hugged each other in greeting, but reminded myself that Miranda had no idea who I really was. I was just a woman whose family had known her grandmother back in the day, and who had ended up in the same city where she now lived. Our conversation that evening was deep and engaging, and as drinks evolved into dinner, I learned that Miranda had her own story of loss. She shared that her teenaged mother had become pregnant while the family was living in South America, where her grandfather was on a diplomatic posting. Her mother had attended the American school there, along with her five siblings. The family had decided that the pregnant teen should return home to California to have the baby, and that Laura should accompany her. The diplomatic assignment would end the following year, when the rest of the family would join Laura and Miranda's mother at their home in San Diego.

Laura's stepdaughter wasn't able to raise Miranda on her own, as she was still in high school and struggling emotionally. And so Laura had taken over Miranda's care, and everyone simply accepted that she was her grandmother's favorite. Miranda recalled a secure and loving childhood with her grandparents, in which she had attended private schools and wanted for nothing. And yet she had wondered about her absent father. Her mother had told her that the boy who got her pregnant had never even known that he had had a daughter, as she had been sent back to America before anyone outside the family even knew she was with child. Miranda didn't ask about him after that, but she never ceased from wanting to know who he was, what he looked like, what traits he had given her, and most of all, would he welcome the news of her existence?

Listening to her story, I was dumbstruck by the parallels to my own, the yearning for a missing parent that had so deeply marked us both. I shared my own story of having been raised by my grandmother, but was careful to stay far from any details that might connect me to Laura. But perhaps Miranda sensed something, because at one point she looked at me oddly and asked, "How do you know my grandmother again?"

"Old family friends," I repeated, and she didn't press for any more.

I invited her to my forty-fourth birthday bash that Marc was throwing for me at a restaurant in the city two weekends later. I remember being pleased that Miranda attended with a couple of her friends and seemed to enjoy herself. We saw each other on a few more occasions after that night, but as time passed, we slowly fell out of touch. I wonder sometimes if she might have worked out the truth about my relationship to her grandmother. Maybe she had looked into my face at one point and seen Laura's eyes. I'll never know, because she eventually stopped responding to my text messages. Perhaps she had called home and asked her grandmother about me, but Laura would have corroborated my story about an old family friendship, protecting her secret at all costs, of this I felt sure.

Whatever the cause of Miranda's withdrawal, our fleeting association had left me with a somewhat more generous view of my mother's life during the years before we had reestablished contact. Her unstinting devotion to her step-granddaughter had undoubtedly helped to secure her, despite her quiet yearning for an absent father. To my mind, the fact that Laura had been a good mother to a child who shared my missing parent story counted as a form of reparation, balancing the ledger of loss for the care she had never offered to me.

Of course, my friendship with Miranda had been constrained from the start, because as simpatico as our initial connection had been, I would never be able to let down my guard and be my authentic self with her, for fear she discover my lie. I had a startling insight that the anxious vigilance I had experienced with Miranda was a lesser expression of the feeling that had stalked my mother for decades, ever since she had conceived me without her family's knowledge in a forbidden affair with her Black married lover, my father.

AS MY OWN CHILDREN GREW OLDER, WHAT SURPRISED ME MORE THAN almost anything else in my motherhood journey was the hunger they both expressed to know their grandparents. They knew and loved Marc's mother, and looked forward to spending time with her in New Orleans every summer. They had also been told many stories about both their grandfathers, as both Dutch Morial and Ross Miller had been history makers in their own right. It became apparent to me, however, that while the Morial family history seemed easily grasped, as so much of it had been corroborated in books and articles, our kids were left with significant gaps in their knowledge when it came to my parents, and not just Laura, but Ross as well.

Margeaux was only four years old when she began asking about my mother. "Where is she?" she wanted to know after determining that her grandmother was still alive. "How come we never go to visit her like we do Daddy's mom. Why don't you ever talk about her?"

I marveled that my little girl was feeling the gaping absence of my mother a whole generation later. How deeply the loss of a parent could slice through a family, all the way down through the years. Remembering all too well how it felt as a child to be given only half-truths, or none at all, I did not withhold any part of the story. "Well, honey, I didn't grow up with my mother," I told her. "She couldn't take care of me, and so she left soon after I was born. I was raised by my grandmother and my dad. I hardly ever saw my mother when I was growing up."

Margeaux was almost six when she asked the most piercing question. "Why couldn't your mommy take care of you?" she said one evening as I was helping her to pick out clothes for school the next day. I remember it was my birthday, and we had celebrated with cake and candles earlier in the evening. Margeaux's birthday would be coming up two weeks later, and perhaps that had her thinking about mothers and daughters.

"My mother could not take care of me because her family did not approve of her being with a Black man," I said plainly. "Some people in our country can be like that."

"Did that make you sad?" my little empath wanted to know.

"Yes," I said. "Sometimes it did."

"I wish I could meet her," Margeaux said, her eyes steady on mine.

"We'll see," I said, cupping her sweet earnest face between my palms. "Maybe one day you will."

Interestingly, my children's curiosity about their maternal grandparents seemed to run along gender lines. While Margeaux regularly questioned me about my mother, Mason periodically pressed for new details about my dad. He wanted to know about the many hats Dr. Ross Miller had worn—as chief of surgery for his hospital and founder of a community clinic serving the marginalized and the poor; as a Democratic Party delegate and one of Compton's first Black city councilmen, fighting against police misconduct; as president of his Alpha Phi Alpha fraternity; as a founder of 100 Black Men of Los Angeles; and as a member of the local Board of Education, working to improve resources at underserved schools.

But the one story that intrigued Mason more than any other was of my father trying to save Senator Robert Kennedy's life. I first told him about that night when he was eleven years old, on an evening when Marc was in his study listening to recordings of Senator Kennedy's speeches. Marc often listened to famous orators the way other people watched the History Channel, and Mason and I could hear Kennedy's distinctive cadence from the living room.

"You know, son, your grandfather Ross campaigned with Robert Kennedy, and he was with him the night he got shot," I said. "In fact, my dad was the first doctor to attend to the senator that evening."

Mason, who was lying on the floor playing a video game, suddenly sat upright. "For real?" he said. I nodded.

"But you were just a baby when Kennedy died," he said, looking at me skeptically. "How do you know your dad was there, and that he was the first doctor on the scene? How do you know all of that really happened?"

"Well, Mason," I said, taken aback by his doubt, "my dad told me the story. He wouldn't make it up."

"I'm not saying Grandpa Ross wasn't there," Mason replied in a long-suffering way. I could see him trying not to roll his eyes. "I'm just asking, Mom, how do you know? Can you *prove* it?"

My son threw down the gauntlet that evening, and I decided to pick it up. Our conversation occurred in the spring of 2013, and the forty-fifth anniversary of Robert F. Kennedy's assassination would be coming up on June 5 of that year. Mason had challenged me to find evidence that the story of my dad rushing to Bobby Kennedy's side after he was shot was more than family lore. I didn't have a shred of doubt that what my father told me about that night was true, but now I was curious to know if any evidence existed that might settle his place in history.

A preliminary Internet search turned up a news story referencing one Dr. Ross Miller being interviewed by a CBS news reporter in exchange for a ride back to the Ambassador Hotel from the Good Samaritan Hospital, where Kennedy had been taken. Armed with that detail, I decided to pitch my producers at CBS a story about how my father had labored to save lives that night, even though he had quickly assessed that no one could save Senator Kennedy. But more than a recounting of the events of the evening that had begun as a victory celebration and ended in tragedy, my story would also be a piece of detective work—probing my family history and publicly sharing the answers, whatever they might be. As the daughter of the trauma surgeon who had first attended to the candidate's mortal wounds, I would seek out proof of my father's presence at the scene, thus correcting his omission from the written record of Senator Kennedy's untimely death, an event that many believed had changed the entire course of American history.

My producer, Joneil Adriano, green lit the story, and for the next several months, along with my news associate Anam Siddiq, I tracked down every scrap of relevant information I could find, and talked to every person I could locate who had borne witness to the events inside the Ambassador Hotel on that fateful night. On June 5, 2013, I shared what I had found on *CBS This Morning*, offering for the first time a definitive account of the role my father had played in the aftermath of the shooting.

"When I was growing up, my father used to talk about how he rushed to Senator Kennedy's side, but not until my own son dared me to prove it did I look for the evidence to back up what my dad had told me," I began the segment, before launching right into footage of my father being interviewed on the night of the shooting. "With calm precision, Dr. Ross Miller described to CBS news correspondent Terry Drinkwater the tragedy that had unfolded backstage hours earlier," I reported, adding, "I never knew this interview existed. Few did. It was buried deep within the CBS News archives."

I remember when Anam had first unearthed the tape, how surreal it was to see my dad that young, to find visual confirmation of his involve-ment in an event that I had only ever heard described. I could hardly take in what I was watching, my father in the first year I was born, the Black doctor my mother had loved, handsome and resolutely composed, who hadn't hesitated to act when history called him. I knew from his later accounts how rocked by the violence he had been, and yet while being in-terviewed by the CBS newsman, he maintained his professional cool, his eyes behind his black horn-rimmed glasses somber. Here was the proof my son had asked me to find, stored for more than four decades in a vault at the very network where I was now employed. What were the chances?

Digging through the archives some more, I became curious about the other five gunshot victims whom my father ministered to that night, including Bobby Kennedy's good friend and labor organizer for his presidential campaign, whom my dad had accompanied to the hos-pital in an ambulance. "I'll never forget his name," my father had told me. "Paul Schrade."

I located Paul Schrade still living in California, a piercingly present eighty-eight-year-old who immediately agreed to meet with me once I explained that I wanted to discover what he recalled of the evening his dear friend Bobby had been killed. I didn't specifically mention that I was curious as to whether he remembered seeing my father in the chaos of the Ambassador Hotel pantry before he himself lost consciousness. A week later, sitting with Paul Schrade in his study, surrounded by folders stuffed with news clippings, court filings, and forensic evidence from the night of June 5, 1968, the one-time union man told me that he refused to die before proving to the world that there had been two gunmen that night, and that it was the second gunman, not Sirhan Sirhan, who had killed Bobby.

Schrade had been on stage with the candidate as he gave his vic-tory speech after winning the California primary. He remembers that Kennedy had finished speaking just after midnight, and that he was supposed to exit stage right, but was somehow diverted off the back of the stage and led into the pantry area of the hotel. He entered ahead of everyone else. Schrade, just steps behind him, recalls thinking, *Where is his security? Why is he alone?* The candidate paused to shake the hands of two Mexican bus boys, which pleased Schrade, because Chicano and Black voters had been critical in delivering the win that evening. Suddenly, Schrade said, the lights in the room became blindingly bright, and he collapsed, convulsing violently, unaware he'd been shot in the crown of his head. He heard sounds like firecrackers exploding in quick succession, and then blackness. He would not learn that Bobby Kennedy had been shot and had died of his injuries until he awoke in the hospital with his own head bandaged late the next day. Schrade had turned his face to the wall and sobbed.

He suffered with survivor's guilt for a while. The last thing he recalled before the world went dark was his friend Bobby calling out, "Is everyone okay? Is Paul okay?" Schrade eventually emerged from his despondency with a new purpose—to create a living legacy to Bobby Kennedy's anti-poverty and Civil Rights work. He became the driving force behind the Robert F. Kennedy Community Schools, constructed on the site of the old Ambassador Hotel. Today, the schools serve a surrounding neighborhood of mostly Hispanic, Korean, and Black students, and on the spot where Kennedy gave his victory speech that night is the Paul Schrade Library.

I shared with Schrade the video I had found in the CBS archive, in which my father, when asked about the other victims who had been shot that night, referred to him by name. Unlike Kennedy, all five would survive. "I also took care of Paul Schrade," my father had told Terry Drinkwater. "He had a deep laceration of the forehead, and although he had a great deal of blood loss, and there was a lot of blood around, apparently his injuries are not critical."

A tall, gracious man, his once dark brown hair now fully white, his clear gray gaze genial and penetrating, Schrade was astonished by the recording, as he had no memory of anything that had happened after the bullets flew. He expressed his profound gratitude to be sitting all these years later with the daughter of the physician who had helped to save his life. "You had a great father," he told me. I thought of my son Mason, and imagined his chest swelling with pride when he watched Paul Schrade's summation of his grandfather in the video segment I was creating for him more than anyone else.

Schrade observed now that in helping him survive, my dad had left him with an assignment not unlike the one I had recently undertaken—to reconstruct what had actually unfolded in the hotel's pantry that night. He later shared reams of forensic evidence, much of it never presented at trial, that he insisted conclusively showed that Sirhan Sirhan, the young Palestinian immigrant whose bullet had shattered against Schrade's skull, could not have killed Bobby. Schrade pointed out that the candidate had been shot four times from behind at point blank range, as shown by the gun powder residue behind his ear, where the fatal bullet entered, and on the back of his suit jacket. Sirhan never got within a foot of Bobby, he insisted. As video footage later revealed, Sirhan had been tackled and restrained after the first two shots, and fired the next six shots wildly.

Further, Schrade continued, all the shots from Sirhan's gun flew in a westerly direction. The four bullets that pierced Bobby Kennedy came from the east. And Sirhan's gun held only eight bullets, while at least a dozen bullets had been fired that night. Schrade did have a theory of who actually killed his friend, but he refused to enter that speculation trap, and relied instead on cold forensic findings to prove his case. (For anyone curious about the leading theory, he allowed, the Netflix four-part documentary *Bobby Kennedy for President* does not shy away from conjecture.)

As I took my leave of Paul Schrade that afternoon, I promised to stay in touch. The man's lightness of spirit after experiencing such tragedy had been inspiring to me, and instructive, too. He seemed to have cracked the code for how to carry the burdens of this world gently, which left me reflecting on how we humans weave in and out of each other's lives, offering support at critical moments, or provoking insights we may have been blind to before. My own reconstruction of that night wouldn't end with Paul Schrade, however. He had shown me a photo essay depicting the night of Bobby Kennedy's assassination in *Life* magazine. A photograph caption in the story had listed "Dr. Ross Miller" as one of the people pictured, but I had peered into that photograph long and hard, and could not find my father's figure anywhere.

I reached out to the man who had taken the picture, photojournalist Bill Eppridge, who was perhaps best known for another iconic image he had taken that night, one of Juan Romero, an Ambassador Hotel bus boy kneeling at Bobby Kennedy's shoulder, one hand under the candidate's bleeding head.

I traveled with my camera crew to meet with Bill Eppridge at his home in Connecticut, where he described to us the depression that descended on him after Bobby Kennedy was assassinated. I will never forget him musing with a sorrow that seemed as present as if the horror at the Ambassador had unfolded only yesterday, that America would have become a far better country if Robert Kennedy had lived to fulfill his early promise and become the nation's thirty-seventh president. When I showed him the image in *Life* that named my dad in the caption, he studied it for a moment before admitting he did not know where in the photograph "Dr. Ross Miller" might be. We both agreed that whoever had provided caption information must have been aware of a physician by that name who was at the scene that night.

Eppridge had later published two books about Robert Kennedy's life and death, and he had hundreds of unpublished images from that night at the Ambassador in his photographic archives. He allowed me to pore through them, searching for my father. "That's when something jumped out at me," I later recounted in the segment's voiceover. "It's a picture inside the Good Samaritan Hospital. There in the corner, standing just outside of Kennedy's room, the good doctor Miller."

I recognized at once the set of his head in three-quarter profile, the way his glasses sat on his face, the blur of his thin mustache.

"Bill, I think we found him," I said, breathless at my discovery.

Eppridge grabbed his photo loupe and peered through its magnifying lens at the small image on a contact sheet printed from several strips of his film negatives.

"Yes, it's him!" he confirmed, sounding as excited as I felt.

"That's Dad," I said softly, speaking more to myself than to Eppridge or anyone else in the room. So much emotion swamped me that my eyes brimmed, and I hardly noticed my videographer moving in for a better angle, his camera capturing it all.

"That's him," Eppridge repeated as I whispered, "Thank you." Hearing the crack in my voice, he patted me on the back in a comforting way as I impulsively hugged him. We had no idea then that the legendary photographer who had captured my father's image inside the Good Samaritan hospital on that tragic night forty-five years ago would pass away after a short illness just four months following our interview. It would be a poignant reminder of just how important it is for us to pursue what matters in the here and now, because if we wait, we may well be too late.

Back at the CBS studio, poring over our hours of videotape, Joneil, Anam, and I chose not to cut my raw human moment with Eppridge from the final edit of the piece. Though I had gone to the photographer's home as a journalist and he was my subject, both producers agreed that my unforced response as a daughter recognizing her much-adored father only served to amplify this deeply personal story.

"Finally the photographic proof that my dad actually did what he said," I had summed up in my recorded voiceover. "My family history forever intertwined with the night that may have changed American history." In my heart, I was speaking directly to my son Mason, as it was he who had sent me on this loving odyssey to restore his grandfather's name to the public record of that night.

TWENTY-FOUR

The Mouth of Babes

My daughter Margeaux, now eight years old, continued to ask me about my mother, and repeatedly expressed a wish to meet her. "I want to know who she is," she would say, "see what she looks like, how she acts."

"But why?" I would ask her, wondering why this person she had never been attached to in any immediate way should be so alive in her thoughts.

"I guess I'm just curious," Margeaux would respond, shrugging.

"We'll see," I would reply, and that would be the end of it—for a while.

Once, when I'd asked Margeaux why she wanted to meet her grandmother so badly, she admitted that she had thought a lot about what had happened to me as a child, and she wanted to look into the face of the woman who had left me, because she didn't understand how a mother could do that. She had added that when she thought about me growing up wondering why my mother wasn't around, it made her angry. I had hugged her close and told her to let go of her anger, it wasn't hers to carry, and besides, everything I had been through in life had brought me to this perfect moment, in which I was a mother of two glorious children of my own.

"Okay, Mommy," she had said obediently as I rocked her against me. She was a considerate child, who never wanted to cause trouble, and perhaps the vigor with which I had enfolded her made her think she had upset me. She hadn't. Yet I was struck anew that my mother was as much a riddle for my little girl as she had been for me when I was her age. I wanted to help make Laura Hernandez less mysterious, so that her absence might weigh less heavily on my daughter, so that it would not hamper her becoming who she wanted to be, as it had sometimes done for me. And so, when our family planned a vacation in Hawaii in the spring of 2014, I scheduled a two-day layover in San Francisco on the off chance that a meeting with my mother could be arranged.

I called Laura a few weeks before our trip to inquire if she might be willing to drive up to the Bay Area and meet my husband and children. I was in shock when she readily agreed to join us for lunch at our hotel. She even offered to show us some of the sights of San Francisco, where she said her older sister had lived for decades. Though I was aware she had a brother—I remembered my father sharing that the brother had been particularly incensed by her dating a Black man—I had not known before this call that she also had a sister. At the age of forty-seven, I was still learning new things about my maternal family.

For days beforehand, I kept saying to Marc and the kids, "We're going to see my mother." I was my old irrepressible self, bouncing with anticipation, and even daring to hope that this might be the start of a more open relationship between Laura and me. Once or twice, I caught Marc looking at me with a furrowed brow, and I knew he was worried that things might not go quite as I hoped, and he didn't want me to be disheartened. But I was optimistic—because how could my mother fail to adore her two grandchildren, and not want them in her life after meeting them?

On the appointed day, my family had just ordered lunch in the hotel restaurant when Laura walked in, a slender, attractive woman in her mid-seventies wearing navy blue slacks and a gray sweater, with an aloofness about her. She held out her arms to Margeaux and Mason and they hugged her politely. She embraced Marc and me, as well, but it was perfunctory, with little discernable warmth. She sat with us at the table but didn't order any lunch. Marc, a master conversationalist, kept the talk flowing, and I was grateful for his social ease, because I found myself slipping into reporter mode, dispassionately observing the interactions around our table and taking mental notes. Mason seemed entirely indifferent to the proceedings as he ate the BLT sandwich he had ordered, but I could see Margeaux studying Laura closely, the barest hint of a frown on her solemn face. Imagining the scene through her eyes, I saw how my mother must appear to her, a thin, anxious woman chitchatting with her publicly unacknowledged flesh and blood about nothing in particular.

"What do you want to call me?" Laura asked the children at one point. It might have been the only occasion after their initial greeting that she addressed them directly. Mason shrugged and Margeaux smiled shyly and said she didn't know.

"How about Grandma Laura?" I suggested.

"That's fine," she agreed with a shrug.

Though her question sparked some hope that she might be envisioning a continuing relationship with her grandchildren, the mildness of her response, coupled with that diffident little shrug, revealed her indifference. It was at that point that I cautioned myself to manage my expectations, to rein in the fantasies of this day turning into anything long term. If that happened, I would be ecstatic, but it was just as likely that after this meeting, our relationship would limp along as before, and I needed to prepare myself to handle that, and to make sure my children knew not to take personally the very real possibility of having no meaningful connection with their grandmother.

When the meal was over, we walked outside to wait for the valet to bring around her car. We piled in, Marc in the front seat beside

Laura, me in the back with the kids. Laura spent the next couple of hours driving us around the neighborhoods of San Francisco, pointing out its distinctive Victorian architecture, including the famous Painted Ladies, stopping to show us Balmy Street in the Mission District with its vibrantly colored murals, and eventually crossing the Golden Gate Bridge, the longest suspension bridge in the world, gleaming red in the afternoon sun.

On the other side of the Bay, Marc and I volleyed back and forth about something insignificant, I don't recall what; perhaps it was nothing more than the route we should take back to the hotel. We weren't arguing; we were just being ourselves, both of us with strong opinions about everything. So I was taken aback when Laura rolled her eyes and tossed out a flip, dismissive comment. "You two need to get it together," I think she said.

I felt a surge of defensive anger. *Lady, you have some nerve,* I thought. How dare she criticize my relationship with Marc, or offer judgment of any sort about my family when she hadn't ever been there to teach me how to be a wife and mother? That sudden flare of resentment clued me in to how wound up I had been feeling all afternoon, how protective of my husband and children. When we pulled up to our hotel at the end of our sightseeing excursion, I found myself exhaling with relief that I would soon be alone again with the three people in this world in whose company I felt most at home.

As we stood outside the hotel saying our goodbyes, Laura pulled a long black jewelry case from her purse and placed it in my palm. Inside was a gold charm bracelet that she said my father had given her, and she wanted me to have it. I thanked her for the piece of jewelry with more enthusiasm than I truly felt, because I knew that my dad had gifted at least two other women with the same bracelet, though each had received different charms from the ones he had given my mother. *That guy, what a player,* I thought, not for the first time. I felt some sadness at the realization that my mother had been trying to give me something of emotional value, but it had ended up being as hollow as our entire relationship had turned out to be.

Laura didn't hug us as she took her leave. She just gave a little wave with one hand and climbed back into her car, hardly noticing Margeaux alone mirroring her wave before letting her hand drop heavily to her side.

Later that night, as I quizzed my family about their impressions, Marc observed that Laura was as beautiful as I had always said; he could see why my father had been attracted to her. But he also noted that she had seemed "nervous" and "high strung," as if perpetually glancing upward to make sure that the sword of lies dangling above her head wouldn't come crashing down. "It's Damoclesian how terrified she is," he reflected. "She's been living this double life, and when people aren't true to themselves, when they're hiding some essential knowledge of themselves, they become inauthentic. They've practiced wearing the mask for so long that the mask becomes who they are, and they don't know themselves apart from it anymore."

Margeaux's impression of the afternoon ran along similar lines. She shared that every moment had felt tense to her, as if Laura and I were doing our level best to keep everything agreeable, and all the adults were putting on a good face for the children.

"She didn't feel like a grandmother," she had added, peering into my face as if to make sure I didn't mind her saying that.

"What do you mean?" I asked.

"Well, a grandmother is someone who loves you, and wants to be around you and know all about you, but she wasn't like that. She felt like a stranger."

The mouth of babes, I thought, kissing the top of my daughter's head.

"Well, she *was* a stranger," I agreed. "You're not wrong there."

For his part, Mason had little to say about the afternoon. "It was okay," he allowed before turning back to a Marvel movie marathon on the hotel room television. But for me, it really hadn't been okay.

Nothing had gone really wrong, but nothing had felt very connected or right either. In fact, the whole visit had been anticlimactic. After that afternoon with my mother, I finally understood that the perfect family scenario that the little girl inside me still dreamed of achieving—with Laura playing fond mother to me, and doting grandmother to my children—was simply never going to be. It was past time for me to accept this truth, to release the fantasy I had been chasing for a lifetime, to allow my mother the grace of living with her secrets while I poured myself into nurturing the beautiful family Marc and I had made.

Laura and I did speak again several times after our afternoon in San Francisco. On one call in early 2016, she shared that she was thinking of moving to the Bay Area permanently to live with her sister, with whom she had always been very close. Perhaps I should have held back what I said next, because it may have been the remark that finally broke us.

"How can you say you're so close to your sister when you've never told her you gave birth to a child?" I asked her. "If you still can't tell her that, then you're lying to her, and she doesn't know you at all."

Laura changed the subject, declining to address my comment. But we ended the call soon after that, and since then, her cell phone has gone unanswered whenever it was my number on her caller ID. After several months of doggedly calling her every other week, I finally decided to let her be, recognizing at last that she would likely never publicly acknowledge me. I realized that I had known this on some level ever since our family meeting in San Francisco, but I had refused to accept that forever being my mother's shameful secret could be a fixed and immutable truth.

As I allowed the reality of our dysfunctional and perhaps irrevocably broken relationship to make a home inside me, I discovered that all I now wanted for my mother was for her to find a measure of serenity. When I included her in my prayers after that, I petitioned for only this. I might have lived the rest of my days with this truce, but when an increasingly toxic social and political environment began inflaming tribal animosities and escalating chaos on a national scale, the world suddenly seemed unbearably brittle, and I wanted nothing so much as to know that, wherever she was now living, my mother was okay. But Laura Hernandez still would not pick up my calls.

TWENTY-FIVE

A Reckoning

In one sense, my relationship with Laura ended in 2016, because I still have not heard from her since our last call. And yet this story continues, because as I have finally understood, it belongs to me alone.

The first years of the 2020s will forever be remembered as a time of loss. As the new decade dawned, an unprecedented coronavirus would claim so many millions across the globe that the toll of the dead became near incomprehensible. In America, the sense of looming apocalypse was intensified by the fact that our country was convulsing in other ways, too. The year 2020 had culminated with the polarizing Republican president trying to win reelection to the Oval Office by intensifying racial conflict and undermining trust in the electoral process. In November, the incumbent president would be trounced at the polls by more than seven million votes, but he would be anything but gracious in defeat. Instead, amid feverish cries of voter fraud, he unleashed a campaign to have the election overturned, going so far, some say, as to incite violent insurrection on January 6, 2021, the day the election was to be officially certified in Congress. Though America would be brought to the very brink of authoritarianism that day, democracy would prevail, and the winning candidate, Joe Biden, would be inaugurated as the forty-sixth U.S. president three weeks later.

Along with the global pandemic and the toxicity of our political reality, our nation was suffering on other fronts, as well. We had lost esteemed gatekeepers of conscience and decency in 2020, women and men like Supreme Court Justice Ruth Bader Ginsburg and Georgia congressman John Lewis, who had made the fight for freedom and equality their life's work. For me, the death of John Lewis from cancer on July 17 felt particularly momentous, as he had been a revered member of my father's Civil Rights circle. As a child, I had met the gentle warrior when I was visiting Big. In fact, she was the one who had introduced John to his wife, Lillian Miles, at one of her famous dinner parties.

Now, assigned by CBS to cover the multiple memorials being held to honor the late congressman, I felt personally bereft as I stood with his family in Selma, Alabama, on Sunday, July 26, to watch his flag-draped casket being pulled by horses across the Edmund Pettus Bridge. The occasion commemorated the many times in his life that Lewis had led marches across that bridge to uplift the cause of racial justice. The first time had been fifty-five years before, when he had been among six hundred brave souls who set out to walk from Selma to Montgomery to shed light on the disenfranchisement of Black voters. When the marchers defied orders to disperse, they were mercilessly beaten by police wielding billy clubs, one of which had cracked Lewis's skull. The brutality of that day, known as Bloody Sunday, had been broadcast across the country, ultimately turning the tide of the Civil Rights movement. Now, in recognition of Lewis's lifetime of fighting the good fight, we stood in silence as his body rolled over a carpet of rose petals strewn across the bridge, marking his final crossing.

I drove from Selma to Birmingham the next day to join my family for a ninety-fifth birthday gathering for Aunt Edna. One day later I was once again on the road, heading toward Atlanta for the home-going service for Congressman Lewis at the famed Ebenezer Baptist Church, where former president Barack Obama would deliver a poignant eulogy. Xernona Clayton would also offer a lively remembrance of Lewis, sparking an avalanche of news stories about the petite and feisty woman who had brought the humble American patriot to life for us one last time. But as keenly as I felt the loss of the congressman, a far more wrenching goodbye came on September 2, 2020, when my beloved Aunt Edna, one of my most magnificent mother surrogates, passed away in her sleep. How grateful I was then to have spent her last birthday on this earth with her and the family, as difficult as it had been for me to get time away from my work assignments that week.

Looking back, I cannot recall another year that left me as emotionally exhausted as 2020 did. As a journalist on the front lines of so much soul-crushing news, I had to fall back on years of training to maintain my professional neutrality on camera, especially as it became clear that communities of color were dying at disproportionate rates from Covid-19. Decades of racially compromised health care, conditions of poverty, and the overrepresentation of Black and Brown people in the ranks of essential workers were taking a deadly toll. And individuals of color were increasingly endangered in other ways, as well, with rising attacks against Asians, whom right-wing voices had incorrectly blamed for bringing the coronavirus to our shores, along with a heartbreaking roll call of Black men and women whose lives were senselessly snuffed out by police and White vigilante violence during the spring and summer of that year.

The whole incendiary mix exploded on May 25, when George Floyd, a Black man in Minneapolis, was murdered by a White cop in broad daylight, his curbside execution captured by a brave teenager's phone camera. The first time I saw the agonizing video of Floyd's death, I was alone in my living room in South Orange, screaming at the television screen. "Get off him!" I yelled, jumping to my feet, my heart hammering inside my chest, my hands beseeching the air. "Get your knee off his neck!"

My cry would be echoed by millions of souls who bore witness to the murder by police officer Derek Chauvin, who had knelt beside an already restrained Floyd and dug his knee into his neck. On the video, it appeared that he had one hand casually tucked into his pocket as he slowly pressed the life out of somebody's father, brother, son, friend. Floyd, who had recently relocated to Minneapolis from Houston in search of a new start, was unarmed and handcuffed as he lay gasping under the White cop's knee. He had been arrested on suspicion of passing a counterfeit twenty-dollar bill in a grocery store, which surely did not warrant death. I noticed with horror that as Chauvin pinned Floyd's neck, another cop knelt on his back, a third cop held his legs, and a fourth waved away a growing crowd of pedestrians begging them not to kill the man and to call for medical help.

As I listened to the bystanders' frantic pleas, Chauvin's demeanor chilled me most of all. His seeming nonchalance as Floyd struggled for breath and called out to his dead mama suggested that he saw the man's life as utterly disposable, and himself as untouchable. A surge of fury and sorrow flashed through me, leaving me shouting at the screen for the full nine minutes and twenty-nine seconds that Chauvin kept his knee on Floyd's neck. "You're killing him!" I wailed again and again, as if George Floyd weren't already dead.

Understand, I had been in the trenches of some of the toughest stories of the past two decades, and in every instance, I had been obliged to maintain my composure and pursue the facts in a manner that was scrupulously fair and accurate. As hard as this had been to achieve when I'd reported on evacuees seeking refuge from Hurricane Katrina in Houston shelters, it had been near impossible seven years later, when I was the first reporter from my network on the scene of a mass shooting at an elementary school in Newtown, Connecticut. My hands trembled and my voice quavered as I spoke into the mic, yet to all outward appearances,

I held myself together as I covered perhaps the most shattering story of my career. Little children were dead, and yet I had no choice but to contain my sorrow as I reconstructed what had transpired inside Sandy Hook Elementary School that Friday morning. The following July, I was outside the courtroom absorbing everyone's shock and sorrow when Trayvon Martin's killer was acquitted of murdering the unarmed Florida teen, and one year later, after a grand jury refused to indict the White cop who had gunned down yet another unarmed Black man, Michael Brown, in Ferguson, Missouri, I was once again in the thick of a news story that tore people's souls. And yet I had no choice but to preserve a professional and impartial stance as I reported on the riots that would birth the Black Lives Matter movement.

I remembered the ABC casting director telling me all those years before that I was too transparently vulnerable. Since then, I had learned not to wear my heart so much on my sleeve. I fully appreciated the tension every news correspondent faced, to cover the most devastating news stories through a dispassionate filter, to sequester feelings and remain open to all accounts, because even the most inconvenient or uncomfortable interpretations might inform the overarching truth of a story.

Yet George Floyd was different somehow. Witnessing his death from the sanctuary of my living room, I was suddenly like every other person on the planet, emotion crashing through me, my careful journalistic filter demolished. As Floyd exhaled his last breath, a nation already caught in a cataract of death had nowhere to escape the news, and so more than fifty million quarantined viewers felt the horror of George Floyd's killing exactly as I did, with the tape looping on one newscast after another.

Across the country, people howled at the injustice, much as they had fifty-five years before when they witnessed the televised violence of Bloody Sunday on the Edmund Pettus Bridge. Within days, hundreds of thousands of protestors poured into the streets to decry not just Floyd's death but also the destruction of other Black bodies during that season of loss: Ahmaud Arbery, Breonna Taylor, Elijah McCain, Rayshard Brooks, each of them doing nothing more than jogging, sleeping, walking home singing, breathing while Black. These deaths in the spring and summer of 2020, on top of so many others that had come before, pushed a face-masked multitude to demonstrate in unprecedented numbers, chanting "I can't breathe" in solidarity with the dead, confronting cops in riot gear lobbing teargas canisters, shooting rubber bullets at deadly close range, and cracking skulls with their batons. The widespread brutality of the police response only spurred more people of conscience into the streets. No longer could they sit safely at home in the face of atrocities committed by those who had taken an oath to protect and serve.

And this time, the demonstrators weren't mostly people of color, as had been the case in Ferguson, Missouri, six years earlier. In the summer of 2020, White people were out in the streets, too, masks in place as they raised fists and chanted alongside their brothers and sisters of color to protest an inhumanity made so gruesomely visible to everyone. It was the power of broadcast news, rallying new forces to the cause of justice and equality, much as it had done at the height of the Civil Rights movement. Now, from New York to Iowa to Oregon, and as far away as Australia, and even Antarctica, allies of all creeds and colors took up the fight in a new way, understanding at last why former NFL quarterback Colin Kaepernick had taken a knee, and why African Americans felt such a burning need to proclaim the obvious—that Black Lives Matter, too.

AS RACIAL JUSTICE PROTESTS INTENSIFIED ACROSS THE COUNTRY, Brian Bingham, my supervising producer at *CBS This Morning*, called me. "Michelle, we need your insights as a Black woman in this moment," he told me. "We need your passion, the kind we hear from you in meetings, when you're fired up about giving voice to the voiceless. We need you to share your story and offer a perspective on the national conversation on race that only you can bring."

I clicked off the call and immediately began dictating notes into my phone, energized by my network's recognition that experiences like mine could help to illuminate how we had arrived at this inflection point in our history, where a Black man could be executed by a White police officer in plain view of the entire world. It occurred to me this was the mantle that my former mentor George Curry had urged journalists of color to take up, one that was exactly the opposite of the instruction that the executive at the Minneapolis *Star Tribune* had tried to impart all those years ago, when he had advised the Black summer interns to "put race aside" when reporting their stories.

Knowing that my segment would be part of a program exploring race in America, and ways to create lasting change, I decided to share my own start in this world, because how could I talk about our nation's racial story without acknowledging how inherent bias against Black people had shaped everything I knew about myself from my first moments of life. "Born into the unrest of the late 1960s, I was raised in South Central Los Angeles," I told viewers, "the product of an interracial union that my father celebrated, and my mother, to this day, does not acknowledge."

My piece, titled "Witnessing History," ran on June 6, 2020, eight years to the day after the network aired my story about Dr. Ross Miller rushing to Robert Kennedy's side on the night he was fatally shot. In this, my second piece for CBS about my family, I didn't hesitate to include as a visual the only photograph I possessed of my family of origin, the one with me as a tearful toddler flanked by my parents, which had languished in an old photo album of my dad's. We blurred Laura's face in the photo, as my goal was not to "out" her or cause her public distress. But after so many years of languishing in the shadows of my mother's life, I had finally decided that I had every right to tell my own story, because the truth of my beginnings belonged as much to me as it did to my parents. No longer would I collude in hiding it, as if my very existence as the Black child of a mother who appeared White was cause for shame.

My children paid little attention to the segment—they were teenagers, after all, and constitutionally uninterested in their mother's working life. Mason and Margeaux had also long-ago moved on from the idea of ever having a relationship with their maternal grandmother, as it had been clear to them on the single occasion of meeting her that Laura Hernandez was not particularly eager to be an ongoing part of their lives.

Marc, on the other hand, had been fully invested, urging me to hold nothing back in documenting my parental story. He thought it particularly important for me to speak as fulsomely as I had about the role my father had played in securing the woman I had become. Here was a strong and accomplished Black man who gave the lie to the stereotype of the absent Black father, Marc pointed out, a man who at every turn had been fully present and devoted to his four children, ensuring we were properly educated and provided for, and that we never had any cause to doubt his commitment to our welfare and his love.

AFTER THE PIECE AIRED, I HALF-HOPED THAT LAURA HAD SEEN IT AND would call to talk about what I had shared and perhaps finally claim me as her own. I should have known better, but hope springs eternal. As the weeks passed with no word from her, I resolved to call her myself, except she still didn't answer the only number she had ever given me.

Seemingly out of options for connecting with her, I reached out to Eric Schubert, a young genealogist I had met when *CBS This Morning* did a segment on his work in May 2019. In the course of reporting that piece, I had sat with Eric in his kitchen and told him my own story, which helped him understand why his unsolicited pitch on tracing one's roots had so resonated with me when it landed on my desk. Now, over a year later, I asked him to help me find my mother.

Eric unearthed multiple phone numbers from different eras of Laura's life. He also turned up vital records for various members of my mother's family of origin, including my maternal grandfather's World War II draft card showing that he and I had been born on the exact same date in December. This unexpected detail hit me hard—to think that Laura had looked into the face of her infant daughter born on her own father's birthday, and had not seen it as a sign that she should bring me home to her people.

Alone in my home office after Eric emailed me digital scans of the records he had found, I printed out each document, stacking the sheets of paper one on top of the other in a forlorn little pile. I then sat at my desk for the next several hours, poring through the documents, studying each one closely, my vision often blurred by tears. There was the certificate listing my grandfather's birthplace in Santa Rosalía, Mexico, and the census rolls showing all the addresses in Los Angeles where my mother's family had lived. I lingered over Laura's birth certificate and high school yearbook photo, imagining how treasured these items must have been to her parents. On another sheet of paper, the names and birthdates of Laura's siblings were listed, each line inked by an anonymous bureaucrat's painstaking hand. Eric had also turned up my maternal grandmother's obituary in a local newspaper, and the burial dates and gravesites of Laura's parents and her husband. Shuffling through the printed sheets of paper, I was forced to confront the stark and unadulterated fact that my existence had gone completely unrecorded in the ledger of Laura Hernandez's life.

Night had fallen as I sat there in my home office with copies of the documents spread like a fan in front of me. I switched on the desk lamp and held up to its glow the faded, sepia-toned headshots affixed to some of the forms. I searched each face for some resemblance to my own and tried to imagine the lives my grandparents had led as hardworking

Mexican immigrants, my grandmother as a seamstress and homemaker and my grandfather as a cook. At some point I realized that I no longer felt any rancor toward my mother for keeping me a secret from these industrious people, only sadness that she had locked herself so deep inside her cage of lies, and all because America had told her family a story about the color of their skin and the color of mine.

I had lately come to see my mother's refusal to publicly acknowledge the Black child she had borne as rooted in America's willful failure to admit the way that systemic racism had splintered our society. But if her rejection of me was emblematic of our nation's marginalization of its communities of color, she herself had also been a victim of that pervasive racial messaging, which had ultimately convinced her not to yoke her life to my Blackness. Ironically, my mother would never be free of the shame she carried until she could embrace me as a part of herself, just as America would never begin to heal its divided psyche until the nation became willing to confront its original sin. Only then could restoration become possible.

And yet, though I too had come of age in our racially fractured homeland, my mother's leaving had not destroyed me—I saw that with complete clarity now. My father, Bigmama, Aunt Edna, Vondela, and so many others had provided a sheltering village in which I had been able to grow into a woman confident in her Black identity; who was fierce and abiding; who had learned to see the road ahead, no matter how pitted, as strewn with lessons and possibilities. Yes, I had missed my mother, but the loneliness of that had helped me to figure out that we must each run our race with fortitude, and that our highest human cause is to appreciate the life we have, not the one we might wish for, while cherishing love and connection wherever it is offered along the way.

This was my new perspective as I called each of the numbers for Laura Hernandez that Eric had provided to me—again to no avail. No one admitted knowing my mother's name.

———————

AS I WRITE THESE WORDS, I HAVE NOT GIVEN UP THE SEARCH FOR MY mother, because I want so much to let her know that I no longer place the burden of my healing on her shoulders. I finally recognize that the choice she made on the day I was born, has led in a direct line to who I am now. I am at last fully content with the life I have managed to create as a wife to Marc, as a mother to our children, and as a working journalist offering my unique perspective on the news. In reframing how I understand my story, in casting light into the shadows, I have become the agent of my own healing. It is a powerful place to stand, because it allows me, finally, to forgive not just my mother, but also my father, these two people so flawed in their own ways, and yet each one had only done the best they knew how. *When you know better, you do better,* Bigmama used to tell me. I now took that to mean that if I wanted to make peace with the two people who had made me, forgiveness was my ticket to ride.

I realized that I would have to take a hard look at a few failings in myself, too, including the way I had left Cheryl's care entirely in the hands of Vondela, then Maria and my brothers, after Daddy died. I had begun to grasp how my birth had unraveled the life my sister might have led had Ross and Laura never conceived me. Cheryl might have been raised in a still intact family, or at the very least with a bright, attentive sister her own age to share her days. Perhaps our lost sister Adrienne might have secured Cheryl in ways that I had never managed—but it wasn't too late for us. Though most of our parental figures had already departed this earth, Cheryl and I were still standing. I could still step forward and do right by my sister, as different as we both were, as fraught with things unspoken and unknown as our sibling relationship had always been.

And so, when my brothers had called to share the sad news that Maria had suffered a stroke and would have to be moved into an assisted-living facility, necessitating the sale of the family apartment, I had flown to Los Angeles to get my sister and bring her back to New Jersey with me. Marc and I found housing for her, conveniently just a few minutes from our home. Cheryl had never held down a job, so I had little expectation of her becoming self-supporting now. I was just happy that she could still lose herself in books and television shows, entertaining herself thus until Marc and I drew her out for social events, which she willingly attended as part of our family. We also started the process of getting Cheryl's social challenges properly diagnosed, resolved that whatever the result, I would be my sister's keeper till the end of our days.

Though it had taken me a while to get there, I finally understood that it was up to me to construct a safe emotional harbor for my loved ones, that it was me—not my father or my mother—who was ultimately responsible for planting my feet in the places where I truly belonged. I also saw more clearly than ever that my most purposeful place was with Marc and our children especially, as well as with the wonderful and supportive community of extended family and friends whose love and constancy had anchored me.

Now, with our eldest Kemah married and a new mother to our first grandchild, I wanted all my beloveds, whether given by blood or chosen by love, to be able to rest in the one assurance I had craved in my motherlessness, the knowledge that by me, they were valued in their very being, that no matter how distracted I might sometimes become, or the slings or arrows we might yet suffer, I would hold them close. I had not grown enough in awareness to give this warranty to Vondela, who had literally saved Cheryl and me after Bigmama passed away. Yet Vondela agreeing to finish raising Ross Miller's girls had left me with perhaps the most valuable lesson of all—to prize the ones who stay by your side, to show them your heart and never let them go.

As for the woman who gave birth to me, I still nurse a flame of hope that I will find her again, or perhaps she will find me. And though this tiny flame may flicker, I now know that it will never be extinguished, because it is fed by the breath of filial love, a bond of nature that resists the quenching of all light. And so I will continue to hold faith in everything that lies ahead, because even if my mother never chooses to proclaim me to the world as her own, I will always be her daughter.

Acknowledgments

Words are my stock in trade, which is why I am so grateful for the people who helped me bring my voice to the page through the stories that describe my belonging.

First, I have to thank my collaborator Rosemarie Robotham, who through many months of sensitive and probing conversations helped me excavate memories buried deep inside and bring them into the light. During our work together, Rosemarie always managed to see the essential *me,* despite the constant flurry of activity and movement that is my life. I am grateful for the love and empathy she brought to the writing of this memoir, and for her warmth, talent, and commitment in helping me tell my truth.

My gratitude also to Dawn Davis, editor in chief of *Bon Appétit* and former Simon & Schuster VP, who saw the potential in my story early on and connected me with Rosemarie, assuring me that she was the one I needed on this journey. Thank you, too, to Caroline Clarke for walking me through the proposal process and asking the big question, "Are you sure?" My agent Will Lippincott of Aevitas Creative Management guided me into the capable hands of the team at HarperCollins, and offered wise counsel, patient encouragement, and steadfast support at every stage.

My heartfelt thanks to Lisa Sharkey, senior VP and director of development at HarperCollins, who was perhaps the first person to believe this book could be. She listened generously as I gave voice to my pain during a *CBS This Morning* segment on my family, and afterward reached out to let me know that I had a story worth telling. Matt Harper, editor extraordinaire, engaged with every word of the manuscript, offering thoughtful suggestions to enrich and deepen the narrative. My thanks to Matt and the entire HarperCollins publishing team, including associate editor Maddie Pillari, attorney Trina Hunn, Leslie Cohen in publicity, Katie O'Callaghan in marketing, and Rebecca Holland in production editorial.

Of course, I wouldn't be here at all without the lifelong devotion and guidance of my family, beginning with my beloved father, Dr. Ross Miller, who promised me a magnificent life no matter the discomforts of my beginning circumstances. Thank you also to my mother for choosing to carry me to term. And how can I ever fully express my undying gratitude for the selfless nurturing of my grandmother, Bigmama, Beatrice Bessie Burson Miller, and my Aunt Edna Gardner, who fixed any problem I ever brought to her. My dad, Bigmama, and Aunt Edna all girded me with strong family values rooted in love, and they live on in my heart always.

Thank you to my cousin Reggie, the older brother I never had, who continually watched over me through life, and to cousins Lynn, Paul, Eric, and Tommy, who taught me about everything from facials to football, poetry to Prince, and the healthful benefits of vegetarianism. I am stronger, smarter, and more well-rounded because of you. My thanks also to my sister Cheryl, who helped me discover my love of reading as a child, and to my brothers, Matt and Jonathan, who showed me the joys of being a big sister.

There aren't words enough in the English language to thank my husband, Marc Morial, who has told me since the day he learned my history that I needed to write a book. He has been my guiding force, my rock, and the person I can always depend on. With him at my side, my life blossomed in extraordinary ways, especially when his family folded me in as their own, including his wonderful mother, Miz Mo, his siblings, Cheri, Monique, Julie, and Jacques, and his beautiful daughter, Kemah Dennis Morial West, who wrapped her arms around her MaMeesh and who, with her husband, Julius, recently gave us the gift of our first grandchild, Audrey.

To my amazing children by birth, Mason and Margeaux Morial, I love you beyond measure, no matter how much I can sometimes embarrass you. You are my life's greatest treasure, and no mother could be more proud than I am of you. And to Judy Lopez Whitt, Hope Zapanta, and Rey Arile, I could not do all that I've done without the care and support you gave to my children and our family.

I have been blessed with a wealth of friends, mentors, and role models. Some of you are mentioned in this book, but many more are not. I want to express how deeply grateful I am for your presence in my life. A special mention to Dr. Thomas and Patricia Gibson, who among many other kindnesses, helped me get into Palisades High, and to Reverend Paul Smith and Reverend Sandye Wilson, for the spiritual sustenance you provided to our family. Pam Carlton, Charles Hamilton, Susan L. Taylor, Khephra Burns, Nadja Bellan White, Gayle Pollard, Mike Terry, Nina and Ted Wells, thank you for welcoming us in.

To my Howard crew—HU, You Know! I would not be who I am today without my unforgettable mentors, including Dr. Lee Thornton, Dr. Olive Taylor, Dr. Victor Pelosi, Dr. Laurence Kaggwa, Dr. Janet Dates, Carol Dudley, and Raymond Archer, and the fellow students who changed my life—Wendy Robinson, Chris Thomas, Rhea Lloyd, Linda Looney, Quay Whitlock, Dawn Hightower Lucas, Arvia Few, Ernest Champell, Kelvin Phillips, Yasmin Cader, James Walker—as well as those alums I didn't know well back then, but who have become incredible shoulders for me and educators in the arts—C. Brian Williams, Mark Mason, and Lewis Paul Long.

To my ride-or-die Jersey girls Annelisa Blake Wasden, Monique

Pryor, Deirdre Duice-Minor, Kim Cockerham, Michelle Swittenburg, Victoria Carter, Carolyn Cookie Mason, and Abigail Osuala, I could not have raised my children without you. It's no exaggeration to say you helped me stay mentally balanced. Thank you also to the late great Heather Holley, my colleague and longtime friend, who invited me to live in a community like no other.

It is my great honor to be a member of Alpha Kappa Alpha Sorority, Inc., following in the footsteps of my grandmother. I will always be grateful to the late soror Jonetta Haley, Bigmama's protégé, and to Staci Collins Jackson and Daria Ibn-Tamas, who embraced me into my honorary status. Thank you to President Dr. Glenda Glover, who gave me the privilege of delivering the commencement address to the graduate schools of Tennessee State University, and to my countless friends and guiding lights in the sorority, including Kuae Kelch Mattox and U.S. vice president Kamala Harris, who were among the Thirty-Eight Jewels of Iridescent Splendor that inspired me in college and beyond.

To the inimitable Hasoni Pratts, Eli Tatum, Terri Gibson, Marcella Maxwell, Betty Obiajulu, and Kim Jefferies-Leonard, thank you for being my sisters in Linkdom.

To my NABJ crew Audra Burch, Neki Mohan, Suzanne Malveaux, and Kevin Fraser, thank you for navigating through thick and thin with me. And to my Jack and Jill family and the Triple Threat/BRWL-ers, thank you for keeping me in shape both physically and communally.

My culinary enlighteners Toni Tipton Martin, Alexander Smalls, Michael Lomonaco, Dawn Burrell, and Chris Williams share with me their exquisite food and delicious company—you bring such joy. To my former Crescent City roomies, Chuck and Jana Grauberger, what a time we had. And Winston and Wendy Burns, you showed me how to close, and were the life—and the buffer—of the party. Also to Tiffany Haddish, thank you for making this Los Angeles girl's Oscar dream a reality.

To my WWL-TV peeps who taught me the ropes, Sally Ann

Roberts-Nabonne, Eric Paulsen, Angela Hill, Karen Swensen, Hoda Kotb, Val Amedee, Meg Farris, Akili Franklin, Mike Millon, Bill Capo, David Bernard, and Willie Wilson, I'm so grateful for you. Dr. Michael Lomax, thank you for giving me my first teaching gig, and to my New Orleans support system, including the Norman C. Francis family, Phillipa Bowers, Justin Woods, Debbie C. Ware, Lisa Fuller, Craig Schwartzenberg, and the entire Rhodes clan, you're the absolute best.

A huge thank you to my CBS family, including Joe Duke, who let me in the door; Marci McGinnis and Byron Pitts, who helped to create space for me at the table; Bill Owens, for putting me out front where I could prove myself; and Rick Kaplan, Chris Licht, Paul Friedman, and Pat Shevlin, for changing their minds and giving me a shot that meant everything. Thank you, David Rhodes, for allowing me to launch CBSN, now the live stream of CBS News. And to Brian Applegate, my deepest thanks for giving me the best job I could ever have asked for, and for widening my musical tastes with your Saturday Sessions. SATMO is a shining light and a dream! We are going to hit Number One—I promise!

My gratitude to my partners at the table Dana Jacobson and Jeff Glor, and to our amazing support team, Tony Dipolvere, Vidya Singh, Greg Mirman, Jessica Haddad, Kelli Casse, Turaya Bryant-Kamau, Marci Waldman, Debbye Chapnick, Brendan Conway, Anjali Patil, Emily D'Alessandro, Mary Ann Keane, Colin Hekimian, and Dan Elias, you always bring your magic to the best show on TV. A special shout out to Sierra Morris for all the effort she put into being my First Aide.

To Randall Pinkston, Mika Brzezinski, Jim Axelrod, Elaine Quijano, Jericka Duncan, Jamie Waxx, Vlad Duthiers, Peter Greenberg, and Dr. Jonathan LaPook, my correspondent crew, thank you for giving advice and stirring fun into the work mix. And to the producers who believed in me from day one, Deborah Camiel, Mikaela Bufano,

Alyse Shorland, Mary Lou Teel, Ramon Parkins, Allison Schwartz Dorfman, Nicole Young, Andy Merlis, Jack Renaud, Warren Serink, Chris Laible, Joe Long, Jen Janisch, Ryan Kadro, Chris Weicher, and Kathleen Seccombe, Natasha Singh, Kira Kleaveland, Maite Amorebieta, Robbyn McFadden, Kathy Black, Alturo Rhymes, Alvin Patrick, Marcie Spencer, Michelle Fanucci, Chuck Stevenson, Lauren White, Guy Campanile, Rodney Comrie, Betty Chin, Gabriel Falcon, and Nancy Kramer, I appreciate you always.

My deep thanks also to Anthony Mason, my big brother at the network, who saw me for who I was long before anyone else did, and to Marva Smalls, my sponsor and mentor, who opened doors in New York beyond my career, and showed me so much that I never saw coming. Marilyn Booker, thank you for keeping me on your A-list; and Charles and Karen Phillips, and Bruce and Tawana Gordon, thank you for having my back.

There are angels who look out for us on our journey yet rarely seek recognition and praise. Among them are Kurt Davis, Sandy Gleysteen, Patrick Lee, and Ingrid Ciprian Matthews, ninja warriors helping others to move forward. Kakesha Ruffin, Rodney Hawkins, Lance Frank, Jonathan Blakely, Muna Moushien, and Sgt. Michael Scott, my mentees who are flying high and are now mentoring me, you are the brightest of stars, and I see you. To the Desk, Terri Stewart and Andre Rodriguez, for the early days of guidance and an open ear, thank you. To Kim Godwin, for choosing me to cover some of the most pivotal stories of my career, including the one that garnered my first-ever Emmy win, thank you. To George Cheeks, Bob Bakish, Shawna Thomas, Neeraj Khemlani, and Wendy McMahon, thank you for always keeping everything on the rails.

My warmest appreciation to Gayle King, Bill Whitaker, Jane Pauley, and Scott Pelley, the best storytellers in the business, who are still somehow never too busy to answer a call or pitch me a story.

To Susan Zirinsky and Judy Tygard, thank you for opening *48*

Hours and long-form documentaries to me. And to Rand Morrison and the rest of the Sunday Morning crew, thanks for holding it down the way you do—through everything!

Last but most definitely not least, to The Glam Squad—many of you have been with me since the beginning. Lena Gjokaj and Yolanda Bracero, you are my aces every Saturday morning. And Kim Serratore, Bilgi Kaya, Rae Dawn Johnson, and Gisele Modeste, thank you for always sending me into the spotlight with your special shine.

Finally, my sincere thanks to all the amazing people whose stories I have covered through the years. Every one of you has inspired me and taught me more about this life we share than you will ever know. Through you and so many others, named and unnamed in these pages, God has richly blessed me indeed.

About the Author

MICHELLE MILLER is a cohost of *CBS Saturday Morning*. Her work regularly appears on *CBS Mornings, CBS Sunday Morning*, the *CBS Evening News*, and *48 Hours*.

From presidential elections to the climate crisis, her area of coverage is wide-ranging, but her reporting on social justice has been particularly groundbreaking. From the killings of George Floyd, Trayvon Martin, Michael Brown, and the Emanuel 9 Massacre in Charleston to sexual assault allegations against Bill Cosby, Russell Simmons, and Harvey Weinstein, Miller has been at the forefront of these issues.

The first CBS News correspondent on the ground at the Sandy Hook Elementary School shooting, she closely followed the movement to change the nation's gun laws, including the March for Our Lives protests. Her coverage has extended overseas to the refugee crisis in the Middle East, the life of Nelson Mandela, and the wedding of Prince William and Kate Middleton. She has interviewed global leaders, politicians, artists, and celebrities, including President Bill Clinton, Oprah Winfrey, former Soviet premier Mikhail Gorbachev, Nobel Peace Prize winner Wangari Maathai, Beyoncé, James Earl Jones, Lenny Kravitz, Carlos Santana, Denzel Washington, violinist Yo-Yo Ma, and immunologist Dr. Anthony Fauci.

Miller's reporting has earned her several prestigious journalism awards, including an Emmy for her series on the National Guard's Youth Challenge Academy, a Gracie Award for *48 Hours: Live to Tell:*

Trafficked, and a Murrow Award for her coverage of a daycare center stand-off in New Orleans. A graduate of Howard University's School of Communications, she was inducted as honorary member of Alpha Kappa Alpha Sorority, and was the recipient of the 2022 University of New Orleans Homer L. Hitt Distinguished Alumni Award.

ROSEMARIE ROBOTHAM is an award-winning author, editor, and literary collaborator. A former senior editor at Simon & Schuster, she also served as deputy editor at *Essence* magazine. She lives in New York City with her husband and two children. For more on her work, visit RosemarieRobotham.com.